Leading Effective Supply Chain Transformations

A Guide to Sustainable World-Class Capability and Results

William B. Lee, Ph.D. ■ Michael Katzorke

Copyright ©2010 by William B. Lee and Michael Katzorke

ISBN-13: 978-1-932159-91-2
Printed and bound in the U.S.A. Printed on acid-free paper
10 9 8 7 6 5 4 3 2 1

Library of Congress Cataloging-in-Publication Data
Lee, William B., 1941-
  Leading effective supply chain transformations : a guide to sustainable
world-class capability and results / by William B. Lee and Michael Katzorke.
    p. cm.
  Includes bibliographical references and index.
  ISBN 978-1-932159-91-2 (hardcover : alk. paper)
  1. Business logistics. I. Katzorke, Michael, 1948- II. Title.
  HD38.5.L4374 2010
  658.7--dc22   2009045637

Direct all inquiries to J. Ross Publishing, Inc., 5765 N. Andrews Way, Fort Lauderdale, FL 33309.

Phone: (954) 727-9333
Fax: (561) 892-0700
Web: www.jrosspub.com

I am most richly blessed with a wonderful family.

To my wife, Jane

To my daughter, Karen, son-in-law, Ric, and grandsons, Barclay and Philip

To my son, Richard, and granddaughter, Abigail

Thank you all.

—WBL

First of all, to Julie, my best friend and wife of 41 years, who is my best
source of counsel, common sense, and perseverance

To Douglas, Ryan, and Matthew, my sons, who are much of the motivation
for all my labors

To daughters, Linda, Karen, and Carrie, wives to my sons

To my grandchildren, Hayden, Danielle, Kaylen, Hailey, and (soon) Caleb

To my parents, who taught me my values

To my sister-in-law, Carolyn

To my country, where we are free to pursue our dreams and where anything
is achievable — may it ever be so

Above all, to Almighty God from whom all these blessings come

—MK

CONTENTS

FOREWORD

This book is needed — now. I enthusiastically endorse it.

Research, published annually in the *Supply Chain Management Review*, shows a mixed bag of supply chain progress. In October 2008, our sixth annual global survey contained the following observation (see Poirier, Charles C., Morgan L. Swink, and Francis J. Quinn. "Sixth Annual Global Survey of Supply Chain Progress: Still Chasing the Leaders." *Supply Chain Management Review* 2008 October. Waltham, MA: Reed Business Information):

> *This year's survey results show that companies continue to make steady supply chain progress across a range of competencies — though some have progressed a lot faster than others. For those companies following the leaders ... you can't afford to be playing catch-up anymore.*

Our studies have shown that the financial and operational performance differences between supply chain management leaders, followers, and laggards are truly stunning. The opportunities for making progress in ways that create competitive advantages are huge. This book should help all companies make faster progress. Even leaders need to move faster — otherwise your competitors will gain on you.

This book's title contains some very effective words: leading, transformations, sustainable, capability, and results. These words are indicative of the book's emphasis and focus. In the seven chapters and three appendices that make up this book, the authors have prepared a well written, lucid, clear, and logical guide to supply chain organizational transformation. The three major segments of the book provide, respectively, the motivation for transformation, the details of managing the transformation, and the tools for transformation. As such, *Leading Effective Supply Chain Transformations: A Guide to Sustainable World-Class Capability and Results* deserves to be read and studied in its entirety.

The book is written with a very practical and useful slant. It also contains sufficient references to high-quality research to give it credibility as more than just the opinions of two (albeit, very experienced and knowledgeable) authors. The authors admit that other good work has been published, and they cite such work in the right amount of detail.

I recommend this book for several audiences. One audience likely will be managers who see a need for transformation in their supply chains. Anyone from a chief executive to project team members can use the insights in this book to make transformation a reality. Non-supply chain professionals who want to know about their relationships with the supply chain components also would benefit from reading the book. A second audience likely will be in academic courses (probably at the MBA level). The book could be used as a supplement to a more standard textbook or as a stand-alone book for an elective course. Case studies referenced in the book could be used to supplement the topics it addresses. Another audience likely will be a hybrid company/academic executive education program. I can easily see the book being used either as primary or secondary material in an executive education program on supply chain management.

> — **Morgan L. Swink**
> Professor, Eli Broad Legacy Fellow of Supply
> Chain and Operations Management
> Eli Broad College of Business, Michigan
> State University
> East Lansing, Michigan
> Co-Editor-in-Chief: *Journal of Operations
> Management*

*   *   *   *

I strongly recommend this book by Lee and Katzorke. It is a must read for all serious leaders, practitioners, and students of supply chain management. Since the late 1970s and early 1980s, people and firms have increased their knowledge of supply chain management strategies and approaches such as supply base rationalization, six sigma and lean, low-cost-country sourcing, and supplier integration. In addition, leaders from firms worldwide discuss and present what needs to be done to improve supply chain performance. However, knowledge of what should be done has not necessarily resulted in implementation of effective worldwide supply chains supporting business and product goals.

Leading Effective Supply Chain Transformations: A Guide to Sustainable World-Class Capability and Results provides holistic insight into those actions that company executive leaders should be taking to achieve effective supply chains. It presents approaches to supply chain transformation that will lead to enhanced firm competitiveness, not only from a cost perspective, but also through growth and revenue enhancement.

My research and experience over the past twenty-five years suggests that organizations typically respond to problems with a set of new initiatives, such as low-cost-country sourcing, supplier risk management, supply base reduction, and S&OP, or tool application, such as spend analytics, supplier lean analysis, and forecasting. The Lee and Katzorke book transcends these approaches by discussing how supply chain competitiveness can be embedded into the overall competitive model of the firm.

The perspectives and approaches discussed by the authors and the need to align and link end customer needs based on their relative value to business and supply chain strategies are carried forward throughout the book. How a firm can achieve business-driven effective supply chains is clearly presented with a framework for readers to follow. This framework includes excellent discussions of actions required for supply chain transformation, such as generating short-term specific results, collaboration within and across supply chains, supply chain segmentation for results, and nine critical initiatives for successful supply chain transformation.

The authors provide an important book for company leaders about how to compete with supply chain strategies as an important element of overall company competitive strategies. There are numerous publications discussing the "tools" and "initiatives" associated with supply chain management. However, there are insufficient guides to achieving real transformation of supply chains that are linked to overall business success and how this can be achieved by company leaders — this book begins to remedy that situation.

— **Robert M. Monczka, Ph.D.**
Research Professor, Supply Chain
    Management
W. P. Carey School of Business
Arizona State University and
Director — Strategic Sourcing and Supply
    Chain Strategy Research
CAPS Research
Tempe, Arizona

*   *   *   *

Like others in this field, I have participated in and led several supply chain transformations. *Leading Effective Supply Chain Transformations: A Guide to Sustainable World-Class Capability and Results* points to several keys to success which I think are critical to creating and sustaining a supply chain organization that brings real value to the enterprise. The book captures many critical concepts and practices, such as a critical focus on improving supplier performance through better understanding the supplier's technology, quality, cost, and delivery. Getting focused on operational excellence is another concept covered in this book. I believe operational excellence to be an important area of opportunity, not just because it is what I do every day, but because of the relevant and important impact it has on the business. Operational excellence requires collaboration across the supply chain — it will enable the enterprise through true value creation that is a result of flawless execution.

This book also points to several other key areas of opportunity when building out a nimble supply chain. One important item is mentioned in a section of the book that speaks to supplier partnerships and collaboration. The discussion is about being selective with which suppliers you consider as a partner. Getting the selection and alignment process right is critical. The discussion clearly points out that every supplier is not a partner and that mutual interest is the key to a genuinely strong partnership. Based on my personal experiences, I could not agree more. The discussion even goes so far as to address the importance of forming "mutual-commitment long-term agreements" and "annual improvement commitments." Both are vital in building a strong long-term partnership and are often overlooked and not well understood.

Another key observation made by the authors in the book is the important use of technology to aid and create velocity in your supply chain. As early adopters of technology, the authors speak through personal experiences about how technology, when used properly, will help drive speed and flexibility into better managing your supply chain. I have found this to be true in my own career and personal experiences.

One of the most significant areas of discussion in this book has to do with the critical focus that needs to be placed on people and talent development. The authors know this well because they have had a chance to concentrate on "people development" throughout their careers. The focus on talent resides in the top three priorities of a chief purchasing officer. This book does a nice job in directing the reader on how to use supply chain staffing and strategy as a tool to transform an organization.

Leading Effective Supply Chain Transformations: A Guide to Sustainable World-Class Capability and Results contains many other practical concepts which have been garnered throughout the authors' careers. These practical concepts steer the reader to how it is really done as opposed to how one thinks it should be done.

The experiences the authors have gained from working at great companies and leading successful supply chain organizations come through very clearly in this book. I believe everyone will benefit by reading and learning from the concepts which have so clearly been put forth.

> — **Shelley Stewart, Jr.**
> Research Chair, ISM Board of Directors
> Sr. Vice President, Operational Excellence and
> Chief Procurement Officer
> Tyco International

* * * *

PREFACE

This is not a book about "what supply chains are" or "how to manage supply chains." Too many books in the market already do that. Rather, this is a book that recognizes the sorry state of the supply chains of many companies — supply chains that are in dire need of transformation. The target audience is C-suite executives, who acknowledge that they need to do something, but are not quite sure what to do and how to go about doing it, and all other executives, managers, and professionals working in supply chains.

Over the last thirty years, numerous books and articles have been written about supply chain management, strategic supply management, and purchasing. These publications have discussed the increasingly strategic importance of supply chain management, strategic supply management, and purchasing processes to the competitive success of enterprises. They also have related the evolution of thought and best practices. For example, in 2006 *Straight to the Bottom Line* (Mike Katzorke's book with three other authors) provided an executive-level roadmap to world-class supply management. In *The Purchasing Machine*, Dave Nelson's 2001 book, he and his co-authors discussed how top companies used best practices to manage their supply chains. *Purchasing Magazine, Supply Chain Management Review*, the Institute for Supply Management (ISM), and APICS: the Operations Management Society provide a continual flow of information on the topic of supply chain management. In the academic world, the *Journal of Operations Management* and *Production and Operations Management* are well recognized publications. These are just a few examples of the myriad writings on the subject. So why write one more? Let us tell you a story.

In our roles in industry, consulting, and academia, we talk with many supply chain experts and other seasoned business executives. We often ask them about why supply chain improvements do not have staying power beyond the initial champion. Many executives and other experts admit that they do not know why sustaining improvement is so difficult.

Our experience has shown that far too many supply chain improvement projects fail to last and sustain improved results because they are too dependent on the strength of the personality of the supply chain leader. Often not enough emphasis is put on gaining ownership across the business. Typically, a number of initiatives are put in place to drive the process change and associated improved results. If executives are not careful, they develop process silos and competing initiatives, which sometimes have led to process optimization and disappointing enterprise suboptimization.

We believe that the process needs to begin with listening — to end customers of the supply chain, to the company's immediate customers, to the process leaders across the business, to suppliers, and to supplier's suppliers — listening that includes everyone who has a stake in supply chain success. (We call them stakeholders for some strange reason!)

Plan linkage is fundamental to success. For us, the term *supply chain* is about linkage and integration and encompasses everything from ore, oil and gas, and seeds in the ground to product obsolescence and recycling. Any given company may have multiple supply chains. For example, at an aircraft company, one supply chain feeds product development; another supply chain feeds manufacturing; another chain feeds the repair and overhaul business; and still another chain feeds fleet spare parts (for example, timeshare customers, fixed base operators, and airlines). Although there are similarities in the supply chain processes, there also are stark differences in the relative value of key success factors such as cost, reliability, quality, technology, and others. The business and process strategic plans must address the *differences* in key success factors for these multiple supply chains and *how to integrate* the transformative initiatives around them.

Plan linkage is essential to avoid competing initiatives. In most cases, a business has a strategic plan that identifies customer desires and stakeholder deliverables along with its relative maturity in achieving those competitively. The strategic plan also prioritizes where the products and processes must be improved to achieve customer and stakeholder satisfaction. We always advise clients that their business strategic plan should also incorporate process strategic plan key initiatives. These should be derived against "what a *good* supply chain looks like," which usually is developed from process and metrics benchmarks. We want to deliver competitive results, not only today, but to do today what it takes to be competitive tomorrow. We also believe we must provide specific incentives for the key initiatives in the compensation schemes of all process leaders and key executives across the business.

> *How can we define a **good** supply chain?*

A lot of water has gone under the supply chain evolution bridge in the last several decades. It may sound arrogant, but we think we have an answer — not the *only* answer, but *an* answer. We cannot take total credit, however, because we have talked with, consulted to, researched, and taught the subject for years and we have learned from the many people with whom we have interacted.

Our answer is not about strategies, although integrated strategies are important. It is not about tactical process change, although this is required. The answer is about *how* transformative changes are led and *who* is engaged in leading them. In short, the answer is about *leadership*. Leadership is the focus of this book. Let us illustrate a little further.

Our experience is that even the most intelligent, astute supply chain design solutions, generated by the brightest leaders, can succeed and sustain only when the more complex human behavior challenges and their solutions are addressed and integrated into the transformation process. *What to do* is relatively easy. *How to get it done* in a large organization, much less across an integrated supply chain, is the challenge — and *the soft stuff really is the hard stuff*. This is why we refer to the soft stuff throughout the text and have included material such as that contained in Chapter 3, *How Can We Convince the Organization*?

Within this book we describe in pragmatic terms, from real-world experience, across many industries, what you actually do, in what sequence, and with whom to create a sustainable world-class supply chain capability and associated results. We tell it "like it was" and "like it is." We believe these situations are almost identical — but have reason to believe the future will be quite different.

The first three chapters in our book set the stage and will be of interest to C-suite executives. We begin by describing the big-picture, macro transformative issues that impact global supply chains. The second chapter provides insights and suggestions for how companies can know that they have problems and opportunities with their supply chains and then shows how detailed assessments can be put to use. The third chapter explores how the "big picture" and detailed assessments can be used to convince an organization to move forward with transformative initiatives.

Chapters 4 through 7 form the second segment of the book, which deals with the details of the transformation. Chapter 4 focuses on the very short term — "stopping the bleeding" — and how to get enough control over the supply chain to provide some breathing room for longer-term fixes. Chapter 5 emphasizes the need for collaboration along and between supply chains. Chapter 6 provides guidance about multiple supply chains and shows that companies with them need to manage multiple supply chains differently. Chapter 7 brings everything together and lays out nine key initiatives for supply chain transformation. These four chapters are written in enough detail so a reasonably experienced supply chain transformation team can implement the ideas successfully.

The third segment of the book is the appendices — on visioning, benchmarking, and a maturity assessment tool. The appendices are presented in a logical sequence and are written as "tools" that can be used in a company's transformation effort. First, visioning is presented as one of the key steps in transformation. This tool is written as a five-step process that leads to a vision of transformative supply chains. The second appendix presents a benchmarking tool in a how-to-do-it format and includes needed and sufficient caveats, which are all too often ignored in practice and thus make a benchmarking effort less than successful. The third appendix contains a very detailed assessment tool to assist readers in assessing where their company stands currently, progress in how far their company has moved, and in what direction their company is moving.

We think you will enjoy the principles, associated stories, and lessons. We want your continual supply chain transformation process to be helped by them. If that happens, all our efforts put into writing this book will have been worth it. After all, this information is for *you*, the executives and professionals in supply chains and the academics who do the research and teaching to develop and pass along the knowledge.

ACKNOWLEDGMENTS

First and foremost, over many years, we have learned a great deal from our lovely and gracious wives, Jane and Julie. Career-wise, we have learned much in our jobs and from our co-workers, bosses, subordinates, and others with whom we have worked. We are truly grateful to all of them. Unfortunately space simply prohibits us from mentioning everyone.

Bill Lee

I have had what you might call three careers after college: industry, academia, and consulting. Each career has been instrumental in my learning. First, what I call my only "real" jobs (tongue-in-cheek) were with Martin Marietta Aerospace in Orlando (as a young engineer just out of college) and with Rockwell. I put my first MRP systems into Rockwell valve plants in the late 1960s when these were new ideas. I learned from Joe Orlicky, Ollie Wight, and the other gurus of the time. At both Martin Marietta and Rockwell, I learned a great deal about leadership from Paul Delacourt, my boss in Orlando and again at Rockwell.

I gave up "working" for a living during the 1970s and became an academic. This was my first retirement. Dick Levin, Curt McLaughlin, and Basheer Khumawala at the University of North Carolina at Chapel Hill were extremely influential in my development as a doctoral student. The critiques from these three men were always on point, sometimes embarrassingly so.

As a young academic, I joined the faculty at the University of Houston. My colleagues there for the next number of years are too numerous to mention and each knows my depth of gratitude. My second retirement was from the University of Houston.

I knew all along that I wanted to consult. Consulting seemed to be a happy medium between being a professor and having a real job, so Earle Steinberg and I founded a small consulting firm, which we called SOM Associates. Jim Schwendinger soon joined us and we had a thriving business for awhile — but we wanted to be bigger — doesn't everyone?

So Earle and I sold our little business to what was then Touche Ross & Co. (later to become Deloitte & Touche and now, simply, Deloitte). We joined the firm as direct-entry partners. Jim came with us and is a very successful Deloitte partner, as we always knew he would be. I spent some exciting years at D&T and was fortunate to serve in several leadership positions — Director of the Manufacturing and Distribution Consulting Practice, Partner-in-Charge of the Houston office, Director of the Change Management Consulting Practice, and National Partner for Education and Research. Terry Seitz, Larry Warder, and other colleagues were invaluable in teaching me how to become an effective consultant. My third retirement was from D&T.

This retirement lasted less than two years. The late Jim Burlingame called from The Oliver Wight Companies. Ollie had been an inspiration to me for years, even though I did not know him well. I admired his creativity, insight, and ability to make things simple so I could understand them. I became president of Oliver Wight Management Consulting and enjoyed immensely working with Bill Mackie and others in the firm. My fourth retirement was from Oliver Wight.

I then joined the faculty and administration of the Jesse H. Jones Graduate School of Management at Rice University where I was Professor of Management Practice and Associate Dean of Executive Education. I am a great believer in lifelong learning for individuals and in organizational learning for organizations. The position at Rice gave me an opportunity to combine my interests in improving organizational performance, teaching, research, and learning. Colleagues such as Al Napier and Pat Hanenberg were terrific. My fifth retirement was from Rice.

Mike Katzorke

My professional experience began in college while working in retail sales and for a brokerage business for two Jewish gentlemen who took a then-Catholic boy in as family. I learned more about business from those mentors than I ever did in my formal education and I was a pretty good student.

With the completion of college, my first job was in purchasing in the computer industry with Sperry Univac. Many people helped me get a solid foundation in the real world of how large corporations do business. I learned how important velocity of change is in the high-tech world; the importance of having a belief in the need to improve; and the importance of having an ability to anticipate needed change and to be out in front of it. Then I moved within Sperry to the very different world of aerospace. At Sperry Flight Systems, I found a far more advanced materials environment where a couple of visionary leaders had actually put those Univac computers to work managing the business in general and materials specifically.

After more than a decade with Sperry, I moved to Motorola when Sperry was acquired by Burroughs. I thought I knew about all there was to know about operations and materials, but after spending some time in Schaumberg, I found a whole new frontier for the subject — *strategic supply management*. My career eventually led me back to aerospace with Honeywell, where there was much to learn from in the arena of soft skills. Then I moved to AlliedSignal and its aerospace, automotive, and chemical businesses where the drum of numbers performance beat loudly.

At Cessna Aircraft, and later at Smiths Aerospace, as a senior executive, I put all the strategic, tactical, and process learning together. Much of what I learned is applied in this book. Today, in the consulting business, it is clear that the same business and process principles and techniques work, without regard to the industry.

So many people helped me along the way, taking my career much farther than I ever imagined as a young man fresh out of college. Paraphrasing Zig Ziglar, many people go much farther in life than they thought they could because somebody else thought they could. For their confidence, I thank Dr. Larry Moore (my first purchasing manager at Sperry Flight Systems), who later became COO of the corporation; Tom Hoogervorst, CPO, who put me in the fast-track rotational program at Sperry and scared me to death with my first operations leadership job; and Mike Smith, ultimately president of Honeywell Commercial Flight Systems, whose patience with and forgiveness of my driving style were of a saintly nature.

Ken Stork, CPO, at Motorola Corporate mentored a brash young, know-it-all until he helped me to see how much I had to learn. Keki Bhote, the design of experiments (DoE) guru at Motorola, taught me how much fun process improvement could be when he taught statistical process control (SPC) and DoE with card and other tricks. Charlie Johnson, COO of Cessna, gave me the support needed to transform the procurement process from traditional purchasing to a supply chain process that won *The Purchasing Magazine Medal of Professional Excellence Award*, which is awarded to one company each year. He exhibited the white-knuckle ride endurance that only a former Air Force Wild Weasel pilot could. John Ferrie, CEO of Smiths Industries Aerospace, consistently provided sage and gentle leadership style coaching to this hard driving yank in a U.K company, albeit sometimes in a thick Scottish brogue.

So many people contributed nuggets of wisdom and knowledge. Although maybe none of them were a mother lode individually, in totality they provided pragmatic answers to the eternal business leadership question: "What are you really going to do today to make this quarter's numbers and to set us up to be and stay competitive next year and the year after and the year after?" I sincerely hope I have added a nugget or two to each reader's leadership toolkit.

A Special Thanks to Our Editor and Publisher

Bill and Mike want to express a special thanks to our editor, Carolyn Lea, and publisher, Drew Gierman. We worked closely with both of these individuals over several months. Clearly, they contributed much, and we learned a great deal from them. We want to say a sincere, "Thanks to both of you."

ABOUT THE AUTHORS

William B. Lee was Professor of Management Practice for several years in the Jesse H. Jones Graduate School of Management at Rice University, Houston, Texas. He also held positions at Rice as Associate Dean of Executive Education and Director of Energy Programs. Bill also spent ten years on the faculty of the College of Business Administration at the University of Houston and was chair of the Department of Systems and Operations Management. He holds a Ph.D. in Business Administration from the University of North Carolina at Chapel Hill, an MBA from Rollins College, and a BSEE from Vanderbilt University. Bill has had careers in academia, industry, and consulting. He is the author of over seventy-five books, articles, and academic presentations. His research and teaching interests are in global supply chain management, primarily for large, complex companies. Bill and his wife, Jane, live and work in Houston and Galveston Island, Texas. Bill can be reached at wbleephd@ymail.com

Michael Katzorke is a business process improvement professional with more than twenty-five years of leadership experience in operations, materials, manufacturing, quality, systems, and strategic supply chain management. He served as vice president of supply chain management with Smiths Aerospace. Prior to joining Smiths in December 2003, he was with Cessna Aircraft Company as senior vice president of supply chain management and with AlliedSignal as corporate director of supply chain management.

Mike has consulted in a broad spectrum of industries and organizations in both public and private sectors and is currently president of Bryce Consulting Group. He has participated and led in the application of Malcolm Baldrige, lean, and six sigma tools in integrated improvement processes at three *Fortune* 100 companies.

Mike is a graduate of the University of Utah and is a private pilot. He co-authored *Straight to the Bottom Line*™, an executive supply chain book. He has also served on the board of directors for Mid-America Manufacturing Technology Center and has been active in the Center for Advanced Purchasing Studies (CAPS), the Institute for Supply Management (ISM), and the Association for Manufacturing Excellence (AME). Mike and his wife, Julie, live Scottsdale, Arizona and Hatch, Utah. Mike may be reached at www.bryceconsultinggroup.com or at mkatzorke@att.net.

Web Added Value™

Free value-added materials available from
*the Download Resource Center at **www.jrosspub.com***

At J. Ross Publishing we are committed to providing today's professional with practical, hands-on tools that enhance the learning experience and give readers an opportunity to apply what they have learned. That is why we offer free ancillary materials available for download on this book and all participating Web Added Value™ publications. These online resources may include interactive versions of material that appears in the book or supplemental templates, worksheets, models, plans, case studies, proposals, spreadsheets and assessment tools, among other things. Whenever you see the WAV™ symbol in any of our publications it means bonus materials accompany the book and are available from the Web Added Value™ Download Resource Center at www.jrosspub.com.

Downloads available for *Leading Effective Supply Chain Transformations: A Guide to Sustainable World-Class Capability and Results* consist of a supply chain leadership checklist, slides describing both an effective sales and operations planning and a demand forecasting implementation process, a supply chain people-development process, and outlines of comprehensive supply chain and project management education and training programs.

MACRO TRANSFORMATIVE ISSUES AND SUPPLY CHAIN DISRUPTIONS

> *It is not the biggest, nor the strongest,*
> *nor the most intelligent that will survive.*
> *It is the species most adaptable to change.*
> — Charles Darwin

Why start with the big picture? Why not just jump right into the meat of the matter? Why worry about macro issues and supply chain disruptions? We have a job to do — so let's get on with it! After all, when we have a problem don't we just roll up our sleeves, wrestle the problem to the ground, and fix it? As some say (or act as if they believe), "ready, fire, aim."

As you read the book, you will probably see snippets of our disdain for this approach. Why? Well, we happen to be analytical people. How would you like to visit a physician who prescribes surgery and/or medication before he or she has even taken the time to diagnose and understand your problem?

We have all heard jokes like *to a surgeon, cutting can fix anything* or *to a chiropractor, manipulation can fix anything* or *to a psychologist, everything's mental.* These jokes are, of course, not fair to those professionals, particularly the good ones, but don't we have the same sort of phenomenon with supply chains? Some will advocate that *lean can fix everything* or that *everyone needs to do six sigma.* Again, we do not want to disparage the advocates of those techniques, just as

> *Diagnose before you prescribe!*

we do not want to disparage surgeons or chiropractors or psychologists. It is just that we need to take a longer, more analytical look at our supply chain problems and not just jump in with the latest buzzword. Paraphrasing an old saying: "Have tools, will travel." As you probably can guess, that is one of the reasons why companies have so much trouble with their supply chains.

So, from where did we come, and how did we get here? Supply chain management has been around for millennia, but not by that name, of course. Let's examine some brief history as a way of setting the stage for the book. This chapter will focus particularly on transformative issues as we consider from where we have come. Chapter 2 will focus on how do we know we have problems and how can we diagnose them? Chapter 3 deals with how to convince the organization that we need to change. Further chapters will dive deeply into the problems and focus on how to fix them.

DRAMATIC CHANGE

In the past, to be an executive of an American company, you could stay in the United States and had only to be fluent in English. The same was true of executives in Dutch, Japanese, or Australian companies. This is no longer the case. Key executives of global companies today need two or three languages and global mobility. It is not unusual for executives to make multiple around-the-world trips in a single year. (At one point in his consulting career, Bill Lee had platinum frequent flyer cards simultaneously on three airlines — he is not proud of that; it is just a fact!)

Time has become a competitive weapon. The level of global competition demands that organizations be quick, agile, and flexible. In the United States alone, thousands of new consumer products are introduced annually and taken quickly around the world. We see the same brands and even some of the same stores in Abu Dhabi, Acapulco, Amsterdam, Atlanta, and Auckland. The Gap is a global brand. A Coca-Cola is the same whether it is in Cairns, Cairo, Caracas, Chicago, or Copenhagen. Virtually the only difference in a Toyota in Toronto or Tasmania is that one drives on the right and the other on the left.

> *It's a cliché to say that dramatic change has occurred and that this change is accelerating.*

Power in the supply chain has shifted downstream toward the consumer. Couple quick-response capabilities with enormous product variety and you have the makings of the customer as king or queen. One might even say that the old virtue of listening to your customer has again become fashionable. The customer pays the fiddler and calls the tune. All companies face increasingly fickle customers and markets that keep changing at lightning speed.

Wal-Mart is a prime example of listening to the customer coupled with fast response. Witness Wal-Mart's explosive growth in the United States and now increasingly in other countries. Executives at Wal-Mart credit their e-business and supply chain capabilities for a substantial portion of this growth. Wal-Mart today certainly is one of the most customer-focused and information-enabled companies in the world.

When embracing a customer-focused, quick-response strategy, you must be very good at the basics, the nuts and bolts, of running a business. To understand this, just look at the current business press to see the number of companies that have stumbled at e-commerce. The supply chain is the Achilles heel of e-commerce.

A SHIFT IN COMPETITION

All this change has caused a shift in the basis of competition. Whereas in the past, most of an item's cost was in manufacturing and upstream, today much of the cost is added after the item is committed to production. For example, inventory today is widely viewed as stated by one executive: "Inventory is the result of lack of information coupled with incompetence." Often, the very fact that a company *has* inventory on its books is viewed as a negative. Inventory is a cost — even though it shows up as an asset on the balance sheet. Inventory consumes working capital, which costs money. Inventory consumes storage facilities and transportation capability, which cost money. Inventory is damaged or becomes obsolete, which costs money. In short, as the cost basis is shifting, inventory is being viewed widely as a negative.

If inventory is a cost, how do we reduce it without killing customer service? After all, the primary justification for inventory in many companies is to get the product closer in time and place to the customer. The simplistic answer is — *with information.* If we have better linkage and visibility into our customers' real needs (i.e., information), then we can plan to meet those needs, and we do not have to guess. We will have much more on this in subsequent chapters.

> *Inventory is the result of lack of information coupled with incompetence.*

With all this focus on customers and costs, companies and industries have tried to gain competitive advantage through mergers, acquisitions, and joint ventures. Daimler-Benz and Chrysler merged to capture the synergies of two well-run companies; but, oops, it did not work out as planned. British Petroleum bought Amoco and Arco to take cost out of the total supply chain; but we have not seen any independent analysis of whether it really worked. Brazil privatized its telecommunications industry because of high costs and lousy customer service; and that seemed to have worked — somewhat. Alcoa computerized its production and inventory control in order to link them more closely with global demand. Cemex from Mexico bought its way into the cement industry around the world and used its technology to establish a leading position, successfully, we believe. Motorola and Philips teamed up in a joint venture for cellular phones to enhance their joint competitive positions — and on and on.

In the global economy, businesses are increasingly forced to shift away from merely having a presence in different countries. The traditional multinational is a national company with foreign subsidiaries. These subsidiaries are outposts from the parent company. There is no question about a subsidiary's national origin. Many companies doing international business today are still organized as traditional multinationals, but this mode of operation is no longer sufficient.

The transformation into global companies has been underway for years, and it is moving fast. The products or services may be the same, but the structure is becoming fundamentally different. In a global company there is only one economic unit — the world. Selling, servicing, public relations, and legal affairs might be local, but planning, research, finance, marketing, pricing, and management are conducted with a focus on the world market. A German company, for instance, might make a critical component for all of its products worldwide in one Asian location. It might have organized product development for the entire world in three places and manufacturing in four. For this company, national boundaries have become largely irrelevant.

POLITICIANS ARE BEHIND (AS USUAL)

You can probably tell that we are not enamored by politicians — anywhere, at any level, doing anything!

Global companies are ahead of the politicians. The global company, however, must adapt to certain controls by national governments, but these adaptations are exceptions to policies and practices decided for worldwide markets and technologies. Successful global companies see themselves as separate, nonnational entities, operating as much as possible without regard to national borders.

Governments get in the way. Laws and regulations drive increased product proliferation and costs around the world. Conforming to different product standards in both the United States and Europe is still a major headache to many companies. Labeling requirements between Argentina and Chile might require changing only a few words; nevertheless, it adds complexity and cost to the supply chain and the consumer ultimately pays.

TRANSFORMATIVE ISSUES

Supply chain management has seen transformations in the past. Let's start about a hundred years ago. Remember Eli Whitney? How about Frederick W. Taylor? Henry Ford? Many people will recall them, at least vaguely, but of course not personally.[1]

Eli Whitney is most famous for his invention of the cotton gin. For our purposes, however, consider that he generally is credited with inventing the concept of the *interchangeability of parts*. None of us remembers Taylor either because he was around about a hundred years ago, but he had a major transformative impact on "the works," as it was called then, in his search for ways of improving industrial efficiency. Taylor generally is acknowledged as the father of scientific management with his ideas of the one best way to perform work. This was an early predecessor of what we today call supply chain management. Taylor's scientific management consisted of four principles:

- Replace rule-of-thumb work methods with methods based on a scientific study of the tasks.
- Scientifically select, train, and develop each employee rather than passively leaving them to train themselves.
- Provide detailed instruction and supervision of each worker in the performance of that person's discrete task.
- Divide work nearly equally between managers and workers, so that the managers apply scientific management principles to planning the work and the workers actually perform the tasks.

The ideas of Whitney and Taylor were keys to Henry Ford's assembly line. Not only did Taylor lay out how to determine the one best way to perform work, but he also was a proponent of the standardization of parts. Ford used both of these concepts in the design of his assembly line. Furthermore, Ford was an advocate of an *integrated* supply chain. For his Model T automobile, he mined the ore, turned the ore into steel, shaped and machined the steel into parts, grew the rubber for the tires, and assembled the automobile in his own factory. This was the first great modern integrated industrial enterprise — assuming we do not count the Egyptians and the pyramids.

Many other developments occurred during the mid-1900s, but let's pick up in the 1960s when Joe Orlicky coined the term *materials requirements planning* (MRP). MRP was an idea whose time had come with the widespread acceptance in industry of the IBM System 360 series of computers. The 360 was the first of the modern generation of computers, with (relatively) large storage capacity and (relatively) fast processing speed — although they do not seem large or fast today.

Joe Orlicky worked for IBM and saw, perhaps more clearly than any other person, how the computer could be used to manage the supply chain. He focused primarily on dependent-demand materials that are a characteristic of manufacturing. If, for example, someone wants to make a finished product that requires multiple components, then a computer can calculate the gross requirements, subtract the available on-hand and on-order quantities, and determine the net requirements for each item in the assembly. Furthermore, it can schedule backward from the need date of the finished product through all levels of the bill of material to the raw material. MRP works off the basic questions of manufacturing:

- What are we going to make, when, and how many (or how much)?
- What does it take to make the products?
- What do we have in stock and on order?
- What do we need to get, or what are we missing?

But, we already know all this, don't we?

Joe's concept took off like crazy. Soon, every progressive manufacturing company was implementing MRP. Although companies still use the basics of MRP today, people soon realized the limitations of Joe's concepts and began adding to them.

One of those people, Oliver Wight, coined the term *manufacturing resource planning* (MRPII) in the 1970s. As the story goes, Ollie did not like acronyms, so he simply added the Roman numeral II to Joe's MRP. Ollie's belief was that the ideas, concepts, tools, and techniques of MRP could be used to plan and control all the resources of a manufacturing firm. Hence the term *manufacturing resource planning* was born. In Ollie's thoughts, the manufacturing resources included **all** the resources of a manufacturing enterprise, including the human resources, facilities and equipment resources, financial resources, sales and marketing resources, and so on. Unfortunately, people misunderstood, as they often do. They saw the term *manufacturing* and immediately thought that MRPII referred *only* to the manufacturing *function* and *not* to the manufacturing *enterprise*. Thus, in the 1980s, the term *enterprise resource planning* (ERP) began to get widespread recognition — as it still does today.

	PLANS	NO PLANS
FOOLS	Second Place	Last Place
GENIUSES	Winners	Next-to-Last Place

Figure 1.1. Fools, Geniuses, Plans, and No Plans.

In addition, the 1980s spawned a whole new alphabet soup of new ideas such as just-in-time (JIT) and total quality management (TQM) which came out of Japanese manufacturing enterprises. Arguably, these too are the result of a natural evolution of management thinking — although they are not generally traced directly to Orlicky's MRP logic.

Along came the 1990s, and another term became popular — *supply chain management* (SCM). SCM is somewhat the same, but essentially different from its predecessors outlined above. Although SCM uses some of the same logic as MRP/MRPII/ERP/etc., the essential difference is that SCM goes beyond the individual enterprise and includes the entire supply chain from customers' customers to suppliers' suppliers. As we say, SCM goes from digging minerals out of the ground to someone's finished Ferrari. It goes from drilling an oil well to putting gasoline in your new Ferrari. As we say, womb to tomb, cradle to grave, and alpha to omega.

FOOLS, GENIUSES, PLANS, AND NO PLANS

Ted Turner has quoted T. Boone Pickens as having said, "A fool with a plan can outsmart a genius with no plan."[2] Neither Ted nor Boone was referring to leaders of supply chains, but the quote can well be applied to such individuals. We both have known fools who had strong supply chain plans and other fools who had no supply chain plans. We also have known geniuses with plans and geniuses without plans. Speculate on who wins (Figure 1.1)!

Guess what? Boone was right! Fools with plans for their supply chains can beat geniuses without plans, but we also will say that geniuses with strong supply chain plans easily can beat fools with strong supply chain plans.

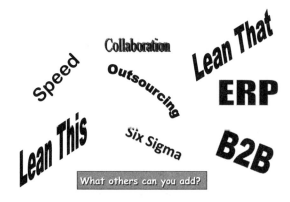

Figure 1.2. Terms We Hear about Supply Chain Management.

In some respects, this is the essence of this book: how to develop strong plans for managing supply chains — plans that can be implemented by either fools or geniuses. We prefer geniuses, but seldom see them, perhaps because there are so few of them. Yet at the same time, there are few fools running supply chains, either. Most people in those positions are neither fools nor geniuses — just ordinary people who perhaps are just slightly smarter than the average. The most successful of them have a vision and know where they are going. Furthermore, as the quote from Darwin at the beginning of this chapter implies, the survivors will be those who best adapt to change.

SILVER BULLETS

So, if we need a vision and we need to adapt, what do we do? As is the case with too many of our solutions to problems, people seek simplicity. We are all in favor of simplicity; nevertheless, people sometimes go overboard and seek the silver bullet.

So what do we hear about supply chains and supply chain plans? Figure 1.2 illustrates some of the key ideas that we hear — usually as silver-bullet solutions.

Do you remember the Lone Ranger, a long-running fixture on radio, television, and other media back in the 1940s, 1950s, and 1960s?[3] The character, a masked Texas Ranger in the American Old West, galloped about righting injustices with the aid of his clever, Native American sidekick Tonto. Departing on his white horse Silver, the Lone Ranger would famously shout, "Hi-yo, Silver, away!" as he raced out of the picture and on to the next adventure.

The Lone Ranger used silver bullets in his guns. We thus have the expression of the silver bullet to indicate a *single* solution for a problem, even though the problem might be very complex and have many elements to its complexity. Silver bullet has become an expression that is derided as being simplistic and out of touch with a complex reality.

Figure 1.2 illustrates some silver bullets for supply chains. Some people say the solution to supply chain issues is *lean* management. The idea of lean originated with the Toyota production system. We are all in favor of companies practicing lean management. Others say that we must *collaborate* within and between the various functions, geographies, and enterprises that comprise the supply chain — and that is true. Enterprise resource planning (ERP) software and business-to-business (B2B) software, although important and useful, are also put forth as solutions.

> One of our favorite thoughtless expressions is used often by software suppliers who label their software as *solutions*. Nonsense! Software is software. It can only be a solution when it is applied with intelligence to a problem. The key here is the word *intelligence* — but more on that later.

How about the terms *speed*, *outsourcing*, and *six sigma*? Have you heard them? Well, they too often are put forth as the silver bullets to solve all our supply chain problems. Now, please do not think that we are deriding the terms in Figure 1.2. We are not. We simply want our readers to understand that people will use a variety of ideas, concepts, tools, and techniques in managing their supply chains. None of these, per se, is the solution to supply chain issues.

So, why do people keep looking for the silver bullet? We think one reason is because a number of transformative issues have driven supply chain management in the past decade and perhaps longer. Companies are significantly affected by these transformative issues, most of which they have no control over. However, we all must deal with these issues or closely allied ones. They affect our decision-making processes as well as the outcomes of our decisions.

The remainder of this chapter addresses these transformative issues. Then, the rest of the book addresses how companies should be (and how some are) transforming themselves.

SO, WHY IS TRANSFORMATION NECESSARY TODAY?

MRP/MRPII and other associated ideas truly were transformative in the history of management thought. Many changes have resulted and many improvements were made, but time marches on, and we continually get new and better ideas (illustrated in Figure 1.3). MRP was invented in the 1960s, MRPII came along in the 1970s, ERP was introduced in the 1980s, and SCM made its debut in the 1990s.

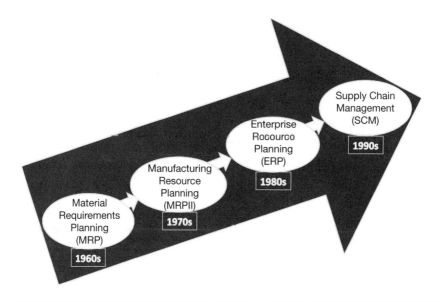

Figure 1.3. Evolution of Supply Chain Management.

Why is SCM transformation needed today? We think that it is a function of people looking for a silver bullet and thus not understanding the complexity of supply chain management. They put forth the silver bullets in lieu of a comprehensive understanding of the issues. Before we go on, let's pause and ensure clarity in some of our definitions:

> The supply chain begins with customers' customers and ends with suppliers' suppliers. The supply chain represents the linkage among all elements of material flow, information flow, and cash flow.

Many (including ourselves) consider the term *supply chain*, however, to be a misnomer for essentially two reasons. First, the word *supply* many times causes people to think automatically of suppliers and hence to think only of one side of the linkage. Some have proposed the term *demand chain* to illustrate the primacy of the demand (or customer) linkages. Others have proposed the term *value chain* to emphasize the flow of value in the linkages. However, although we believe the term *supply chain* is too restrictive, it nevertheless is the accepted terminology, and we will not mess with it in this book. We will continue to use supply chain in our writing and speaking while acknowledging its limitations. Our own personal preference is Porter's term *value chain* which we believe actually is the most descriptive,[4] but that term never really caught on, except perhaps in some academic circles. Second, the word *chain* many times causes people to think automatically of a linear series of links in the relationships. We often use the saying, "A chain is only as strong as its weakest link." This is true. However, the problem with the word *chain* is that it implies a one-to-one linear relationship, when the real metaphor is more like a web with multiple-to-multiple relationships along the supply chain. So, our definition is:

> *Supply chain management is the process through which customers' needs are identified and met by developing, producing, and distributing products and services. Customer-focused supply chain management begins with assisting a company's customers to better serve their customers and to better compete against their competitors. The same is true from the ultimate customer (and the recycling or return process) back to the ultimate supplier.*

The real measure of success in supply chain management is how well the *entire* chain works. Companies continuously try to improve their performance, which has led to a multitude of attempts to accomplish this.

A number of transformative issues have driven supply chain management in the past decades. Companies are affected significantly by these transformative issues, over which most have no direct control. However, companies must deal with these issues — they affect their decision making and the competitiveness of their businesses. So, what are some of these issues with which we will deal in this book?

- Globalization
- The global idea market
- Giant wealth transfer
- Wall Street's short-term focus
- Innovation

Transformative Issue One: Globalization

It is the same Coca-Cola, Nestlé, Volkswagen, and Sony anywhere you go. You can walk into a Lone Star Steak House in Australia and an Outback Steakhouse in Texas. Boeing and Airbus sell and support their airplanes all over the world. Consumer fads travel, seemingly in days, around the world, but how can companies keep their global supply chains in sync with this change? This leads to the deeper implications of globalization: namely, the problem of balancing — balancing demand with supply with financial issues — across geographies, functions, and even businesses.

Globalization has been a major transformative issue for companies with worldwide supply chains. Globalization also is a major transformative issue for an individual's life style. Consider this little snippet of everyday life:

She drives home through the heavy Mumbai traffic, thinking about her job with a Swiss bank. She listens to music by a Russian composer played by a Canadian orchestra with an Austrian conductor. She loves her European car, but does not know that it was made using Brazilian steel, Argentinean leather, and Japanese electronics. Her tires are from Italy. Her suit was designed by a French designer and made in Hong Kong from Italian silk. Her shoes are British. Her watch is Swiss. Her shawl is New Zealand wool.

At home, she steps onto her Persian carpet and sits down at a Danish table. She turns on her Korean television and watches the world news on CNN International. She starts a load of clothes washing in her new Swedish washing machine. She pours a glass of Australian wine into Irish crystal and prepares to go out to a Chinese restaurant to discuss a deal with an American energy services company. Throughout all of this, she never thinks about the global supply chains on which her lifestyle is based. Frankly, she could care less!

Sound familiar? Sure — the details will vary, but the essence is there. We are all affected by globalization. It is not just some far-off, abstract term that economists and politicians use. It is real. It is here. And we all know it, whether we like it or not.

Information technology, communications, transportation, and the *idea market* have enabled globalization. The old business model was "the big eat the small." Today's business model is "the fast eat the slow." Innovation in information is just beginning, even though we have seen gigantic strides in the last four decades or so. To talk about the rapid advances of the Internet and e-commerce is a cliché today.

The Internet is just another hot topic in a more general and substantive subject. That is, how can companies use information technology, including the Internet, to enable integration all along the global supply chain — from suppliers' suppliers to customers' customers — be they in Abu Dhabi, Amarillo, Amsterdam, or Auckland? Yet, focusing only on the Internet is just the tip of the iceberg. Integration still depends on people operating with effective business processes *and* information technology.

Global information technology and communications enable companies to seek out the most cost-effective labor, wherever it may be located in the world. Product design can take place 24 hours a day simultaneously in the United States, India, and Scotland through the use of computerized databases, satellite communications, and engineering protocols.

> *Speed kills the competition.*
>
> *Information enables speed.*

"Engineering never sleeps," remarked a senior executive in a company where speed to market with new products is a key competitive advantage. At times videoconferencing is used with minimal inconvenience whenever there is a need for face-to-face conversations.

Of course, great distances separate markets around the globe and generally add considerable complexity to managing the global company. Jet lag is real — a common phenomenon faced daily by thousands of executives. Global networks of interconnected airline schedules make planning easy, even if the travel is not. You can even keep your frequent flyer miles on your favorite (read, *least objectionable*!) airline.

As much as we like to talk about global communications and transportation, the fact remains that, as the old song goes, it is still "a long way to Tipperary." (DHL, FedEx, and UPS can deliver a package quickly anywhere in the world and could deliver even quicker absent governments' customs regulations and bureaucracies.)

Transformative Issue Two: The Global Idea Market

There is nothing mysterious about this phenomenon. In the long run, the globalization of the idea market perhaps will do as much as anything to increase supply chain effectiveness and efficiency throughout the world. The globalization of supply chains has significantly increased the rate of technology and information transfer. The transfer of new ideas among companies throughout the world has also greatly speeded the productivity increases necessary for global competitiveness. Ideas rub off among competitors in the same industry, among suppliers and customers, and even among nonrelated companies. Executives throughout the world read the same business press, attend the same conferences and trade shows, and even talk to each other on airplanes.

Consider the Japanese automobile companies. Witness the effect that these companies had in the 1980s when they moved into the United States. Prior to that movement, U.S. companies were able to discount many Japanese manufacturing techniques as being "unique to the Japanese culture and won't work here." That argument has long since been debunked.

Information systems linkages within companies and with their networks of relationships make much of the global economy work. B2B (business-to-business) e-commerce quickly gained plausibility as a significant driver of productivity increases. At first, this was limited largely to giant companies setting up websites to purchase automobile components, steel, and chemicals; but this changed as smaller firms combined their buying power through third-party enablers of e-commerce and did it themselves.

But everything is not, and will not be, information enabled. All is not totally rosy for the techno-geeks of the world. National and ethnic cultures and languages add to the complexity of communications. Knowing not to show the bottom of one's shoe in the Middle East is still essential to good communications. Much of the world subscribes to differing business practices. The importance of family and relationships in much of the world still drives how business is conducted. Simply being allowed to do business in many countries requires some type of joint venture or partnership with a local company.

Complex networks of customers, joint ventures, partnerships, third-party alliances, suppliers, and so forth are now common ways of dealing with these different business practices. Still, coordinating performance and aligning objectives among these different entities is a major issue. Simply put, even with the vast array of enablers of globalization, coordination is still a frightfully complex endeavor.

Worldwide brand names, super-efficient production and logistics, strong management, and articulate commitment to shareholder value are the definitions of excellence in today's marketplace. Let's look at some examples. Some are thriving. Some are not.

We generally think of supply chains beginning with mining, agriculture, and drilling for oil and gas. These products move along the value chain to finished products such as automobiles, clothing, food, and plastics, but where are the drivers? What drives global trade among the United States, Europe, Japan, China, India, and so forth? Additionally, trade flows both ways — from the U.S. to China and vice versa.

Companies have moved manufacturing to China and India to gain lower costs. Mattel has a constant flow of toys from China to the United States that is driven by designs produced in the United States for U.S. consumers. A well-known Stanford Business School case study illustrated vividly, however, some of the problems and issues with these global supply chains with Mattel's recalls as the case focus.[5]

Addressing the entire global supply chain in the context of global market demand and supply is necessary. Companies, regardless of where they are located in the world, have learned that they must appropriately access a global supply base. The global idea market, however, is impacted significantly by how (and whether) intellectual property is protected and shared around the world. We all have heard stories concerning the rampant availability of knock-off consumer products (and, perhaps, have participated ourselves) — videos and movies, DVDs, clothing, ladies' handbags, and many more. As important as this is, the problem goes deeper than just knock-offs showing up in retail outlets. It concerns how intellectual property is viewed around the world — it is different depending on where you go and what is happening.

For example, governments might feel they have the most incentive to limit intellectual property rights if they perceive that heavy-handed firms use it to suppress competition and innovation that is built on a particular idea. Governments might consider that dominant firms are using their ideas to eliminate or at least to curtail their competitors — or governments might seek to limit intellectual property rights if their objective is to assist their own companies to grow and/or hire and train more of their country nationals. There could be all kinds of reasons for governments to allow piracy of intellectual property.

One of the authors was consulting several years ago with a high-tech medical equipment manufacturer that absolutely refused to sell or allow to be sold any of their advanced technologies in certain countries. The manufacturer knew that if it did, the technology would be stolen and used to their detriment. The result to no one's surprise, of course, was that the citizens of those countries did not get the benefits of the life-saving, advanced technologies on which the company had spent many years and a great deal of money. The manufacturer would sell only older, obsolete technologies to these countries.

The message here is that there really is a global idea market, but it works in different ways around the world.

Transformative Issue Three: Giant Wealth Transfer

All of this global trade has caused a giant wealth transfer among the countries of the world. The balance of payments is a concern for many countries. The balance of *international payments* is the value of all goods, services, capital loans, government aid, and payments — coming in and going out — from one country to another. The *current accounts* balance perhaps is the most widely cited statistic among those comprising the balance of international payments. Also, from a supply chain standpoint, the *merchandise trade* balance is important. However, do not forget the *services trade* balance, which is also a part of the current accounts balance.

For the United States, the U.S. government keeps track of the various statistics in the balance of international payments. These statistics are published in various outlets, including the Internet and *The Economist* magazine. The statistics in Table 1.1 were published in the May 9, 2009 issue of *The Economist* along with those from over 30 other countries. Some statistics to notice are as follows:

- The United States has run a negative (i.e., more merchandise coming in than going out) trade balance month after month for years. The same is true for Britain and the Euro area. These countries have eviscerated their manufacturing bases.
- Japan, Germany, and China typically run positive (i.e., more merchandise going out than coming in) trade balances. These countries

Table 1.1. Trade and Current Account Balances

Country or Area	Trade Balance Latest 12 Months (U.S. $B)	Current Account Balance	
		Latest 12 Months (U.S. $B)	Estimated 2009 GDP (%)
United States	−$761.0 (Feb 2009)	−$673.3 (Q4 2008)	−3.3
Japan	+$21.0 (Feb 2009)	+$131.8 (Feb 2009)	+1.6
Britain	−$163.1 (Feb 2009)	−$44.6 (Q4 2008)	−1.7
Germany	+$234.6 (Feb 2009)	+$206.2 (Feb 2009)	+4.4
Euro area	−$59.4 (Feb 2009)	−$150.9 (Feb 2009)	−1.0
China	+$316.9 (Mar 2009)	+$400.7 (Q2 2009)	+6.9
India	−$109.0 (Mar 2009)	−$37.5 (Q4 2008)	−3.0

have strong manufacturing bases and particularly have targeted export industries to keep their economies strong.

- India, although its economy is growing strongly, has not developed its manufacturing base to the extent that, say, China has.

Notice also that the current account balance typically (although not always) follows the trade balance into positive or negative territory.

Countries (primarily Western) that have traditionally had a strong manufacturing base have transferred much of that capability to others. These countries have moved from primarily being manufacturing and technology economies to being primarily service economies. What specifically has been happening? Are some countries simply gradually spending their inherited national wealth? (As American authors who have researched, consulted, and held executive positions in manufacturing companies, we are distressed at what has happened to the American tradition of manufacturing. We think there is some linkage with this point to our next transformative issue, Wall Street's short-term demands.)

Transformative Issue Four: Wall Street's Short-Term Demands

Short-term demands by investors (dare we call them that or should we just call them *short-term speculators*?) have distorted decision making within companies. For example, both authors consulted with a large, well-known company and visited a number of their business units. We were told, almost unanimously, by the division heads that they would not take needed supply chain actions because the payoffs would come too late for them to "make their numbers." Clearly, this issue has transformed how companies view needed investments.

Quarter-by-quarter decision making just does not make sense. Short-term decision making drives long-term mayhem. One CEO told us that he must see a

6-month payback before making a major decision. The problem is that long-term transformative changes sometimes take much longer than that to play out.

> Bill Lee is an outside director on the board of directors of a large privately held, family-run business (not his own family). Before he and the chairman of the board came to agreement on whether Bill should join the board, a long discussion was held on the value of public versus private ownership of large businesses. We found ourselves to have a high degree of alignment that being able to take a long-term view of decisions allows management and the board to much more effectively run the business. Simply put, we do not have to put up with Wall Street analysts (so-called) who want to see quarter-by-quarter results. The authors feel strongly that this short-term focus is one of the main drivers of the silver-bullet syndrome about which we spoke earlier. Management too often simply is looking for that one thing that will transform their supply chains.

Transformative Issue Five: Innovation

A 2009 cover article in *Business Week* explored innovation, primarily in the United States, and concluded:[6]

> *During the last decade, U.S. innovation has failed to realize its promise — and that may explain America's economic woes. 'We live in an era of rapid innovation.'*

We're sure you've heard that phrase, or some variant of it, over and over again. Innovation is multifaceted. Innovation occurs in product technology, manufacturing process technology, business process technology, and so forth. For example, try to think of all the different advances in technology that went into today's communications capability. Consider technology and innovation that moved capability for the past 50 years or so and included general electronics, computers, telephones, space technology and satellites, and many others. All of these, together, contributed.

But *innovation* is different from *technology*. Companies typically describe the two terms somewhat as follows. Clearly, different companies and people will use different definitions, but these are very descriptive:

- *Technology* is what we know. It is the know-how, basic and applied science, mathematics, and engineering to make things work better, easier, faster, and/or cheaper.
- *Innovation* is how the technology is applied. It is harnessing the imagination, originality, inventiveness, creativity, imagination, ingenuity, and energy of people to apply technology. The objective of innovation

is to break new ground and to meet the needs and to solve the problems of customers, processes, and employees.

There have always been skeptics. Maybe *Business Week* is one of those skeptics?

Yet technology and innovation leadership is often suboptimal — optimizing at the wrong levels — optimizing subprocesses — suboptimizing the business:

- Understand the necessity for product strategy to be supported by the appropriate supply chain strategy.
- Appreciate the need to integrate beyond the organization (i.e., customers and suppliers) for the supply chain to be totally effective.

For example, the first oil well was drilled by Colonel Edwin Drake near Titusville, Pennsylvania in August 1859. The well was 59 feet deep and produced 25 barrels a day which sold for $20 a barrel (over $450 in today's money). Consider today's oil and gas wells that are drilled in thousands of feet of water and then thousands of feet underneath the water. Clearly, innovation and technology beyond one company's capabilities were required for these developments.

WHAT IS HAPPENING IN TODAY'S MARKETPLACE

We generally think of supply chains stretching from mining, agricultural, and oil and gas companies to retail establishments and the ultimate consumer. The chain includes companies in basic industries, industrial companies, and consumer products companies, among others. The annual *Fortune* Global 500 issue makes for interesting reading on this subject. Of course, these rankings are based on the magazine's definitions of *industries* plus their classification of individual companies into these industries. This can be tricky. For example, Mitsubishi is identified as a trading company, but the company clearly also manufactures in several industries, not the least of which is automobiles. The same is true of several others on the list.

Different industries, of course, will have different supply chain characteristics and different operating philosophies, but they all have certain things in common. One example of a global supply chain is Royal Dutch/Shell. Go anywhere in the world, practically, and you can buy gasoline from a Shell station. Royal Dutch/Shell is big. It has about 100,000 employees. Royal Dutch/Shell operates in over 100 countries around the world. It explores for and produces oil worldwide, refines oil in more than 40 refineries, transports crude oil and its products, and sells gasoline through about 45,000 gas stations in over 90 countries. Competitive prices and widespread product availability are its keys to success in the consumer markets.[7]

Now consider the global fashion industry — nimbleness and lightening speed are important because fashions and fads can change overnight. The typical item takes several months to be designed, presold, sourced, and manufactured. Yet quick response (in days or, at most, weeks) on hot items is a key to success, which obviously requires an ability to listen intently to the voice of the customer and then to translate that message throughout the supply chain without missing a beat. If the supply chain is managed well, then fashion houses can respond quickly to an increasingly short product life cycle.

One popular example is Zara, which has become one of the world's preeminent popular-priced fashion retailers with stores all over the world.[8] The following quote from 1904 is in the Zara case study and illustrates one of the reasons for Zara's success:

Fashion is the imitation of a given example and satisfies the demand for social adaptation. The more an article becomes subject to rapid changes of fashion, the greater the demand for cheap products of its kind.
— Georg Simmel, *Fashion* (1904)

Food and beverages also are global industries. Nestlé, Mars, and Coca-Cola are known worldwide for their products. New Zealand lamb and Australian beef are eaten throughout the Middle East. We drink coffee made from beans grown in Brazil, Africa, Columbia, and elsewhere. French wine is sold alongside wines from California, Chile, and even Texas. Foster's, Budweiser, Heineken, and Kirin beers are global brands. We can eat fresh strawberries anywhere in the world at anytime of the year.

The automobile industry is another frequently cited example of global supply chains. The merger between Daimler-Benz and Chrysler was a seminal event a few years ago in the automobile industry, combining two of the largest players on the world stage. Chrysler was once thought of as one of the most innovative auto manufacturers in the world. Daimler-Benz, on the other hand, was cash rich and debt free at the time of the merger. In combination, they were in a position to put considerable pressure on the other top automobile companies as they consolidated internal operations, coordinated their product development processes, and leveraged global economies of scale. Today, we see that these objectives have not worked out at all! The merger was taken apart and, as of this writing, Chrysler is in bankruptcy and being bought by Italy's Fiat. We will see what happens next.

By no means was DaimlerChrysler the only event of its type. General Motors grew originally by buying other automobile companies. Ford purchased Jaguar and later Volvo's car unit. Today, mergers, acquisitions, and joint ventures seem to be a way of life in the car business. Unfortunately, so is bankruptcy.

In an article written several days after the bankruptcy of General Motors in 2009, Larry Lapide, a professor at the University of Massachusetts at Boston, made the following observation:[9]

> *Now that GM has declared bankruptcy, the post-mortem begins. A big problem may have been the misalignment of the supply chain and the corporate strategy.*

The supply chain and the corporate strategy are issues of paramount importance in most global industries, not just automobiles. The pressure to merge, or at least to form strategic joint ventures and alliances, is overwhelming. *In no industry do customers want to pay more or wait longer or settle for less than they can get elsewhere. Incremental approaches just will not suffice anymore.*

Regardless of the industry, we are seeing vast amounts of cross-border investment. Multinationals invest globally. The DaimlerChrysler combination is just one example of massive German investment abroad. Companies such as Mercedes, BMW, Hoechst, Siemens, and Bertelsmann are examples of other German companies that have invested heavily abroad.

Some have argued that German companies have been fleeing some of the highest labor costs in the world combined with high unemployment and excessive spending on social programs. In addition, German companies have been looking for large, dynamic markets such as the United States. Increasingly, if a company wants to be a player in a given market, it must invest and have a presence in that market. Yet, at the same time, Germany has geared its economy to the export trade. Go figure. Why?

The same is true in newly industrializing countries such as Brazil. Ford, General Motors, Volkswagen, and Fiat had Brazil all to themselves for a long time. Brazil's local content laws made importing cars uneconomical, and strict governmental controls made building new factories prohibitive. Now, however, all that has changed and other automobile companies have moved into Brazil.

Brazil's steel industry is another example. Brazil has all the ingredients for a world-class steel industry. Brazilian labor, energy, and iron ore are all extremely cheap and plentiful. The real winners will be global steel buyers as well as consumers who will benefit from cheaper durable goods such as appliances and automobiles.

The point: every industry has its stories. They are all globalizing, computerizing, focusing their supply chains on their customers, and improving the economics of doing business.

WHERE TO FROM HERE?

Where do we go from here in this study?

First, think about the customers. Delighting customers is the goal. Serving customers better than anyone else is the means. Identifying, meeting, and sometimes even creating customers' needs are important roles in most companies.

Focus on your customers' customers and your customers' customers' customers.

For consumer product companies such as Procter & Gamble or Unilever or Sony, their ultimate consumers purchase the product at a retail outlet. That retailer might be a mass merchandiser such as Wal-Mart in Boston or a small retail outlet in the suburbs of Buenos Aires or Beijing. For a giant energy company such as Exxon or Shell or BP, the consumer might fill up at tens of thousands of gas stations throughout the world.

This notion of customer focus has a deeper meaning, however, than just a focus on the ultimate consumer. Customer focus is the *total chain* of customers. Every company is someone's supplier and someone else's customer. The call is to help your customers serve their customers better — something we call focusing on your customers' customers.

Second, think about the supply chains that support the customers and the customers' customers. The supply chain is all about linkages, a very popular concept today — and for good reason. If competition is no longer company to company, but supply chain to supply chain, then the rallying cry must be: "My supply chain can beat your supply chain!" or "I had better take the weak links out of my chain."

The action is at the intersection of people, processes, and technologies. Supply chains run on all three. Leave out any one of them and you are in trouble. The profound issues lie in how to gain the synergies of knowledgeable and committed people, linking cooperatively with others in well-structured and well-designed business processes, and using appropriate information technologies.

Whether the products are consumer products or petroleum products, the concept is the same — linkages exist between successive entities in the chain. These linkages can be internal (e.g., between sales and manufacturing) or external (e.g., between different companies). The linkages are enabled electronically as companies increasingly use information to connect key supply chain activities.

Just look at Dell Computer. Global stock markets conduct a referendum daily on the relative performance of companies' supply chains. Michael Dell made his mark by devising a better way to build and sell computers, i.e., a better supply chain. He is now one of the world's richest people even though Dell has stumbled in the last several years.

> *Competition is no longer company to company, but supply chain to supply chain.*

Recognize, please, that citing companies in this way can be a dangerous practice for authors. From the writing by the authors to the reading by the customers, much can change. Please take this as a caveat to what we say here about specific companies.

WHAT IS THE RESULT OF THESE CHANGES?

One predictable result when dramatic changes occur is *hype*. We have surely seen it with the Internet, e-commerce, and globalization. All kinds of wild predictions have been put forward and repeated endlessly as if truth were already here. Is this just another management fad?

If it is a fad, then it certainly is a *value-added* fad. Management consultants and others are often accused (sometimes rightly so) of being solely interested in hyping the latest management fad. We certainly have seen a continuing flood of articles, books, and speeches about the topics that are the subject of this book, but what if they are a management fad?[10] How should executives react? Should they embrace and move headlong into e-commerce and globalization? Should they treat them with skepticism and even stay away? What to do?

We know historically that management ideas, trends, and fads have their own product life cycle. They were born, grew, matured, and declined. The successful ideas that became popular usually responded to some need, problem, or opportunity shared by many organizations. These ideas seemed to have been timed correctly for the marketplace need. We could say that the idea seed was scattered on fertile ground, took root as a fad or a buzzword, and grew into a mature addition to the managerial body of knowledge.

So, what happens to the ideas, concepts, tools, and techniques associated with fads when they are no longer fads? They do not just go away. The good ones become part of the mainstream body of knowledge. They become accepted practices — the eternal truths of management. Looking back on the long history of movements, the familiar adoption curve is well known and has been cited in all sorts of publications. The adoption curve can be used to understand the life cycles of fads and how different organizations respond to them. It was put forth as a generic concept and has been applied for countless purposes. We certainly have seen it applied to supply chains. Consider the following examples:

- *Innovator* organizations are always looking for new ideas. They have an ability to understand and apply new knowledge. Innovator organizations take pride in being in the forefront of new management ideas. In this case, the innovators have long since globalized their supply chains and gotten on the electronic communications bandwagon. They "get it."
- *Early adopter* organizations tend to be successful users of new ideas. They do not jump on every fad that comes along; however, they are quick to evaluate and apply new ideas that will be valuable to them. Early adopters can be called *fast-follower* organizations. They also "get it."
- *Early majority* organizations adopt new ideas just before the average organization. They participate actively in professional activities, but rarely are leaders. Early majority organizations tend to want to be shown why and how others have used the ideas successfully. They will "get it," but just more slowly.
- *Late-majority* organizations can be convinced, but they have to be shown. They always want to know who else in their industry is doing it. Late-majority organizations are definitely followers.
- *Laggard* organizations just do not seem to get the message. By the time they finally get around to adoption, the idea usually has been superseded and another one has come along. Laggard organizations have been described as *has-been* or *bankrupt* organizations.

A 2009 article in *The Economist* illustrates these points for the global automobile industry. The global automobile industry is an interesting industry — just compare GM with Toyota. GM probably deserved to die, but it was "too big to fail" and the U.S. government rescued it with massive amounts of taxpayer money. We will see how this works out in the next several years. But what about Toyota? Toyota is known as one of the world's best and most innovative manufacturing companies — certainly no GM. Much of Toyota's manufacturing capability is in the United States — the same as GM. Can it be said that Toyota's management beats GM's hands down? One certainly and easily could come to that conclusion. So, what did *The Economist* say? In protecting Detroit:[11]

> ... *they made it vulnerable to less-coddled competitors from abroad. By trying to keep their car industry big, America's leaders ended up*

preventing it from becoming good. There is a lesson in that which all governments would do well to learn.

One point from *The Economist* deserves to be repeated: "By trying to keep their car industry big, America's leaders ended up preventing it from becoming good." This conclusion plays into an opinion that the two authors have had for some time: namely, governments have no business messing with competitive markets to try to keep poorly performing companies afloat.

We tend to see the same companies consistently in the same category — although as we have seen, General Motors, for example, went from being an innovator to being a laggard. The challenge is that innovators need to continue to be innovators. Intel, HP, and Dell Computer have been recognized for many years as innovative companies. Innovators even seem to originate management ideas that become generally accepted, witness Dell's direct-sales model that was first introduced several years ago in their industry. Yet witness the later fall of Dell, based some would say on their slavish adherence to that business model. We will see if Dell can recover.

Sadly, laggards appear always to be laggards. They never seem to have a new idea. They evidently do not take new ideas seriously, especially those from outside their own organizations. For a list of laggards, one only has to look at the bottom of the annual *Fortune* list of most admired companies.[12] The companies at the bottom tend to lag in a whole host of areas, not the least of which are their approaches to management.

Successful organizations adapt ideas, trends, and fads into their own body of knowledge. They tend to be able to look at new ideas, cull what is important and adds value for them, and incorporate these ideas into their everyday practice of management. Some of you are in innovative and early adopter organizations. You are already on the bandwagon. For you, this book hopefully will help crystallize your thinking and perhaps give you a few new ideas or new ways of looking at things.

Some of you are in early majority organizations. For you, we will have examples from different companies and different industries so you can see others who are adopting these ideas, concepts, tools, and techniques. Some of you are in late-majority organizations. For you, we hope to convince you to begin looking around at what is already happening. Read the book carefully, read the citations and references, and think deeply about the very real possibility of being left out.

Some of you are in laggard organizations. For you, our best advice is to get another job! Your colleagues probably are not reading this book so we do not have much hope for your company.

We hope you will approach this book in this manner: not everything here will apply to you. Obviously, we think the ideas are sound and the tools and techniques work. You have to choose what is right for you.

So, where are we now and what is coming? Chapter 1 has set the stage with a brief discussion of how we got to where we are with supply chains and some macro issues with supply chains. Chapter 2 will discuss how companies can know they have problems with their supply chains. Chapter 3 will focus on convincing the organization that transformation is in order. Chapters 4, 5, and 6 will focus on essential elements of the supply chain transformation. Chapter 7 will bring everything back around with a discussion of initiatives for supply chain transformation.

CONCLUSION

Some key points from this chapter are worth remembering:

- Dramatic change is happening worldwide that is enabled by tremendous growth in information technology of all kinds: hardware, software, and communications. Information has enabled companies to globalize, gain efficiencies of integration, and focus better on the customer. To see what is happening, just pick up any issue of the business press. *The Wall Street Journal* has a front-page article on a related subject almost daily.
- The result of supply chain evolution is like any other innovation: there are innovators and early adopters as well as laggards, who still have not gotten these words of change. Our advice: run *toward* change, not *away* from it. Embrace new ideas, identify those that are applicable, and get on with the process of implementing them. That is the idea of this book — transforming your company's supply chains.

REFERENCES

1. See *Wikipedia* articles on Whitney, Taylor, and Ford for more information. Accessed May 2009.
2. "The Time 100: The World's Most Influential People," *Time* 2009 May 11.
3. See the *Wikipedia* article "The Lone Ranger" for more information. Accessed May 2009.
4. Porter, Michael E. *Competitive Advantage* 1985. New York: The Free Press.

5. Hoyt, David, Hau Lee, and Mitchell M. Tseng. *Unsafe for Children: Mattel's Toy Recalls and Supply Chain Management.* Stanford Graduate School of Business Case # GS-63, September 15, 2008.

6. Mandel, Michael. "Innovation Interrupted." *Business Week* 2009 June 15.

7. See www.shell.com. Accessed July 31, 2009.

8. Chemawat, Pankai and Jose Luis Nueno. *ZARA: Fast Fashion.* Harvard Business School Case # 9-703-497 Rev. December 21, 2006.

9. Lapide, Larry. "GM Was Out of Alignment." *Supply Chain Management Review* 2009 July/August.

10. Lee, William B. and Gary Skarke. "Value-Added Fads: From Passing Fancy to Eternal Truth." *Journal of Management Consulting* 1996 November.

11. "Detroitosarurus Wrecks." *The Economist* 2000 June 6.

12. See www.fortune.com. Accessed July 31, 2009.

2

HOW DO WE KNOW
WE HAVE PROBLEMS?

> *If all you've got is a hammer,*
> *nearly everything looks like a nail.*
> — Anonymous
> *There are no problems we cannot solve together,*
> *and very few we can solve by ourselves.*
> — Lyndon B. Johnson

These quotes make sense in light of the objectives of this chapter — how can a company know that it has problems? This chapter discusses using an assessment of the supply chain so a company does not just go around with a hammer looking for nails — and so employees can work together to solve supply chain problems.

In a word, an assessment of the supply chain can be conducted, but what will the assessment tell? Why is an assessment needed? How is it used? How about the following:

- To assess maturity in the journey toward business excellence
- To identify strengths, weaknesses, opportunities, and threats in supply chains
- To study the organization and supply chain processes
- To clarify supply chain responsibilities and accountabilities
- To benchmark against other businesses and world-class organizations

- To focus action plans
- To measure progress in supply chain improvement projects

A periodic (perhaps once a year), formal supply chain assessment is a useful exercise. But you ask: "Isn't that a lot of work? Doesn't it waste a lot of time? Don't I need a lot of data? Are the results of the assessment likely to be worth the effort?" These are fair questions. An assessment is a reasonable amount of work, and it needs some (but not too much) data. Based on experience, however, the results almost always justify the effort required.

Many times, a company does not discover that it has supply chain problems until customers start complaining and then defecting or until suppliers start being more difficult to deal with, complaining: "You're not paying me on time." Or maybe they say, "Quit jerking my schedule around." We prefer to head off situations like these.

To know if there are problems with the supply chains in a company, we recommend three major pieces of information: a framework for analysis, an appropriate assessment questionnaire, and a formal assessment. To answer the question *how do we know we have problems*, we begin with the framework for analysis.

A FRAMEWORK FOR ANALYSIS

A framework for analysis builds a model of the supply chain so that people can "see and feel" what the supply chain looks like. In our opinion, one of the best supply chain models has been developed by the Supply Chain Council (SCC).[1] As of this writing, over a thousand organizations are members of SCC. Many of them have contributed to the development of the SCC model (Supply Chain Operations Reference®, SCOR). Many organizations have used the model successfully to help understand and communicate about their supply chains. Others have used the framework as a basis for actually conducting the assessment.

Figure 2.1 illustrates our adaptation of the SCC model. This model is known as a process reference model, which integrates some well-known concepts of business process reengineering, benchmarking, and process measurement into a cross-functional framework. In our adaptive model, SCOR is composed of five basic components: plan, source, make, deliver, and return. SCOR begins with suppliers' suppliers. In our adaptation, beginning with suppliers' suppliers goes back to the original supply, which we define as digging ore out of the ground, drilling for oil and gas, and growing of plant and animal life. The model continues through customers and customers' customers on to the ultimate consumer. In the adaptation in Figure 2.1, OUR COMPANY is in the middle of the chain and

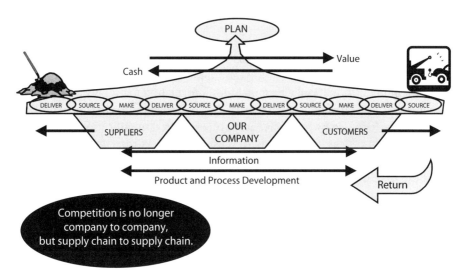

Figure 2.1. Supply Chain Operations Reference (SCOR®) Model. Adapted from www.supply-chain.org.

the assumption is that of the automobile industry, starting with digging for ore and ending with a new automobile. Recycling of the car after its useful life can be considered as the RETURN component of the model.

We have depicted the PLAN component as spanning the entire chain, from ore to automobile. However, practically speaking, that is not true. At best, at today's level of sophistication, PLAN spans OUR COMPANY and its immediate suppliers and customers. However, as supply chains get more sophisticated, we believe that PLAN will encompass more and more of the chain.

Although not in the formal SCOR model, we have depicted value moving from left to right and cash moving from right to left. In this view, value is created as the product moves from successive suppliers to customers and cash is returned. Clearly, the faster product moves through the supply chain, the faster cash also can move. This is a basic rationale for emphasis on inventory reduction — to speed up cash flow.

The cash-to-cash cycle is one of the most useful metrics for supply chain performance. Cash-to-cash means the time from cash being paid out to suppliers until cash is received from customers. This metric is *negative* for the best-in-class performers today — meaning, they receive cash *from* customers *before* they pay cash to suppliers; but they do not do this by stiffing suppliers or making them wait longer for their money. Suppose a company is in a make-to-order business in which it receives payment from customers before purchasing material and components from suppliers. Clearly, its requirements for working capital are significantly reduced.

In our adaptation of SCOR, we also have added information and product and process development as spanning the supply chain. Information is of several types. Planning information, which includes information for supply and demand management, has already been addressed, but information for product and process development — new products, new processes, and modifications of existing products and processes — should also be considered. Best-in-class product development, for example, requires companies to include both suppliers and customers in the development activities. We also should add that product development increasingly includes design for recycling.

We have also included a tag line: "Competition is no longer company to company, but supply chain to supply chain." This expression has become common among companies with leading supply chains. To many companies, we have said that the primary reason is: "Your suppliers are your suppliers because they can do things you cannot or do not want to do. Treat them accordingly as valued members of your supply chain." (We will have much more about this later when we argue for better treatment of suppliers.)

So, how can we use SCOR? SCOR assists in three tasks:

- To capture the *as is* state of supply chain processes and to derive the desired *to be* future states
- To quantify the supply chain operational performance of similar companies and establish internal targets based on best-in-class results
- To characterize the management practices and software solutions that result in best-in-class performance

As we have already mentioned, the SCOR model is composed of five components: plan, source, make, deliver, and return. SCOR contains the following for each of the five components:

- Standard descriptions of each of the five management processes
- A framework of relationships among the standard processes
- Standard metrics to measure process performance
- Management practices that produce best-in-class performance
- Standard alignment to features and functionality

Now, let's address each of the five components in turn:

PLAN. Plan the supply chain, including demand and supply:
- Balance resources with requirements and establish/communicate plans for the whole supply chain, including RETURN and the execution processes of SOURCE, MAKE, and DELIVER.

- Manage business rules, supply chain performance, data collection, inventory, capital assets, transportation, planning configuration, and regulatory requirements and compliance.
- Align the supply chain plans with financial plans.

SOURCE. Source stocked, make-to-order, and engineer-to-order products:
- Identify and select supply sources when not predetermined (as for engineer-to-order products).
- Manage business rules, assess supplier performance, and maintain data.
- Schedule deliveries; receive, verify, and transfer products; and authorize supplier payments.
- Manage inventory, capital assets, incoming products, supplier network, import/export requirements, and supplier agreements.

MAKE. Make make-to-stock, make-to-order, and engineer-to-order products:
- Schedule production activities, issue products, produce and test, package, stage product, and release product to DELIVER.
- Finalize engineering for engineer-to-order products.
- Manage rules, performance, data, in-process products (work in process), equipment and facilities, transportation, production networks, and regulatory compliance for production.

DELIVER. Order, warehouse, transport, and install all types of items:
- Manage order steps from processing customer inquiries and quotes to routing shipments and selecting carriers.
- Manage warehousing from receiving and picking product to loading and shipping product.
- Receive and verify product at customer site and install, if necessary.
- Invoice customers.
- Manage DELIVER business rules, performance, information, finished product inventories, capital assets, transportation, product life cycle, and import/export requirements.

RETURN. Return raw materials and receipt of returns of finished goods.
- RETURN defective items.
- RETURN maintenance, repair, and overhaul items.
- RETURN excess items.
- Facilitate and manage recycling of products.
- Manage RETURN business rules, performance, data collection, return inventory, capital assets, transportation, network configuration, and regulatory requirements and compliance.

The SCOR model goes much deeper, however, than the outline presented here. For example, the SCOR model goes to four levels:

- *Level 1* (the top level): defines the process types (as we have just done)
- *Level 2* (the configuration level): focuses on the resources required for the supply chain components
- *Level 3*: decomposes each of the processes into its elements
- *Level 4*. focuses on implementation of each of the elements

These levels, as we have said, are beyond the scope of this book. Readers who are interested can go to the SCC website or (preferably) get your organization to join the SCC if it has not already. We recommend it.

AN ASSESSMENT QUESTIONNAIRE

After determining the framework for analysis, the second step is to decide on an assessment questionnaire. Questionnaires can come from several sources. Three of the best are:

The Oliver Wight Checklist. This checklist is one of the better assessment tools. It is published in book form and, at the time of this writing, is in its sixth edition.[2] To our knowledge, this is the oldest and most widely accepted checklist. It is, however, not limited to supply chain activities; it covers the whole spectrum of business excellence activities, including:

- Managing the strategic planning process
- Managing and leading people
- Driving business improvement
- Integrated business management (sales and operations planning)
- Managing products and services
- Managing demand
- Managing the supply chain
- Managing internal supply
- Managing external sourcing

The Baldrige checklist. The Malcolm Baldrige National Quality Award is given each year by the U.S. government.[3] A few companies apply formally for the award, but a very few will win it. Although the primary emphasis of the award is on quality, nevertheless, the award criteria and checklist provide a good structure for an assessment. Each year, many U.S. organizations use the Baldrige Award criteria and checklist to assess their performance on a range of topics. The Baldrige Program publishes several documents to assist companies understanding of the award and its criteria. Perhaps the most popular is the *Criteria for Performance Excellence*, which contains a series of questions in checklist format so companies can assess their performance. There also is a self-analysis worksheet for use as its name implies. These materials are available free on the Baldrige website. The Baldrige Award criteria are in the following categories:

- Leadership
- Strategic planning
- Customer focus
- Measurement, analysis, and knowledge management
- Workforce focus
- Process management
- Results

Although these criteria do not address supply chains specifically, they, nevertheless, all have an impact on a company's supply chains and all are relevant to supply chain management.

The SCC framework. The Supply Chain Council, as already mentioned, is a global, nonprofit association with methodology, diagnostic, and benchmarking tools that help nearly a thousand organizations make improvements in supply chain processes.[1] SCC has established probably the supply chain world's most widely accepted framework for evaluating and comparing supply chain processes and performance. As discussed in some detail earlier, the SCOR model is one of the best and most comprehensive frameworks for understanding supply chains. It contains five components — plan, source, make, deliver, and return — which can form the basis of an assessment.

AN ASSESSMENT METHODOLOGY

The third component of our process is to perform the actual assessment. But first you ask: "How should I go about the assessment?" Many have found a six-step process to be useful. This process is illustrated in Figure 2.2.

Step 1. Plan the assessment. A primary component of the assessment planning step is to define clearly the objectives of the assessment. It is important to ensure alignment of the organization's leadership team with solid support for the objectives of the assessment. The assessment *should not be used* in a punitive manner. Communicate to everyone that this assessment approach is to identify opportunities for improvement and not to pin blame on anyone for supply chain

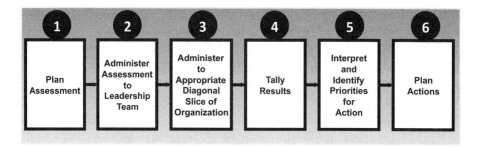

Figure 2.2. Six-Step Assessment Approach.

failures. Furthermore, it also is important for all key individuals to understand these objectives along with the process and tools for performing the assessment and the resources that will be required.

Every organization will, of course, set its own objectives. We have developed the following as an example of how the objectives might be stated:

- Clearly identify and agree on the applicable scope of the checklist as a means of gaining alignment on the objectives.
- Set a clear and independent benchmark that is consistent throughout the entire organization and to which the entire organization can agree and rally around.
- Set a manageable program of excellence-focused activities throughout the entire organization that allows the total organization to advance, together with clear deliverables that benefit the organization's stake-holders.
- Establish at the outset the work and deliverables that will qualify for each substantial improvement achieved.
- Create a meaningful plan that can be resourced and afforded for the entire journey.

Planning the assessment includes identifying the targeted audiences. For example, the business leader, his or her direct reports, and a few other key leaders likely will constitute the first round of the assessment. Next will be a slice of the functional organizations that includes key professional and management people in sales and marketing, product development, operations, finance, product support, and so forth.

Education and training are important elements of the assessment planning process. In our experience, people often *think* they understand supply chain management — but really they do not unless they go through formal education

Level	Time Required	Prerequisite	Content	Education or Training	Attendees
1	3 hours	None	Overview of the total supply chain processes	Education	Everyone except those attending Levels 2 and 3
2	2 days	None	Overview of the total supply chain processes in more detail than Level 1 education	Education	Supply chain process participants
3	5 days	None	Detailed examination of the total supply chain processes	Education and training	Key supply chain process leaders
4	1 to 3 days	Level 3	Detailed module on each individual supply chain process or activity	Training	Participants in each supply chain process

Figure 2.3. Framework for Supply Chain Management Education and Training.

and training. We suggest something like the framework shown in Figure 2.3 for education and training for supply chain management:

- *Level 1:* Level 1 is a brief 3-hour educational overview of the total supply chain processes. It is designed to teach everyone about what supply chain management is all about, why the organization is embarking on a supply chain initiative, and what it means to them. It is intended for those who do not need an in-depth study — they simply need a brief overview.
- *Level 2:* Level 2 is a 2-day educational overview of the total supply chain processes that is in more detail than the 3-hour Level 1 overview. The Level 2 overview is designed to teach supply chain management to process participants who need more than the brief Level 1 program.
- *Level 3:* Level 3 is a 5-day detailed examination of the total supply chain processes. Level

Education and training are different.

*Education teaches the **what** and the **why** and training teaches the **how**.*

Both are needed.

3 is designed to teach supply chain management to key supply chain process leaders. It is *both* education and training.

- *Level 4:* Level 4 is a series of 1- to 3-day modules, each focusing on a particular component or element of the supply chain. For example, there might be a 3-day education/training module on procurement that is designed specifically for participants in that component of the supply chain.

Step 2. Administer the assessment to the leadership team. Target the right leadership team audience for the assessment. Our suggestion is that the audience include, at a minimum, the business leader (CEO or equivalent) and the C-suite executives (chief financial officer, chief marketing officer, chief engineer, chief manufacturing officer, chief information officer, chief procurement officer, and so forth). We further suggest that most if not all of the direct reports to the C-suite be included in the first assessment group. For most business units, this group should include roughly 25 individuals. A sample assessment questionnaire for supply chain integration is shown in Figure 2.4.

We also suggest that the assessment begin with two or three focus groups of about five to seven people each. These focus groups can be conducted in an informal roundtable fashion — with the objective of learning enough about individual opinions to fashion a meaningful assessment process and questionnaire.

Step 3. Administer the assessment to an appropriate diagonal slice of the organization. The target audience for the second assessment administration is key professional and middle management people throughout the organization. This group would include supply chain, product development, sales and marketing, distribution, operations, finance and accounting, aftermarket product support, and so forth.

The example in Figure 2.4 is for an assessment category which we have chosen to call *supply chain integration*. The sample questionnaire includes characteristics of best in class for this category. It also includes three classifications of maturity of supply chain integration: beginning, transition, and advanced. Notice that there are six statements for supply chain integration. Notice also that each of the six statements is worded slightly differently moving from BEGINNING to ADVANCED. For example, notice the first statement and how it is worded differently as the maturity increases:

BEGINNING: The organization's strategic plan reflects supply chain management as *a key strategy.*

Supply Chain Integration	In best-in-class supply chains: • Supply chains are customer focused, integrated end-to-end, and globally competitive. • Supply chain management is a core competency and is managed at a high level in the organization. • Supply chain metrics are standardized and focused across the entire business.	
MATURITY OF SUPPLY CHAIN INTEGRATION		
BEGINNING (0–30 points)	**TRANSITION (40–60 points)**	**ADVANCED (70–90 points)**
Approach: A systematic approach is just beginning. The transition from reaction to prevention is just beginning. **Deployment:** Deployment is beginning in some areas, but major gaps exist.	**Approach:** A sound, systematic approach is in place that addresses the key requirements. An improvement cycle is in place. More emphasis is placed on improvements than on reaction to problems. **Deployment:** The item is deployed in all key areas. The approach is mature and refined in most key areas.	**Approach:** An excellence approach that addresses the item's requirements is in place. The approach integrates an improvement cycle with focus on prevention. Little reaction to problems is necessary. **Deployment:** The item is deployed in all areas. The approach is highly refined in all areas.
1. The organization's strategic plan reflects supply chain management as a key strategy. 2. Top leadership understands integrated supply chain management. 3. Strategic customer and supplier relationships are identified and growing. 4. Planning is underway to conduct a competitive analysis of key supply chain processes. 5. Improvement processes are being developed to simplify, standardize, and synchronize across the supply chains. 6. Planning for statistical supply chain modeling is underway.	1. The organization's strategic plan reflects fully integrated, globally competitive supply chains with end-to-end customer focus as a strategy. 2. Top leadership understands integrated supply chain management and its importance. Leadership should monitor its improvement/deployment. 3. Strategic customer and supplier relationships are growing and are increasingly supportive of supply chain integration. 4. A competitive analysis of key supply chain processes has been completed. 5. Improvement processes to simplify, standardize, and synchronize key processes across the supply chain are expanding. Speed and cost are key focus areas. 6. A supply chain model reflecting actual performance data of processes and suppliers across the supply chains is being piloted.	1. The organization's strategic plan reflects fully integrated, globally competitive supply chains with end-to-end customer focus as a core competency. 2. Top leadership understands integrated supply chain management and its importance. Leadership should visibly lead its improvement. 3. Strategic customer and supplier relationships are developed, supportive of supply chain integration, and managed at a high level across the supply chain. 4. The organization regularly conducts a competitive analysis of key supply chain processes in terms of customer satisfaction and cost. 5. Improvement processes to simplify, standardize, and synchronize key processes across the supply chain are mature with speed and cost as key focus areas. 6. A supply chain model reflecting actual performance data of processes and suppliers across the supply chains is utilized actively in managing the business.

Figure 2.4. Supply Chain Integration: Sample Assessment Questionnaire.

TRANSITION: The organization's strategic plan reflects *fully integrated, globally competitive supply chains with end-to-end customer focus as a strategy.*

ADVANCED: The organization's strategic plan reflects *fully integrated, globally competitive supply chains with end-to-end customer focus as a core competency.*

Clearly, the meaning of the ADVANCED statement reflects more advanced supply chain integration than the meaning of the BEGINNING statement. As we say, the *maturity* increases.

Participants are asked to rate the company from BEGINNING to ADVANCED on each of the six statements, depending on which statement most closely represents the company's status. Notice also that each stage of maturity has a point spread attached to it:

BEGINNING: 0 to 30 points (If no activity is associated with the statement, then zero points would be appropriate.)

TRANSITION: 40 to 60 points

ADVANCED: 70 to 90 points (The highest number of points is 90, not 100, which is intended to indicate that some improvement always is possible.)

Participants are asked to assign a number of points to each statement from the appropriate maturity level. For example, assume a participant answers the first statement: "The organization's strategic plan reflects supply chain management as a key strategy." Suppose the participant thinks that this statement is about "half right" because the strategic plan does have supply chain management listed as a key strategy, but it is a weak statement in the strategy. The commitment is not really strong, but it is in the strategic plan. So, the participant may assign, say, 20 points to that statement — not the least amount of points, but not the most either.

Step 4. Tally the results. Tallying the results simply means averaging the scores assigned to all six statements in the *Supply Chain Integration* section of the questionnaire. Say, this section averages 23 points for the 6 statements from all participants in the assessment. Figure 2.5 illustrates how the results might be posted.

As shown in the chart in Figure 2.5, each section of the assessment will have its own score averaged from all statements in the section with the results from all participants. Notice also that a range is indicated for each section, with supply chain integration showing a range of 10 to 59.

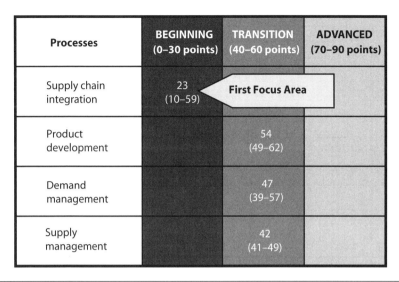

Processes	BEGINNING (0–30 points)	TRANSITION (40–60 points)	ADVANCED (70–90 points)
Supply chain integration	23 (10–59) **First Focus Area**		
Product development		54 (49–62)	
Demand management		47 (39–57)	
Supply management		42 (41–49)	

Figure 2.5. Supply Chain Integration Assessment Questionnaire: Results.

Step 5. Interpret and identify priorities for action. The process is to tally and plot the results in the chart, both the average and the range for each section, because both are of interest. We are looking for both *low* scores and scores with a *wide variance*. For example, in Figure 2.5, supply chain integration has both the lowest score and the widest variance of scores. The low score indicates that participants do not think the company is doing a very good job with the statements in the section. The wide variance indicates that disagreement exists about just how poor a job the company actually is doing. Both of these are cause for concern. Both might require further interpretation, clarification, and discussion.

After interpreting the results from the assessment responses, the next step is to identify priorities for action. One strong and well-known approach is a SWOT analysis (strengths, weaknesses, opportunities, and threats) as shown in Figure 2.6. A SWOT analysis should be performed for the organization as a whole plus the functions and/or processes that were contained as sections in the assessment. The goal is to determine the effectiveness of the total organization and its functions and processes, which leads to the real deliverable of the assessment: a prioritized plan for action.

Step 6. Plan actions. The action plan will come from several sources combined: the assessment questionnaire, the focus group discussions about the assessment, the tallied results, and the SWOT. Figure 2.7 illustrates one way of displaying the results and priorities for action. The 2 × 2 matrix in Figure 2.7 shows the impact on the business and supply chain maturity arrayed against the

Strengths	Weaknesses
•	•
•	•
•	•
•	•
Opportunities	**Threats**
•	•
•	•
•	•
•	•

Figure 2.6. Strengths/Weaknesses/Opportunities/Threats (SWOT) Analysis: Sample Analysis Chart.

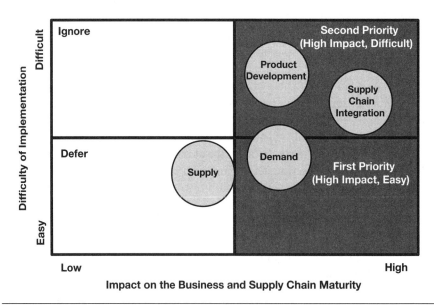

Figure 2.7. Interpretation and Identification of Priorities for Action: Display of Results from Analyses.

difficulty of implementing the solutions. In this example, the top priority likely would be improvements in demand management because it is in the lower right-hand quadrant (high impact/easy to implement).

The action plans would be used to drive higher levels of supply chain maturity based on the relative priorities. Action plans need to answer six questions:

- What needs to be done?
- Why does it need to be done?
- Who needs to do it?
- Where does it need to be done?
- When is it needed?
- How should it be done?

> *Hopes without plans remain hopes.*
>
> — Dr. W. Edwards Deming

Why develop an action plan? We have found that companies are more efficient with their implementations when they have a well-crafted action plan that answers the above questions. A well-crafted action plan also helps with the following:

- Ensures active management of the supply chain transformation process
- Builds confidence in the transformation process
- Sets roles and responsibilities
- Clarifies accountabilities
- Tracks and demonstrates progress

What are the roles in developing the plan?
- The business leader owns the implementation plan.
- The supply chain process leader develops the macro plan with input from key stakeholders.
- Process owners for product development, demand management, supply management, finance, and so forth will own their detailed subplans.
- The supply chain process leader monitors execution of the plan and reports progress to the leadership team.

A good action plan:

- Identifies all key actions and milestones
- Exists at both the macro and detail levels
- Clarifies roles
- Ensures that elements of effective change management are included
- Is sequenced by time

The bottom line is this: identify specific goals for the supply chain transformation, create a process that moves it toward those goals, and install a system to make sure it gets there.

There is real value in knowing where your company and its expertise fall. This gives you insight into the kinds of issues you need to be addressing. This chapter has presented a more extensive assessment methodology. We will now provide some example sample metrics. The chart in Figure 2.8 shows some sample supply chain metrics as one more way for readers to understand better how they are doing. These are sample metrics for a supply chain integration assessment. Notice that the chart has the same format as the assessment questionnaire in Figure 2.4.

DEMAND REVIEW

Demand management is one of the most difficult elements of supply chain management to get operating well. As an example of how to perform a demand management assessment, we present several questions that must be answered for an effective demand review.

Definitions

How does the company define certain terms? Definitions are important. We have found that even among people who work together that there often are misunderstandings of the exact meaning of terms. We suggest that a company develop a corporate supply chain dictionary. We suggest using the *APICS Dictionary* as a prototype.[4] Some companies choose to modify the standard definitions from the *APICS Dictionary* for their own purposes; nevertheless, they find APICS to be a useful starting point. How does your company define the following?

- Demand
- Delivery
- Order
- Sales
- Backlog

Requirements

How should the company identify demand requirements? From where does demand come and why? What are the drivers of demand — what makes demand go up or down?

Supply Chain Integration	In best-in-class supply chains: • Supply chains are customer focused, integrated end-to-end, and globally competitive. • Supply chain management is a core competency and is managed at a high level in the organization. • Supply chain metrics are standardized and focused across the entire business.	
SCORING MATRIX		
BEGINNING **(0–30 points)**	**TRANSITION** **(40–60 points)**	**ADVANCED** **(70–90 points)**
Approach: A systematic approach is just beginning. The transition from reaction to prevention is just beginning. **Deployment:** Deployment is beginning in some areas, but major gaps exist.	**Approach:** A sound, systematic approach is in place that addresses the key requirements. An improvement cycle is in place. More emphasis is placed on improvements than on reaction to problems. **Deployment:** The item is deployed in all key areas. The approach is mature and refined in most key areas.	**Approach:** An excellence approach that addresses the item's requirements is in place. The approach integrates an improvement cycle with focus on prevention. Little reaction to problems is necessary. **Deployment:** The item is deployed in all areas. The approach is highly refined in all areas.
Metrics • Fill rate = 95% • Cumulative product lead time = 120% of industry benchmark • Perfect order = 95% • Free cash flow = 80% of industry benchmark • Total supply chain cost = 120% of industry benchmark • Working capital turns = 80% of industry benchmark • Days of sales in receivables = 120% of industry benchmark • Collection days = 120% of industry benchmark • Cash-to-cash cycle = 120% of industry benchmark	**Metrics** • Fill rate = 97% • Cumulative product lead time = 100% of industry benchmark • Perfect order = 97% • Free cash flow = 100% of industry benchmark • Total supply chain cost = 100% of industry benchmark • Working capital turns = 100% of industry benchmark • Days of sales in receivables = 100% of industry benchmark • Collection days = 100% of industry benchmark • Cash-to-cash cycle = 100% of industry benchmark	**Metrics** • Fill rate = 100% • Cumulative product lead time = 80% of industry benchmark • Perfect order = 100% • Free cash flow = 120% of industry benchmark • Total supply chain cost = 80% of industry benchmark • Working capital turns = 120% of industry benchmark • Days of sales in receivables = 80% of industry benchmark • Collection days = 80% of industry benchmark • Cash-to-cash cycle = 80% of industry benchmark

Figure 2.8. Supply Chain Integration Assessment: Sample Metrics.

How should the company segment customers? What difference does it make and why? How does demand vary from segment to segment and why? By the way, we think that it is important for companies to segment customers. We have seen some companies with a highly heterogeneous customer base to just give up on segmenting, saying: "We treat all our customers alike. All our customers are important, and we do not want to discriminate among them." This can be a *huge* mistake! The fact is that some customers *are* more important than others, and some customers *should* be treated differently from others. We have seen several ways for customer segmentation:

- Who are customers for which we are a *strategic* supplier or perhaps a *sole* supplier? Companies that are strategic or sole suppliers need to know that so they do not inadvertently cause difficulties for those customers when those difficulties might be prevented.
- Who are customers that purchase in *large* annual volumes versus *small* volumes? Why are they different? What is the effect of consistently getting large orders from certain customers versus consistently getting small orders from other customers? Do small customers grow to become large customers, what are the growth drivers, and how should growing customers be managed?
- Who are customers that place *large* individual orders versus *small* more frequent orders? Do some customers order, say, once a year in large quantities versus other customers who order weekly in small quantities? Can and should these customers be managed differently? Some companies, for example, give price discounts for large orders when they really should be giving price discounts for consistently ordering in smaller but more predictable volumes.
- Who are customers that have *large volatility* in their ordering patterns? Do some customers order in large quantities followed by small quantities? Or, do some customers place frequent orders for a while followed by a time of no orders?
- Who are customers that have a *stable frequency* in their order patterns? This might indicate, for example, a weekly or monthly ordering pattern that reflects a fixed periodic review of the inventory position.
- Who are customers that have *linked* versus *transaction-oriented* relationships with suppliers? For example, some companies allow suppliers to have access to their inventory position and perhaps even to production or usage plans. One company (making large, expensive capital equipment) with which we are familiar allows certain suppliers to have complete visibility to their production plans, and thus usage

plans, for these suppliers' products. They simply tell these suppliers: "We don't ever want to run out, nor do we want more than x number of days of supply in stock. You manage the inventory." Transactions-oriented relationships might indicate that all orders come with RFPs (requests for proposal), and the proposal-generating process might be required each and every time the customer buys. We suggest that companies with customers like this might try to get the customer to receive proposals for annual orders and not individual transactions.

- Who are customers that have *special requirements* for their products? Some companies always want, say, special engineering changes to their product. These easily can disrupt the engineering, material, and manufacturing schedules if not managed well. They also should be priced accordingly for the extra requirements.

How should the company identify different demand streams for its products? For example, is the product an OEM (original equipment manufactured) or a non-OEM product?

OEM products. OEM products can be used *as is* or as components:

- An OEM product can be a major purchase for customers that purchase the product and use it *as is*. For example, a company such as Cessna will sell its business jets primarily to major companies and government agencies and a few wealthy individuals. The aircraft almost always is considered to be a major purchase, and the purchasing decision is not a simple one.
- OEM products can also be used as a component in another company's product. For example, Pratt & Whitney sells its aircraft engines to manufacturers to become part of their business jets. P&W is a major and important supplier, and these manufacturers are major and important customers for P&W. There are only a few suppliers of engines for business jets. The relationship is strategic both ways. The overall purchasing decision is also not a simple one. Although the overall purchasing decision is not simple, the two companies might work out a strategic agreement whereby each individual purchasing decision could be relatively simple. This agreement could specify all the applicable terms and conditions, including which ones are standard and which ones will vary from product to product.

Companies purchase many small and relatively *unimportant* items for their products that are considered to be OEM components. Clearly, airplanes probably cannot fly without these items, but in the total scheme of things, these items certainly are not as important as jet engines. Although these unimportant items are considered as *minor* OEM items, many suppliers are likely to exist for these items.

Non-OEM products. There can be numerous demand streams for non-OEM products. Sometimes these products can be the same products that have OEM demand streams. Some examples of demand streams for these items include:

- Many times spares/service/aftermarket products can be the same products that go into OEM products, but they are also used as service items. Continuing with the aircraft example, P&W has a very large and active product support organization that is staffed with engineers, supply chain people, maintenance people, finance and accounting people, sales and marketing people, and so forth. P&W also has many spares on the shelf because aircraft owners and operators usually want fast turnaround when maintenance and spare parts are needed. Aircraft on the ground (AOG) is a term in the service and maintenance industry that indicates the need for immediate availability of service items.

- Items for rework and remanufacturing could also be OEM items that are used in these types of applications. The demand stream could come from any company that reworks or remanufactures products.

- Interplant requirements could be either OEM or non-OEM items. Many companies have feeder plants that supply intermediate products to other plants in the system. For example, one of the authors was consulting with a large pharmaceutical company in its Mexico City plant. The plant made finished products for distribution to Latin America. He was involved in a discussion about an intermediate product that was manufactured in one of the company's European plants. The Mexico plant was having difficulty obtaining sufficient quantities of this intermediate because most of the output from the European plant was being sent to the European finished-products plants. The problem essentially was an organizational one — the European intermediates plant reported to the Europe-Africa-Middle East (EAME) regional head who had dictated that "his" plants were to be supplied first. Ironically, profit margins at the Mexican plant were substantially higher than at the European plant. Nevertheless, organizational alignment took precedence over margin issues.

- Product development requirements are demand streams for products required to support the product development activities with prototypes.

How should product families be defined so that they make sense simultaneously to marketing/sales people, to the marketplace, and to manufacturing? So-called *product families* frequently are used for aggregate-level planning activities such as sales and operations planning and budgeting. Product families represent an intermediate level of product aggregation — between the individual-item SKU (stock keeping unit) and the total business. Why manage at the aggregate level? The answer is because it is just *not* practical for top management to manage every item. Managing at the aggregate level means grouping products into logical families, which may be straightforward *if* all parties can agree what the families should be. Very often, however, sales and marketing view things in aggregate differently than manufacturing does. Sales and marketing naturally look at their products the way customers look at them — from the standpoint of function and applications. Manufacturing, in contrast, tends to look at products in terms of manufacturing processes. Gaining agreement many times is not a trivial exercise.

How should future demand be forecasted or estimated? Some people will argue that forecasting is obsolete — that it has been superseded by *linking*, one of the latest buzzwords. They will say (correctly), "The only thing you know about a demand forecast is that it is wrong!" Linking gets demand information more accurately by getting it directly from the customer. However, that is not always possible: Wal-Mart cannot possibly link with (perhaps) hundreds of millions of customers. That is one reason why Wal-Mart collects massive amounts of data — to allow the company to get a better handle (read, *demand forecast*) on their demand patterns. However, Wal-Mart goes further. They have made immense changes in their supply chain that get the product to the stores much more quickly. Nevertheless, demand forecasting is still extremely important for a certain class of companies and we would be remiss in leaving it out of this discussion:

- What is the purpose of forecasting demand?
- Where and how should companies get the data required?
- How can the data infrastructure be understood? For example, data infrastructure can refer to, say, demand streams or data aggregation into product families and so forth.
- How does the current process work? Clearly, almost all companies must do some kind of demand forecasting; otherwise, they cannot adequately manage their business. Some are highly informal and subjective, and others are very formal and quantitative. Understanding *how* the current process works (the *as is*) is important before trying to improve on it.

- How should the new process work? This is the *to be* for demand forecasting. The company's ability to design, implement, and operate a new *to be* process depends a great deal on answers to the other questions in this series. Additionally, other important questions include whether (or not) the company has the requisite capabilities for demand forecasting.
- What are the key output deliverables from the demand forecasting process? We believe there are several deliverables: short-, intermediate-, and long-run forecasts for critical individual items, product families, and the aggregate business of the supply chain.
- How should accuracy in the forecast be measured? The answer, in a word, is *carefully*. Seriously, there are two key measures and numerous variations on these two. The first element of forecasting accuracy is relatively easy to calculate. It is simply the difference between the actual demand in the period and the forecasted demand for the same period. Consider the following simple example:

Forecast for October	=	500 items
Actual demand for October	=	600 items
Forecast error		= +100 items

The second element of forecasting accuracy, bias, is also relatively easy to calculate. A forecast is considered to be unbiased if the forecast errors are as equally likely to be positive (under-forecasting) as negative (over-forecasting). In the example above, if the forecast error for September was -100, then the forecast would have been unbiased for the 2 months. The simple calculation for bias is to keep a running cumulative total of the forecast errors. If the cumulative total is approximately zero (that is, positives cancel out negatives), then the forecast is considered to be unbiased. If the cumulative total builds up in the positive direction (becoming more and more positive), then the forecasting system is systemically under-forecasting. If negative, then it is over-forecasting.

How should special demand requirements be identified? Special demand requirements would include special engineering or special documentation or something else that is out of the ordinary:

- Special requirements from a customer constitute the most frequent issues. Sometimes, and with some customers, these special requirements are well known in advance. Some customers always require something special. Others never do. The objective is to have a relationship with these customers so that their special requirements become ordinary and "not special."

There is a story about Red Adair, legendary oil well firefighter (played by John Wayne in a movie). When an oil well blowout occurred, Red would order sometimes very complex and unique equipment. Price was no object — delivery was. No matter which company received the order for equipment, the company had to scramble around to get the parts, free up manufacturing capacity, make, and then ship the product, sometimes in hours. Clearly, these were special requirements that caused disruption. As the story goes, whatever Red was charged (remember, price was no object), it just never seemed to be enough, given the disruption. This situation went on for years, until one company decided to work with Red to determine what parts and capacity might be needed, just in case Red called with a blowout somewhere in the world. Problem solved — even though the special requirements did not go away.

- How should a company recognize the impact of special requirements? The answer: *it cannot* unless the company performs a detailed analysis of the whole process step by step, which is what happened with Red's requirements. The company knew (or at least hoped) that Red would continue to call them. The question, then, was not about making the special requirements go away, but about how to handle special requirements in the most expeditious manner.
- How should a company capture data on customer behavior and changes to that behavior? Nothing beats a strong customer information/intelligence system. There are many sources of information about this subject — but it is too big a topic for us to cover here.

The next chapter deals with how to convince the organization of a need for change and to move forward with a supply chain transformation. Once that has been done, Chapter 4 focuses on "stopping the bleeding" with short-term fixes in preparation for long-term systemic transformation.

CONCLUSION

Some key points from this chapter are worth remembering:

- *Know the as is*. The key to a successful supply chain transformation is to know what the *as is* is. We strongly suggest a formal assessment. The assessment starts with a framework for analysis and a questionnaire that has a basis in *good* or *best in class*. We suggest using the

Supply Chain Operations Reference® (SCOR) model for the framework along with several references for an assessment. We think that the best overall assessment questionnaire is the *Oliver Wight Class A Checklist*, but we also consider the Baldrige award criteria and the framework from the Supply Chain Council.

- *A six-step work plan.* We have provided a suggested six-step work plan for the total assessment process.
- *A demand review assessment.* We have also provided a set of suggestions for a demand review assessment.

REFERENCES

1. Supply Chain Council. See www.supply-chain.org. Accessed June 2009.

2. Oliver Wight International. *The Oliver Wight Class A Checklist for Business Excellence, Sixth Edition* 2005. New York: John Wiley & Sons.

3. National Institute of Standards and Technology, Technology Administration, U.S. Department of Commerce, Gaithersburg, MD. *The Malcolm Baldrige National Quality Award.* See www.quality.nist.gov. Accessed June 2009.

4. James F. Cox and John H. Blackstone. *APICS Dictionary* 2008. Chicago: APICS.

3

HOW CAN WE CONVINCE THE ORGANIZATION?

Give me a place to stand,
and with a lever I will move the whole world.
— Archimedes

> *Change would be easy if it were not for people!*

In Chapter 2 we focused on how we can know that we have improvement opportunities. The answer: perform an assessment. But that is not good enough. What do we do now? How can we convince the organization that we need to move forward? This really is a *change program.*

To ensure successful implementation of any supply chain transformation, we have found that building a formal change program into the project is needed. Although we do not have the data to support this finding, we think that probably two-thirds to three-fourths of supply chain projects fail to achieve their initial objectives — not because of a lack of good ideas, but because of a failure to implement and sustain them.

Figure 3.1 illustrates some types of supply chain projects. Downsizings, restructurings, and automation projects have been tried — many to no avail and most without meeting the project objectives. We think this is because the focus has been on rationalization of suppliers, organization, and information systems and *not* on the supply chain business processes. We also think that the focus has not been on management of the change process and the people involved.

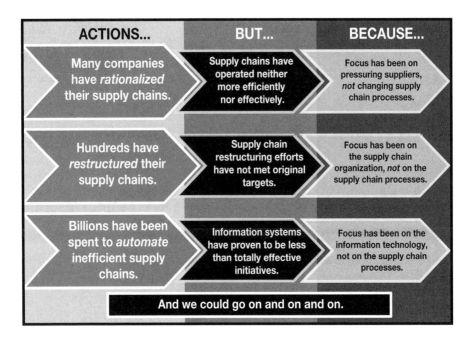

Figure 3.1. Supply Chain Projects: Reasons for Failure.

SO, WHAT DOES IT TAKE?

We know that implementation of sustainable transformations requires a three-level approach. Management of the change process includes people-oriented strategies, tools, and techniques which can be applied in a coordinated and integrated fashion. The three levels are the organization as a whole; groups that make up the functions and business processes; and the individuals who generally work in groups:

The organization as a whole. We believe that organizations fail to implement sustainable transformations of supply chains for a number of reasons. Sustainable transformation needs:

- *A strong change imperative:* Simply put, the case for a supply chain transformation must be made. This is the "push" for change. It includes dissatisfaction with the *as is* situation and is one result of the supply chain assessment discussed in Chapter 2.
- *A vision:* The organization needs a vision of what can be achieved. This is the "pull" of the *to be* situation that grabs the attention of people. The vision also comes from the assessment — when people

begin to see the possibilities in their supply chains by stacking themselves up against best-in-class companies.

- *A process:* The organization needs a process for managing the transformation. This is the "path forward" that people can see. (One thing we are attempting to build with this book is a view of the possibilities for movement toward the transformation.)
- *A commitment:* The organization needs a commitment to make the transformation happen.

Enrollment of the organization in the supply chain transformation process cannot be effective until these have been addressed.

Groups that make up functions and business processes. The supply chain encompasses a number of the functions and processes in the company. Most obviously, procurement, manufacturing, and distribution are the three most-often-cited functions. Other, perhaps less obvious, business processes sometimes might be called inquiry-to-cash (from a potential customer's inquiry through all the stages of production and/or distribution on to the actual collection of cash) or procure-to-pay (from initiation of the procurement process to payment of the supplier). In addition to the obvious functions and processes, companies frequently include the sales and marketing, engineering and product development, finance and accounting, human resources, legal, and perhaps other functions in their definition of supply chain. The following questions are valid:

- What does each business process need to deliver for the business to successfully achieve its strategic plan? When do the processes need to deliver them?
- What will need to be done to successfully achieve these deliverables on time?
- How can the key elements of the strategies for this achievement be included in the strategic plan?
- How can ownership by enterprise leadership be ensured for each of the key deliverables and strategies of the processes?
- How will cross-process ownership and performance be incentivized?
- How will progress be measured and managed?

Individuals who generally work in groups. As individuals:

- We are rational — we analyze, we understand, and we decide.
- We are emotional — we feel, we commit, and we act.

Effective management of change in supply chain transformation projects needs to address both of these sides of our nature. Individuals fail to complete the transformation process for a number of reasons:

- They do not *contribute meaningfully* to the transformation process — a process which begins with an assessment to determine the *as is* situation and to lay the groundwork for the vision of the *to be* possibilities.
- They do not *believe* that transformation is possible. (The authors have heard the old lament, "We've tried that before, and it's never worked." Simply put, individuals must get over this kind of thinking if success is to be achieved.)
- They do not *accept* as true that the transformation is in their own best interests. (They are preoccupied with WII-FM, our favorite FM station, or "what's in it for me?")
- They do not *break* the awesome power of habit. ("We've always done it this way.")

Enrollment of individuals in the transformation process cannot be effective until these points have been addressed.

SO, WHAT *ARE* THE STRATEGIC IMPERITIVES FOR SUPPLY CHAIN TRANSFORMATIONS?

A CEO deals with the problems of satisfying customers and meeting the financial numbers in the strategic business plan. Addressing questions such as the following is key:

- What must the business deliver to the stakeholders (i.e., shareholders, customers, employees, suppliers, and so forth), and what is the role of the supply chain in this delivery?
- What are the key success factors for customer satisfaction and market share growth for the enterprise, and what is the role of the supply chain?
- How will the enterprise achieve these in the required time frames, and what is the role of the supply chain?
- How will satisfactory progress be measured, and how will the supply chain measurements fit in?

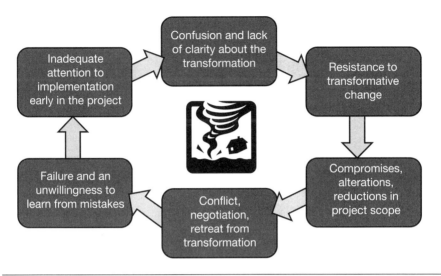

Figure 3.2. Transformation: a Losing Spiral.

THE PROCESS OF TRANSFORMATION

Sometimes we get trapped in a losing spiral as shown in Figure 3.2. Transformative change needs to occur through a combination of one-time and continuous improvement. Consider Figure 3.3. A real issue for organizations is how to make step-function change sustainable so that they can continue to make improvements. In reality, as illustrated in Figure 3.3, change usually entails an accumulation of incremental and radical change with some setbacks along the way.

The supply chain almost always exhibits flat or erratic performance before the change. This is the primary reason for transformation in the first place. The desire is for a real step-function change in performance. Transformation efforts, however, do not just get there in one fell swoop. It takes active management of the transformation and changes that are being made to get the process back on track when the inevitable setbacks occur. It also takes putting into place the capability for continuous improvement after the transformation, so as not only to sustain the changes, but also to improve on them.

We know that transformative changes have been effective when three measureable criteria have been satisfied:

- HOW MUCH has supply chain performance improved?
- HOW FAST have the changes occurred?
- HOW SUSTAINABLE are the changes?

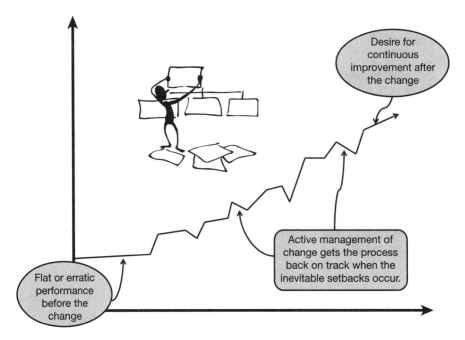

Figure 3.3. Transformative Change: an Accumulation of Incremental and Radical Change and Setbacks.

Of course, these criteria should be considered in relation to how much actual improvement was achieved vis-à-vis how much was needed in the time frame under consideration to remain on plan to competitiveness.

A PHASED APPROACH TO TRANSFORMATIVE CHANGE: USING BEHAVIORAL CHANGE LEVERS

Change management literature contains a number of models of planned organizational change. Figure 3.4 illustrates an adaptation of four of these models. We have not tried to be complete or completely accurate in these representations — each one is much more complicated and extensive and neither space nor motivation permits us to be exact — yet each has something to offer to our understanding.

Consider Figure 3.4 with TIME going from top to bottom. The simplest model is the *Unfreeze → Move → Refreeze* representation. Something must cause the *unfreezing* to take place. It is the push for the project in the first place and is similar to our assessment as described in Chapter 2. The *refreezing* must take place at the project's end to solidify the changes implemented in the transformation.

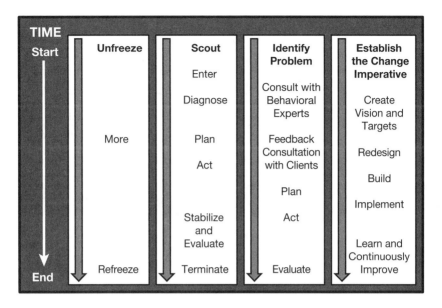

Figure 3.4. Four Models of Planned Organizational Change.

The second model is a little more complicated and puts more emphasis on the *Scout → Enter → Diagnose* phases in the beginning of the project. At the end, similar to the *Refreeze* model, are the *Stabilize → Evaluate → Terminate* phases.

Some people call the third model the *action research model.* This approach puts more emphasis on consultation with behavioral science experts and feedback and consultation with client personnel.

The fourth representation is closest to our approach with its emphasis on *As Is → Vision → Path Forward → Continuously Improve.*

Clearly, we take something from each of the models in the change management literature. In any case, the theory to which we subscribe incorporates behavior-based programs. Individuals, groups, and organizations must behave differently if performance of the supply chain is to improve. Research has shown that *failure* to achieve behavioral change is the *primary cause* of failure in planned large-scale transformative change.

Behavioral change and performance improvement do not just happen either — programmatic change management almost always is required. Frequently, the impact of the coming transformation is not obvious to everyone in the early phases of the project, so resources are not devoted to managing the changes that inevitably will be required. Research and practical experience, however, demonstrate that change management must begin early in the project for it to be effective. Yet organizations often end up doing too little, too late.

Change happens quickly.	Time takes care of everything.	The weak people are the ones who leave.
There will be no emotional reaction to the change.	Pressures that caused the change will be viewed rationally.	People "hear" what management communicates.
Our people are used to change.	During the change, those who appear "OK" really are.	Change just takes some strong leadership.
Change always goes according to plan.	Senior management behavior during the transition is invisible to the rest of the organization.	Everyone is willing to accept good ideas.
If change is easy, then why is the press so full of stories about organizations which cannot achieve it?		

Figure 3.5. Widespread Misconceptions about Change at the Beginning of a Major Supply Chain Transformational Program.

Unfortunately, a number of misconceptions about transformative change reinforce the thinking of leaders that a significant change management program is unnecessary. Consider the chart in Figure 3.5. We have heard these quotes from numerous people in companies embarking on a major supply chain transformational program. Our reaction is at the bottom of the chart: "If change is easy, then why is the press so full of stories about organizations which cannot achieve it?"

Although we dislike pointing fingers, all the same, sometimes it is illustrative to do so! People may argue whether the difficulties in the U.S. automobile industry in the first decade of the 2000s were, strictly speaking, supply chain induced. (The industry clearly had more difficulties than just the supply chains.) In any case, change was not easy. Change did not happen quickly. Time did not take care of everything. There was significant emotional reaction to change and so on.

We have used the term *program* when describing the management of change, but what is a *change management program*? Maybe we could describe it by changing the words around: a programmatic management of change. How about something like this? Programmatic management of change is:

1. The *use* of people-oriented levers, involving:
   - Leadership
   - Communications
   - Commitment
   - Education and training
   - Organization and workforce transition
   - Results orientation

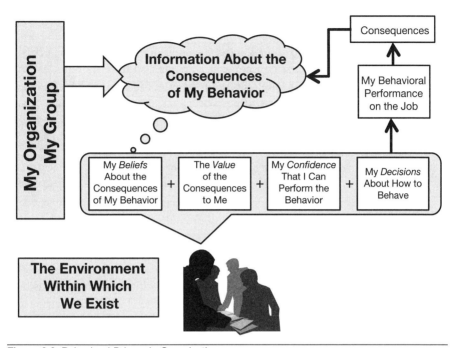

Figure 3.6. Behavioral Drivers in Organizations.

2. Which are *executed* at three levels:
    - The organization as a whole
    - Groups which comprise functions and/or processes
    - Individuals
3. In a *coordinated and integrated* manner:
    - Leadership, communications, commitment, education and training, organization and workforce transition, and results orientation ...
    - Driving with a consistent message to ...
    - The organization, groups, and individuals ...
    - To change behavior
4. So that *changes can be achieved* and *performance can be improved*.

Perhaps a picture will help. Consider Figure 3.6. People exist within their environment. For our purposes, think about the relevant portions of the environment as being *My Organization* and *My Group*. From their organization and their groups, people glean information about the consequences of their behavior. We all do this. People who are successful in their organizations learn to behave in ways that enhance the positive consequences and reduce the negative consequences of that behavior.

Each individual develops *beliefs* about the consequences of his or her behavior and places *values* on those consequences. People also have more or less *confidence* that they can perform the required behaviors for the job. Beliefs, values, and level of confidence contribute to their decisions about how to behave. Their decisions then drive behavior performance which, in turn, drives consequences of their performance, which, again, contributes to feedback to the individual.

> Some people may simply say, "It's not worth it." For instance, perhaps a person does not want to travel (for any number of reasons). He or she will likely behave in ways that minimize the travel requirements of the job. Sometimes, in some jobs, this will not be a problem. For others, it will. An individual makes his or her choices accordingly.

So, what does all this have to do with supply chain transformation? Good question. People have to change the way they behave if they want to transform the supply chain. Think, metaphorically of a lever, somewhat like the quote from Archimedes that began this chapter: "Give me a place to stand, and with a lever I will move the whole world." What are the levers for our supply chain transformation? What are the opposing forces? Where are the force fields? Think in terms of six behavioral change levers and five negative behavioral impacts of the supply chain transformation:

Behavioral Change Levers	**Negative Behavioral Impacts**
1. Leadership	1. Doubt
2. Communications	2. Mistrust
3. Commitment	3. Confusion
4. Education and training	4. Apprehension
5. Organization and workforce transition	5. Uncertainty
6. Results orientation	

The six levers can be used proactively against the negative impacts on behavior. The results of these force fields will be either desired or undesired behavior. The relative impact will depend upon how skillfully the levers are used, coupled with people's beliefs, values, and confidence. Recognize that the objective is to transform the supply chain from low performance into high performance. People may have doubts about the effort, mistrust management, be confused about what is going on, feel apprehensive about their own situation, and possibly be uncertain about the results. Or, perhaps they have other concerns.

LEVER ONE: LEADERSHIP

The first lever for change is leadership. Leadership plays a unique, central role in a change management program. It likely is the most important lever that organizations have. Three leaders have some interesting views on their roles:[1]

- *It was more difficult than we ever imagined, but it was worth it.*
- *When you start to implement, there will be nights when you go home and get sick.*
- *You can survive the old way. You can survive the new way. It's the transition that kills you.*

Leaders:

- Send strong signals to individuals through their communication messages about behavior change
- Send stronger signals through their actions about which behavior change messages are "real"
- Sometimes need to change their styles to match the new processes
- Must personally work the communication and commitment processes to secure support for the change
- Must make the tough "people decisions" required to make the workforce transition succeed

So, how do we use leadership as a behavioral change lever? When Bill Lee was a young manager in a manufacturing plant and was just beginning one of his earliest supply chain transformation efforts, a major piece of the project was going to directly affect the manufacturing shop floor. Through sheer dumb luck, Bill went to the plant manager and asked that the assembly foreman (we will call him George) be assigned to his team. The plant manager said something like, "You're crazy." (Actually it was somewhat stronger language, but we cannot repeat it in this book!) "Don't you know that George has sabotaged every improvement effort we have ever tried?"

As we said, by sheer dumb luck, the plant manager reluctantly agreed. So George was sent off to computer school. He came back convinced that supply chain transformation was the way to go. He became the informal leader of the project with the people in manufacturing. The project was a roaring success — thanks mostly to George. That is real leadership (George, *not* Bill).

Tools and techniques can support supply chain transformation. The following are a few:

- Brainstorming and other creativity exercises
- Leadership assessment tools to help leaders identify and manage their own behavior
- Leadership training
- Force field analysis to help understand the forces arrayed for and against the project
- Mediation and conflict resolution techniques
- Feedback mechanisms from the organization on the messages that leaders are sending
- Planning the management of change process to assist leaders in developing personal action plans
- Coaching, counseling, and mentoring from senior leaders

Consider the six-step change management model presented in Figure 3.4: establish the change imperative; create vision and targets; redesign; build; implement; and learn and continuously improve. This plan will unfold perhaps over several months or a year or so. What does leadership do along the way? There are two primary tasks with several subtasks:

- Visibly show commitment to the project
- Align organizational leadership

Visibly show commitment to the project. It is important that leaders throughout the organization are active and visible in support of the project:

- *Allocate appropriate resources of people, money, and time:*
  - Allocate appropriate human resources. The wrong thing to do is to say, "Joe and Mary don't have anything else to do, so let's put them on the transformation project." Whether that is said verbally or by actions, it sends the wrong message about the importance of the project. A better approach is saying, "Julie and Sam are the best people we have, so we'll put them on the project." Allocating appropriate resources means both the right people and the right number of people.
  - Allocate the appropriate monetary resources. Companies can both overspend and underspend on transformation projects — both are a waste of money. Many people do not recognize that underspending is a waste of money, but it is. Underspending communicates

a leadership message that the project is not worth spending the appropriate amount of money.

- Allocate adequate time. Giving the project enough time to be successful is important. People often joke that their approach is "ready, fire, aim." In their eagerness to get the project finished, they skimp on planning time and resources. They jump directly into the reconfiguration of the supply chain processes without adequately thinking through *what* should be done and *how* it should be done. The results are unintended consequences.

- *Empower teams:* We often say, "Supply chain transformation is a team sport," but what *kind* of teams? What do they need? There are some terms associated with team dynamics: forming, norming, and performing. Teams need to be *formed* well and they have to take time to develop their *norms* of interaction before they can *perform*. (It is beyond the scope of this book to give teams their full due because enormous volumes of work have been written on the subject. Let it suffice to say at this point that teams need to be empowered to make change.)

- *Inspire confidence:* Inspire confidence in the project as it progresses and in new processes as they are developed and implemented, which means that leadership must have and show confidence in the project *throughout* its life cycle.

Align organizational leadership. Organizational leadership alignment takes place at all levels of the organization, from top to bottom. Recognize that *informal* leaders also exist throughout the organization:

- *Senior leadership:* Clearly, the senior leadership team must be aligned and committed. Furthermore, champions must be identified within senior management to lead specific initiatives during the transformation.

- *Informal leadership:* The story we told previously about George, the assembly foreman, is an example of organizational leadership alignment. One can say that it was pure dumb luck, but in reality there was recognition that George was an informal leader on the shop floor. There was a realization that without George's alignment, the project likely would not be a success.

- *Resistors:* Aligning organizational leadership means identifying resistors and getting them persuaded and aligned with the rest of the organization. As some often say, "Either change the people or change the people!"

In his book, Katzenbach makes many points that are worth internalizing.[2] Four are paraphrased as follows (with some editorial license applied):

- The organization likely does not have a track record of success in changes of this type.
- For supply chain transformations, the organization has to get very good at one or more basic things — things which it is not very good at now.
- Relatively large numbers of people throughout the entire organization have to do things differently from what and how they have done in the past.
- People throughout the organization may or may not understand the implications of the changes in their own behaviors and may or may not urgently believe that now is the time to act.

The responses to these four points can help companies determine the degree to which they face major change to which their teams will have to react.

LEVER TWO: COMMUNICATIONS

An effective communication program requires a sound overall plan, effective execution, and continued feedback and revision as the transformation unfolds. Figure 3.7 illustrates the process, including principles of a sound communication program, goals and objectives, plans, activities, and feedback and evaluation.

Communication programs embody principles of sound communication. Communications must be *clear*, so that everyone in the organization can understand them. Communications must be *consistent*, so that everyone from the top to the bottom of the organization receives the same message. Communications must be *timely*, so that people receive the messages in reasonable time proximity to whatever their needs are. Communications must be *frequent*, so that too much time does not elapse between messages because people will forget or remember only certain aspects of the messages. Communications must be *honest*, so that people believe the messages. In addition, communications must be *open*, so that people feel free to express their opinions, including their agreements and disagreements.

What is the purpose of a communications message? Sound communications must have sound goals and objectives. A communications message should contain:

- *Action:* People are being asked to *do* something.
- *Commitment:* People are being encouraged to really *believe* and to be *committed* to something.
- *Expectations:* People are being told what they are *expected* to do.

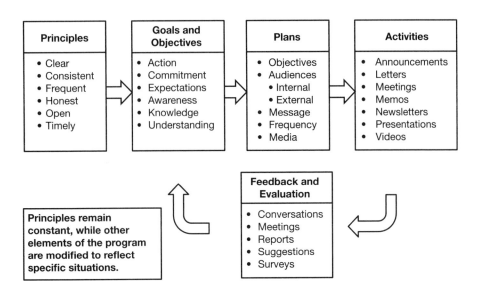

Figure 3.7. A Process for Developing an Effective Communication Program.

- *Awareness:* People are being helped to become *conscious* of the subject matter.
- *Knowledge*: People are being helped to raise their *comprehension* of the subject matter.
- *Understanding:* People are being helped to deepen their *ability* to be able to use the subject matter.

Communications goals and objectives are important so as to move individuals and the organization upward in the hierarchy of the subject matter.

Consider again the six-step change management model we presented in Figure 3.4: establish the change imperative; create vision and targets; redesign; build; implement; and learn and continuously improve. This plan will unfold perhaps over several months or a year or so. How does the *communications program* unfold along the way? There are several tasks and subtasks:

Develop and implement a detailed communications plan:
- What messages need to be communicated?
- To whom?
- When?
- How (what media)?

Communicate information about the project. Communicate its purpose, scope, and timetable as well as project status and progress:

- Use letters, memos, newsletters, meetings, presentations, videos, and so forth.
- Personalize the messages by showing "what's in it for me" (WII-FM) for people, groups, and the organization.
- During the project, coordinate the communications messages with the project status. For example, communicate:
  - Change imperative during and after Phase 1.
  - Vision and targets during and after Phase 2.
  - Redesign plans and progress during and after Phase 3.
  - Build plans and progress during and after Phase 4.
  - Implementation plans and progress during and after Phase 5.
  - Continuous improvement plans and progress during and after Phase 6.

Support the change program. Use selected tools and techniques which support the change communications program:

- Communications audit
- Communications mapping
- Communications planning
- Communications education and training
- Special events planning and execution

LEVER THREE: COMMITMENT

Enrollment in and commitment to the supply chain transformative change program is achieved through targeted participation and involvement:

- People take more responsibility for implementing ideas they helped to create.
- When people are actively enrolled in and participate in the process, they feel more "in the loop" and trust the organization and the supply chain transformation process more.
- Engagement helps people to feel more control over their lives in times of change.
- Allowing many people to participate results in more creativity in the alternative solutions.
- People either participate in change or they anticipate change and speculate on it. Anticipation and speculation usually are incorrect.

Consider once again the six-step change management model presented in Figure 3.4: establish the change imperative; create vision and targets; redesign; build; implement; and learn and continuously improve. This plan will unfold perhaps over several months or a year or so. How does the *commitment program* unfold along the way? There are several tasks and subtasks:

Project teams. Increase participation by establishing and utilizing project teams:

- Change imperative team(s)
- Creativity and visioning team(s)
- Redesign team(s)
- Build team(s)
- Implementation team(s)
- Continuous improvement team(s)

Key people. Involve key people in creating the change imperative:

- Use informal influence leaders and key resistors.
- Identify targets for the supply chain change.
- Build strong consensus for the vision.
- Involve process owners and participants in process redesign, build, and implementation.
- Utilize creative focus groups.

Diagnostics. Perform organizational and cultural diagnostics:

- Analyze, assess, and identify major issues and common themes in the supply chain transformation.
- Conduct challenge sessions with senior management and project teams.
- Begin commitment process early in the project.

Support the commitment process. Utilize selected tools and techniques to support the commitment process:

- An organizational cultural diagnostic instrument
- Commitment charting and planning
- Employment planning
- Employee interviews and opinion and attitude surveys
- Mediation and conflict-resolution techniques
- People-enabler techniques

LEVER FOUR: EDUCATION AND TRAINING

Education and training programs are designed with specific objectives for specific audiences. *Education* is different from *training*. We think that too many people confuse these two terms. Education builds awareness, knowledge, and understanding. Training builds skills. These are different, yet supply chain transformations need both.

The chart in Figure 3.8 illustrates the essence of an education and training program for supply chain transformations. Notice that program elements are in place for senior management, core process team members, and supply chain participants. Content and methods for each are outlined briefly.

Consider once again the six-step change management model presented in Figure 3.4: establish the change imperative; create vision and targets; redesign; build; implement; and learn and continuously improve. This plan will unfold perhaps over several months or a year or so. How does the *education and training program* unfold along the way? There are several tasks and subtasks:

Education and training programs. Develop, update, and refine process-focused education and training program plans throughout the project.

Executives. Conduct executive education.

Project teams. Conduct education and training for project teams:

- Core team education and training
- Creativity and visioning education and training
- Process redesign education and training
- Process and system build training
- Process and system implementation training
- Continuous improvement training

External education and training. Identify, design, and implement external education and training:

- Customers
- Suppliers
- Others

Outside providers. Identify appropriate outside providers of education and training services:

- Companies providing education and training services
- Universities and colleges

Education and Training Program			
AUDIENCE	**PHASES**	**CONTENT**	**METHODS**
Senior management	All	Transformation program education; visioning and creativity workshop; change management education and training	Facilitated discussion; case studies
Core team members	All	Transformation program education; transformation skills training; visioning and creativity workshop; change management education and training	Facilitated discussion; case studies; lectures; exercises
Process participants	All	New roles and responsibilities; systems functionality and operation; customer service	Facilitated discussion; classroom training; on-the-job training; job rotation; self-study

Figure 3.8. A Sample Education and Training Program for Supply Chain Transformation.

- Professional associations
- Individuals

Support the education and training program. Select tools and techniques to support the education and training program:

- Job skills analysis
- Education and training needs analysis
- Education and training program planning
- Executive education programs
- Project teams training materials
- External education and training program providers

LEVER FIVE: ORGANIZATION AND WORKFORCE TRANSITION

When organization, business processes, and jobs are redesigned, people need to be "rematched" with the organization:

- Some people will lack the required new skills. Training will be required.
- Some new capabilities will be needed. Hiring programs will need to be adjusted.

- Some people will not desire or will not be able to adjust to the new environment and will need assistance to find alternative career paths.

Consider once again the six-step change management model presented Figure 3.4: establish the change imperative; create vision and targets; redesign; build; implement; and learn and continuously improve. This plan will unfold perhaps over several months or a year or so. How does the *organization and workforce transition program* unfold along the way? There are several tasks and subtasks:

Issues and planning. Identify "first-cut" organization and workforce transition issues and begin implementation planning from the initiation of the supply chain transformation project:

- "Rightsizing"
- Capability enhancement
- Career-path modification

Updating. Update organization and workforce transition issues and continue throughout the project:

- Seek to close gaps between *as is* situation and *to be* vision and targets.
- Identify specific requirements for specific target populations.
- Begin planning for and continue working with high-potential "survivors."
- Begin working on organization and workforce issues for the "learning organization."
- Develop implementation plans.
- Begin implementation.

Support the organization and workforce transition program. Select tools and techniques to support the organization and workforce transition program:

- An organizational cultural diagnostic instrument
- Management contracts
- Severance planning
- Career paths
- Outplacement counseling in conjunction with professional outplacement firm

LEVER SIX: A RESULTS ORIENTATION

Consider once again the six-step change management model presented in Figure 3.4: establish the change imperative; create vision and targets; redesign; build; implement; and learn and continuously improve. This plan will unfold perhaps over several months or a year or so. How does the *results orientation program* unfold along the way? There are several tasks and subtasks:

Consensus. Develop consensus around the *as is* and *to be* performance measures as a result of the supply chain transformative program.

Leadership. Align leadership around performance expectations.

Communication. Communicate performance vision and targets.

Measure and report. During the early phases of the project, begin measuring and reporting against the vision and target performance.

Support the results orientation program. Select tools and techniques to support the results orientation program:
- Customer satisfaction surveys
- Cause and effect analysis
- Pareto analysis
- Decision tree analysis
- Balanced scorecard (a strategic performance management tool)
- Implementation scorekeeping

CONCLUSION

Successful supply chain transformations need:
- Committed, visible leaders
- Constant two-way communication
- New organization structures and job designs
- Massive education and training
- Better performance management approaches

The focus of the management of change in supply chain transformations thus is on capability development and culture change, explicitly planned from the outset, and integrated into each phase and critical area of the project.

Remember that successful management of complex supply chain transformations includes extensive collaboration within the organization, leverages experience both internal and external to the organization, creatively tailors the approaches, and produces both improved results and new capabilities.

REFERENCES

1. "Reengineering: The Hot New Managing Tool." *Fortune* 1993 August 23.
2. Katzenbach, Jon R. and Douglas K. Smith. *The Wisdom of Teams: Creating the High-Performance Organization* 1993. Boston: Harvard Business School Press.

4

STOP THE BLEEDING

It's very difficult to drain the swamp
when you're up to your neck in alligators.

— Anonymous

Many years ago in first aid training we were taught to help people by evaluating and applying first aid in the following sequence: make sure the person has a pulse and that he or she is breathing and then stop the bleeding. That is what we want to do with our supply chains. Do we have a pulse? Are we even breathing? If so, the patient organization is alive! That is good!

Now, let's stop the bleeding. Many companies are hemorrhaging money through their supply chains, and it needs to stop. That is what this book is all about.

If the first decade of the 21st century has shown us anything economically, it is that cash is king. In industry, this translates to measureable cash flow. In their 2009 book, Darrell Rigby and Davis Sweig stated:[1]

Until recently, most senior executives regarded managing cash flow and liquidity as tactical functions. No more. As the financial crisis choked off credit, cash management became strategic. Companies with weak cash flows find it difficult to secure funding, just when flows are harder than ever to generate.

The sustained continuous improvement of the velocity and volume of cash flow in a business is both its competitive imperative today and its lifeblood now and in the future.

Supply chains are important elements of the cash flow outflow and inflow process. It is both impossible and imprudent to attempt to get an enterprise to rally around the strategic improvement of its supply chains while the enterprise is bleeding to death for cash flow. First, stop the bleeding. Doing this requires an understanding of the causes of cash flow problems (usually not just *one* cause) and an immediate focus on corrections.

Process leaders (ultimately the senior staff) in a business often are very involved in making the near-term financial and nonfinancial objectives and goals for their areas of responsibility. They very often need to refresh their thinking on how their objectives and goals link to those of the enterprise. Experience has taught that this often is best achieved by understanding linkages and levers from a financial perspective.

SHOW ME THE MONEY

A number of years ago, Mike Katzorke worked for a company where the CEO required monthly reports. In his early days in the job, Mike was trying to determine just how many hours people were involved in the monthly reporting process. He knew it was taking many hours, and he wanted to find a way to streamline the reporting. So, Mike asked for all the reports from the previous month. He laid them out across a conference table in sequence from the lowest level to highest. As he looked over these reports, he was struck by the fact that the reports went from talking about *things* to talking about *money* as they moved higher in the organization. He also noticed that the work emphasis at the lower levels was not always synchronized with the financial issues at the upper levels.

> *The bottom of the organization talks about **things**.*
>
> *But, the top of the organization talks about **money**.*

Mike saw that this situation was an understanding, alignment, and communications issue and decided to begin to solve it. His review linked the enterprise objectives and goals financially with those of the supply chain organization. The learnings about how all activities of the company related financially and the improved day-to-day work alignment with enterprise strategy were amazing and lasting. So was the supply chain process contribution to business objectives and goals. The whole improvement process began with cash flow education for the organization.

Element	Data Source
Net Income	Current income statement
+ Depreciation or amortization	Current income statement
± Changes in working capital	Prior and current balance sheets: current assets and liability accounts
— Capital expenditures	Prior and current balance sheets: property, plant, and equipment accounts
= Free Cash Flow	

Figure 4.1. Free Cash Flow: Elements and Data Sources.

Free cash flow. Smart investors seek out companies that produce significant amounts of free cash flow (FCF).[2] Free cash flow shows the capability of a business to repay debt, pay shareholder dividends, buy back its own stock, and fund growth strategies. Free cash flow simply responds to the "show me the money" slogan — cold hard cash. Free cash flow generally is defined as illustrated in Figure 4.1.

As the chart shows, to get from net income on the current income statement (often called a profit and loss statement) to free cash flow, three adjustments need to be made:

- First, depreciation or amortization is a *non-cash* entry on the income statement that affects net income, so it needs to be added back to net income.
- Second, the free cash flow measurement deducts increases (or adds decreases) in working capital. Typically, a growing company will require increasing amounts of working capital to finance it — working capital that "cannot be taken home" because it would cramp the enterprise's operations. Working capital is current assets minus current liabilities and generally is considered as the amount of capital to keep the firm running. Analysts usually think that a year's supply of working capital is desirable.
- Third, capital expenditures are represented by changes in the property, plant, and equipment accounts. Capital expenditures generally are required for the long-term viability of the firm — typically considered as being for replacement of fixed assets.

Working capital. Difficult economic times (as was the case when this manuscript was being written) put a premium on working capital:[3]

> *Working capital performance is a good indicator of discipline and overall rigor within a company. ... Hard times have inspired companies to wring*

lots of cash out of working capital. How much better can they get? ... Plato called necessity the mother of invention.

CFO Magazine annually publishes an analysis of the *Working Capital Scoreboard*, which shows working capital performance of individual companies and industries. Days working capital is their primary metric. Days working capital is calculated as follows:

$$\text{Days working capital} = (\text{cash} + \text{accounts receivable} + \text{inventory} \\ - \text{accounts payable})/(\text{total revenue}/365)$$

We believe there remains room for improvement. If companies in the bottom three quartiles of working capital performance matched those in the top quartile for their industry, they could extract $776 billion in cash from their balance sheets. Clearly, companies are putting more emphasis on working capital management — good news for savvy supply chain executives who understand the linkage between superior supply chain performance and superior working capital performance.

Sources and uses of cash. When the focus is on cash flow for supply chain activities, executives need to understand sources and uses of cash in a business. Some sources of cash are:

- Investors
- Lenders or creditors
- Retained earnings

Some uses of cash are:

- Property, plant, and equipment (capital expenditures)
- Production and distribution expenses
  - Wages and salaries
  - Materials
  - Supplies
  - Selling expenses
  - Administration
  - Research and development
- Interest expense
- Reduction of debt
- Income and other taxes
- Dividends paid

The chart in Figure 4.2 depicts a simplified example of the sources and uses of funds in an enterprise (an actual manufacturing and distribution company

CASH ON HAND, END OF YEAR, 2007	$1,841.8
Net cash from operations	$2,294.1
• Decrease in accounts receivable	−$625.9
• Decrease in inventories	−$643.0
• Other cash impact from operations	$1,025.2
Net cash used in investing activities	−$2,473.3
Net cash used in financing activities	−$74.0
Effect of exchange rates on cash	−$45.8
CASH ON HAND, END OF YEAR, 2008	$1,542.8

Figure 4.2. Statement of Sources and Uses of Funds: $14B Manufacturing and Distribution Enterprise.

with about $14B in annual revenue that serves the global oil and gas industry). Two areas of opportunity for supply chain organizations to impact cash flow are shown: accounts receivable and inventories. This company reduced each by over $600 million in the year depicted.

In many businesses, the opportunities for improvement in cash flow lie in the minimization of trapped cash in the overall process. The more cash trapped in the denominator of return on invested capital (ROIC, in common parlance) for property, plant, and equipment, production and distribution, inventory (at all stages in the conversion of cash to profitable revenue), and in accounts receivable, the greater the opportunity for financial results improvement.

To reiterate, in most businesses, cash gets trapped in inventories, property, plant and equipment, and receivables. Often, businesses accept with little question the amount of cash tied up in the business. They focus improvement initiatives at operational levels on various performance parameters which generally are right and generally are good things about which customers care very much. Yet, often cash flow improvement initiatives get worked into the organization without clear understanding. Too often, individual contributors only hear: "We have to reduce inventory." They wonder: "Why? We were told we had record sales last year."

Management responds: "We have too much inventory based on what the industry benchmark is today." Individuals think: "What's that got to do with anything in our world? We're unique — we're different — that doesn't apply in this case. We'll give it lip service because we're told to, but we think it's ridiculous. After all, aren't we number 1 in our industry?" And, guess what, many management personnel have a similar level of understanding and focus.

Pragmatic enterprise financial education for the masses is important. When people understand the linkage of cash flow improvement to their job security and compensation, they will bring their creativity to bear on improving it —

rapidly. When they can see clearly the linkage of plant and equipment spending to possibly having their job outsourced, a sense of urgency generally will develop around removing waste that requires less trapped cash in the business. When people in accounts receivable and their counterparts in sales and marketing can see the possibility of their functions being outsourced to third parties or distributors, their creativity should begin to focus on getting the cash to the business in days and not weeks and months.

INVENTORY
Good
Bad
Ugly

It has been said that all inventory masks waste. In the purest sense, that is true; but in getting from where a business currently is to the vision, the business has to deal with the realities while the waste issues are being solved.

Inventory can be divided into three categories in the early stages of cash flow improvement — as we like to say: the good, the bad, and the ugly:

- *Good* inventory is planned on purpose with analytically determined specific requirements to satisfy customers and users and to generate revenue.
- *Bad* inventory is created by poor planning and execution inside the business. Bad inventory is the "just-in-case" inventory that a business has just in case someone might want it. There is little or no rhyme or analytical reasoning behind the selection or amount of bad inventory.
- *Ugly* inventory results from poor design, poor yields from production processes, lack of standardization of components on projects, and so forth. Ugly inventory has been created systemically and built into the business in ways that make it difficult to remove.

People who have some control over inventory (that is, nearly everyone in most businesses) need to see the linkage of their jobs to the ultimate success of the business. Jobs are being outsourced because the profit paid to a third party becomes less expensive than keeping the inventory and paying for all the people to manage it. Inventory needs to become as *important* as revenue and profit. Return on invested capital needs to become an understood priority for the whole organization. *So what are we saying?* Financially educate the whole team and link financial improvement initiatives to operational ones. (The next chapter will deal with how to achieve this important linkage in much greater depth.)

Figure 4.3 shows a simplistic inventory/cash flow pipeline, distinguished from the concept of inventory as a stock. Don't people often talk about *how much* inventory or the *level* of inventory or the *stockpile* of inventory or the inventory *reserve* or the *supply* of inventory? All of these terms denote a static supply of

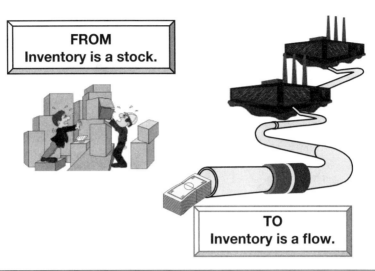

Figure 4.3. A Sample Inventory/Cash Flow Pipeline.

inventory. How about the concept of a pipeline of inventory that moves or flows? Isn't that closer to the concept we want?

In a healthy enterprise, the volume and velocity of cash flow is improving continuously. As a result, the business is able to invest the faster cash flow and continuously improve market share and operational effectiveness and efficiency. Yet we often find very leaky cash flow; that is, poor processes and subprocesses create waste relative to what *could be* in terms of cash flow speed, yield to the treasury, and the amount of near-permanent trapped cash put into the cycle to compensate for all this waste as Figure 4.4 illustrates:

Orders. As orders are entered into the business, they often contain errors (customer or internally created) in quantity, item number or description, specifications, delivery requested or promised, quality requirements, documentation requirements, and so forth. All these create rework — and the process is slowed along with cash flow.

Requirements. As an order is converted to requirements, a variety of issues can be created, such as incomplete or inaccurate bills of materials, inaccurate inventory positions, inaccurate lead times, long administration times, and poor or nonexistent capacity planning. Once again, the result is rework, slowed processes, and greatly diminished cash flow result.

Supply base. The supply base is an environment for cash flow leaks. Slow conversion and inaccurate and incomplete communication of requirements from

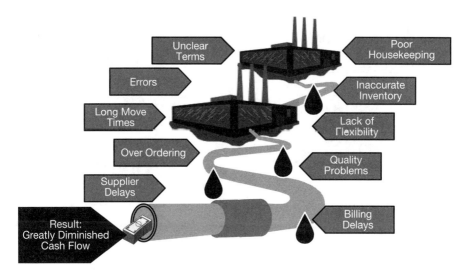

Figure 4.4. Leaks in the Inventory Pipeline: Things that Can Go Wrong.

the business to all tiers of its supply chain is the first (and often the greatest) impact to optimal quality, cost, delivery, service, and flexibility — all effecting cash. The so-called *bullwhip* effect (that is, a small change at the top often causes a huge change further along the chain) magnifies up-front slow communication and accuracy issues:[4]

> *Distorted information from one end of a supply chain to the other can lead to tremendous inefficiencies: excessive inventory investment, poor customer service, lost revenue, misguided capacity plans, ineffective transportation, and missed production schedules. How do exaggerated order swings occur? What can companies do to mitigate them?*

Support functions. Unresolved design problems, supplier selection and relationship problems, collaboration and communication shortfalls, supplier process maturity and commitment problems, and supplier overall performance problems effect product flow and cash flow significantly.

Direct labor. Businesses also have been known to experience issues with the application of direct labor to cash flow. Issues with incorrect and incomplete work instructions; schedule volatility and its management; inadequate training, facilities, tools, fixtures, jigs, and test equipment; and just plain human resources issues impact cash flow negatively.

Support labor. All the people supporting the direct workers and the cash flow process, such as quality, finance, human resources, information systems, and general administration, often work in processes fraught with waste, error, poor linkage, poor communication and sometimes parochialism which leads to rework, delay, and suboptimal cash flow.

Order fulfillment. To state the obvious, cash flows in when orders are fulfilled, so removing waste and rework (which of course is waste) and improving overall process cycle time help to speed product and the resulting cash flow.

Improving overall operational efficiency is what tools and processes like six sigma and lean are all about. Yet few businesses apply them in a visibly linked fashion to cash flow — some initiatives and improvement process priorities would be greatly altered if viewed from a cash standpoint.

In supply chains, plugging the cash leaks often involves what is expressed as doing the "right wrong things" in the short term to permit doing the "right right things" for the long term. Experience has taught a set of actions that rapidly addresses the short-term causes that are not 180 degrees off the long-term direction — more of a zigzag course in the short term (6 to 9 months). These are the *levers* for stopping the bleeding.

Enterprises improve cash flow with the application of four key principles:

- Input less
- Input later
- Output more
- Output sooner

By inputting less, inputting later, outputting more, and outputting sooner, the average investment is reduced and additional cash is created in the business; but what specific levers are needed in the short term to achieve these results? How can improvements result in faster cash generation for the enterprise in the short term without jeopardizing the long term competitive posture? How do we satisfy the near-term immanent issues of the business while still achieving the longer-term important strategic priorities? As we said earlier, how do we fend off the alligators while draining the swamp?

THE SUPPLY CHAIN CHALLENGE

Companies easily can get themselves ensnared in financial and customer issues. Not making the financial plan — either the top line or the bottom line — causes the CEO to bring in a new supply chain leader to help out (maybe with a few other new leaders as well). We have seen this situation at several major corporations.

Each time (and in varying industries), the enterprises had some similar symptoms of an immature supply chain process:

- Deliveries were late and unreliable and customers and users were disappointed (if not angry).
- Too much of all the wrong stuff was in inventory.
- Excessive shortages occurred.
- Costs were escalating.
- Scheduling was highly volatile with many surprises.
- Supplier quality was poor and deliveries were late.
- The supply chain was inflexible with long lead times.
- Logistics performance was inconsistent.
- People were frustrated and burned out in their jobs.
- The blame game ran rampant among customers, internal processes, and suppliers.
- Revenue, profit, and ROIC targets were missed.
- Shareholders were unhappy with their returns.
- The workforce mostly was doing fire fighting.

People like to complain of poor marketing forecasts resulting in schedule volatility, severe materials shortages, and disappointed customers and users. They wonder what they could have achieved if they had had a good sales or usage forecast and thus had had the materials. And, of course, many operations executives cannot understand why sales and marketing people just did not sell what manufacturing produced or what distribution had in stock instead of asking operations to move the schedules around to accommodate what was being sold.

> People in supply chains and associated functions have been known to perform many miracles. In fact, many of us can remember years when an organization boasted of a substantial increase in output and concurrent improvements in nonfinancial metrics such as utilization and efficiency.

But, seriously, manufacturing entities really do incur heavy cost and schedule impacts when they have material flow and schedule volatility problems. These impacts, of course, translate to revenue, profit, cash, and return on invested capital shortfalls.

As Figure 4.5 shows, supply chain costs are often a very large element of the sales dollar in manufacturing enterprises. As such, often the greatest opportunity for profit improvement is in supply chains.

Because production and material planning, supply base management, sometimes manufacturing, and usually logistics fall into supply chain responsibilities,

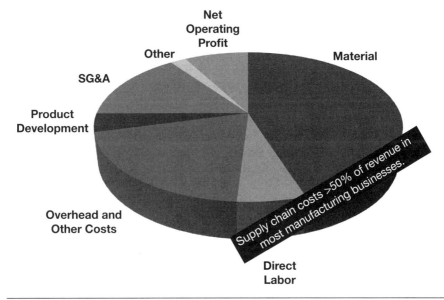

Figure 4.5. Typical Breakdown of Income Statement Expenses.

the supply chain team is often looked to as the group with the largest opportunity for customer satisfaction and associated financial improvements. The supply chain leader often is the person whom the CEO asks to lead the cross-functional improvement efforts. It is a challenging opportunity.

So, a new supply chain leader is often given an immediate challenge:

- Fix the material flow problem immediately.
- Shrink the focus of the problem.
- Fix the cost escalation immediately.
- Get the enterprise and the supply chain to play together as a team — internally and externally.
- Do these things as consistently with the long-term strategic direction as possible in the short term.

WHAT ARE YOU *REALLY* GOING TO DO?

Several years ago, Mike Katzorke was asked to make an assessment of the supply chain process in a large, global enterprise. As the head of the corporate supply chain, he also was asked to lead the planning and deployment of world-class supply chain processes across the enterprise. After the assessment, Mike was asked to brief members of the senior staff on the findings and to propose a deployment strategy. The presentation and discussion went well. After the session, Mike was politely taken aside by Jim, his boss's boss. "Mike," he said, "Great presentation — super job. But, what are you really going to go do?"

Jim's question and the ensuing discussion led to lessons of prioritization and timing of transformations. The basic lesson from the question, however, was simple. A patient cannot get excited about diet and exercise for health improvement and longevity while bleeding to death. The bleeding has to be stopped before the organization can be aligned and rallied around a strategic improvement plan and transformation process. Yet, the planning for the transformation should be done in parallel with the application of process first aid.

So, what are you really going to do first? Fix the material problem immediately.

Step 1. Fix the material problem immediately. If the causes of material shortages were displayed on a cause-and-effect diagram (commonly called a fishbone), the diagram would cover at least two white boards. Most of the causal issues of material shortages are not a 90-day fix — most of them are process related, systemic, and cultural:

- Information for sales, shipment, or usage forecasting often is not well linked and flows are inconsistent, which slows down the supply chain from suppliers to customers or users.
- Planning processes are often immature and there is weak linkage between the sales plan, production plan, inventory plan, materials plan, and financial plan.
- The internal and external supply base is not strategically defined.
- The supply chain is weakly aligned with the business plan.
- The supply chain performance capability is inadequate for the competitive and financial needs. It is not integrated into the business processes of design and manufacturing.
- Logistics processes are not optimal.
- The overall culture is one of acceptance of the status quo, which results from all the above factors.
- The best firefighters become company heroes.

Concerning material availability, the culture issue is one of the places to start. It has to be made *not OK* to be late or to receive over- or under-receipts. *Not OK* does not mean that fingers are pointed and people are fired. It does not mean that individuals receive gold stars and glowing write-ups in the company newsletter for firefighting a problem that they helped create in the first place. It does mean people are visibly recognized for problem prevention — by analytically and

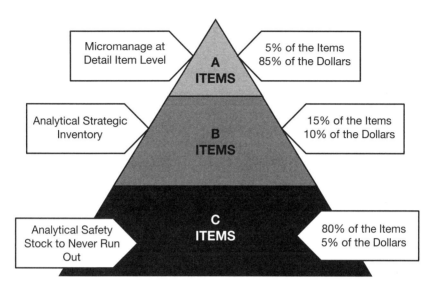

Figure 4.6. Shrink the Focus of the Problem.

creatively working toward avoiding shortages rather than fixing them after the fact — both inside the company and at external suppliers.

Step 2. Shrink the focus of the effort. The second course of action is to shrink the focus of the effort. (Figure 4.6 provides a quick conceptual grasp of the approach using one of the oldest analytical techniques in the book.) In supply chain turnaround efforts, many companies have taken a quick and dirty approach. Yet, time-allocation studies frequently determined what people were actually working on and the relative proportion of their time that was being spent on each activity. Invariably, some were spending 65 to 75% of their time *expediting* (broadly defined) — in all functions, processes, and most levels in the organization — but they still were failing in time commitments, inventories were increasing, and costs (direct and overhead) were escalating. The following is a typical example:

> Many companies have tried to *get along* with a superficial approach. Often, all inventories were treated as *bad* instead of being segmented. Too frequently, safety stock, if any, was provisioned in the master production schedule that was used to determine materials requirements; but manufacturing worked to a lower-volume schedule. This situation, of course, created excess inventory for every single item. Because schedules were volatile in the near term, suppliers paid no attention to them. Suppliers simply waited for the next telephone call to load their production each day. The internal production team simply waited for

POLICY	A ITEMS	B ITEMS	C ITEMS
Percent of items	5%	15%	80%
Percent of dollars	85%	10%	5%
Management approach	Just-in-time	Scheduled through the ERP system	"Never run out!"
Frequency of resupply	Individual item planning	Individual item planning	Approximately twice per year

Figure 4.7. ABC Segmentation Analysis.

the day's hot list complete with its red, yellow, and green tags — *hot* lists, *hot hot* lists, and *super hot* lists — and the organization spent +60% of its time working a small percentage of the problems and the dollars that were impacted.

Systemically fixing volatility and the ability to respond to it, as well as the myriad of other causes for shortages, is not a 3-month project. But what happens if change is made in the *way* with which the problem is dealt? That is, the population of items can be reduced and improvements can still be made on overall inventory investment and cost in the meantime.

One approach is to segment the inventory into some form of A, B, and C items (not a new idea!). There are many ways of performing ABC segmentation, with monetary value being the most common — but this is not the only way. Inventory policy then can be set for the near term using some form of ABC segmentation as illustrated in the chart in Figure 4.7.

Multiple analyses have consistently shown in diverse businesses and industries that C items account for about two-thirds or three-quarters of the shortages being pursued in supply chain transformation scenarios. So, for C items, set a safety stock policy across the board to *never* run out — *ever*!

Start (often) with setting a policy to keep *enough* of each C item available so that an entire order cycle can be missed, but there is still adequate time to recover from the missed order cycle before operations are affected. Then, order and expedite replenishment inventory. Generally, this should not take more than about 90 days to fix. Having this policy eliminates the need to expedite a large number of items as well as eliminates the opportunity for 80% of the items to become a shortage.

What can be done with all the resources that were chasing a large number of the C-item shortages? Simplistically, we say: "Micromanage the A items which account for 80% of the dollars that need to be minimized in inventory." How will that help? The best thing is to keep the A item inventory to a minimum, virtually "just-in-time" for the need — but, of course, any shortages are not good, not one. Add expediting strength, but also free up time for people to analyze these items — determine what safety stock is needed for chronic problem items (due to poor quality, poor suppliers, and so forth). If A items are scheduled to be available just-in-time, and the causes of shortages still exist, shortages will occur. Planners, however, can make provisions for certain chronic problem items in the short term and inventory investment can still be reduced.

With the B items, do the same type of chronic problem item analysis as for the A items, but only after the A items are complete.

So, in 90 to 120 days, 80% of the items should no longer be a shortage issue: 80% of the dollars are being micromanaged for both on-time and inventory and 10% of the items, 15% of the dollars, are being managed more analytically with more resources. The shortage and inventory picture vastly improves as does on-time delivery to customers or users as well as a cleanup of trapped material — often a huge part of the total money tied up in working capital.

One company's actual results, linked directly to the above approach, were as follows:

- 52% reduction in shortages
- 6% reduction in inventory
- 1.5% improvement in the cash position
- 32% improvement in on-time availability

At that point, the problems were not totally solved, but the severe bleeding from shortages had stopped.

Step 3. Fix the cost escalation immediately. The short-term approach to cost escalation is *cultural* and often initially executed in a somewhat heavy-handed style. It is cultural in that people's expectations and standards of what is "reasonably acceptable" have to change to become and remain competitive. Historically, much of industry thought like this:

> *Inflation was at 3% last year. Certainly people have to be given salary increases that let them stay ahead of inflation. So, set a compensation budget increase of, say, 4.5%. As for key suppliers, they have to keep up with inflation, unless the volume goes up enough that by spreading the increased volume over their overhead results can be better than the inflation rate. This looks like a 5 to 6% price increase this year will safely cover and protect the margins. So notify the customers that prices are being raised effective immediately. Customers do likewise, and the increases are passed throughout the supply chain. Everyone understood.*

The problem: no productivity improvements were deemed needed or invested in. The price simply was raised to maintain an adequate return for investors. For the economy as a whole, the inflation cycle kept going. All of this worked pretty well for about 20 to 30 years after World War II.

But then the game changed. An observation was once made that there was just about no way to "mess up" in a U.S. corporation in the 1950s. Then this thing called *global competition* began to rear its ugly head in an increasingly serious fashion. First Japan, then Korea, India, and other Pacific Rim countries became more and more competitive. Western Europe rose from the ashes of war with technological innovations. The Soviet empire fell and lots of cheap labor became available in central Europe.

Wall Street was not happy with single-digit returns anymore either — they could do better with their money by investing it elsewhere.

Oh, yes, and customers did not want long waits for products *or* to hold inventory anymore to offset delivery and forecast glitches. They wanted exactly what they needed exactly when they needed it and with very short lead times. They also did not see why the price should be going up. Enough productivity increases should be generated to offset inflation as a minimum. Really, companies should be outpacing inflation with productivity increases and costs should be going down, not up.

After World War II, corporations became vertically integrated. Competition was largely domestic. Then growing global competition began to force a paradigm shift in how *good* was defined in the customer satisfaction elements of quality, cost, delivery, service, product life cycle, financial performance, and so forth. The definition was also highly dynamic, getting more stringent all the time. *Speed of improvement* in these parameters became the new name of the game, which drove changes in the supply chain as well.

We mentioned earlier that the outside supply chain accounts for greater than 50% of the sales dollar in most companies today. Historically, direct labor accounted for up to 50% of the sales dollar of a business. This was the situation when businesses were very vertically integrated. As competition drove ever higher standards of performance, however, scarce resources of capital and people had to be limited to those things that provided core competitive advantages to a business for competitive financial performance — both short and long term. So businesses began to shed products, processes, and operations that someone else could perform more competitively and that were not core to their strategic competitive advantage. Return on invested capital and free cash flow requirements became more competitive. Businesses began to realize that ROIC had a numerator *and* a denominator. Simplistically,

ROIC = return/invested capital

Previously companies had been focused more on *profit generation* to gain return and less on the *investment* required to support that return. The more companies focused on core products, processes, and operations, the less investment was required in plant and equipment, human resources, and so forth. Everything that was not *core* became *context*. Companies sought to place this context with others who could provide the products and services more competitively. Ultimately, these *others* were found globally. *The supply chain processes became more strategic and more of a competitive differentiator.*

Remembering back to the early 1970s, the term *supply chain* did not exist. Companies had customers and vendors — marketing, sales, engineering, production planning and control, purchasing, quality control, shipping and receiving, accounting, personnel, and so forth. When the term *supply chain* began to surface, people's minds went, "click, click" — *supply, supplier* — thinking "this must have something to do with purchasing." So, they said, "You purchasing people go take care of this." We now explain this with a little tongue-in-cheek scenario (but all too true):

> Engineering told Purchasing what to buy and picked the suppliers. Production Control told Purchasing how many to buy and when to have them delivered. Accounts Payable paid the vendors. (*So what's so tough about typing a purchase order and having the items delivered on time or at least most of the time?*)
>
> Obviously, the company needed more suppliers to get a better price and delivery. But they were told: "Don't worry. If a few get rejected, that just means the Quality Department is doing its job in inspection. After all, nobody is expected to be perfect. And, by the way, inflation is normal, so the price should go up every year — after all, didn't we get a raise last year?"

This scenario worked pretty well after World War II. Then companies recognized that status quo performance and the processes and expectations of people that created it were not going to be competitive any longer   people had to be convinced that things were broken before they would work to get them fixed.

As it turns out, people just cannot be shown a presentation and at the end be convinced that they are standing on a burning platform and are about to become fuel for the fire. People have to touch it — feel it — smell it. Here is an illustration using a well-documented story as we understand it:

> Xerox bought Fuji Xerox back in the early stages of this industrial transformation. When some of their top executives went to Japan, they discovered that Fuji had listened to Dr. W. Edwards Deming about quality management. Fuji could

produce machines that were feature-for-feature competitive with Xerox products and still have profitable selling prices below Xerox costs — something that was not explainable solely as a wage-rate differential.

When the Xerox team got back to Rochester, they could not get the team there to believe Xerox's competitive disadvantage. It was not until the Xerox executives sent teams over to Japan to see the numbers and processes for themselves that transformation domestically began in earnest.

Every time we have been engaged in a transformation effort, we have heard the same words from business leadership and often from the rank and file: "We're unique — we're different — that stuff doesn't apply in this case — you just don't understand our business and our constraints" — blah, blah, blah.

Bill Lee was even told by the CEO of a large, well-known company: "You don't understand. We're the best in the industry." Less than 3 years later, the company was acquired by a much smaller competitor.

Einstein once said: "Imagination is more important than knowledge." It has since been said that "the limit to innovation is not technology." Limitation is the *mindset* in which we operate — if we think we are the best, or at least good enough, we are not going to take transformation seriously.

So, what can really be done to stop the bleeding in cost escalation immediately?

A supply chain organization first needs to understand the problem. At a minimum, the margins will shrink if escalation in the incoming supply chain is greater than that being allowed by customers on the output of the supply chain. The rate of improvement by key competitors in supply chain costs also creates a limit. Today, in most industries, for the most part, expectations are that either more value is delivered for the same price or the price is actually being decreased. These expectations drive supply chain costs and value in both directions.

We have seen one heavy-handed approach work. Of course, senior staff and key stakeholders should have been engaged for consensus in this vision and policy action *before* it is moved forward with the supply chain team and the supply base:

- Set an immediate policy with the supply chain organization (both external and between operations) that does not allow *any* price increase of *any* kind for *any* reason without the approval of the chief supply chain officer. The supply chain organization can implement this policy with suppliers (both internal and external) and blame the boss. No supplier wants that kind of visibility, so suppliers begin to drive processes to take cost out and foster productivity increases.

- As rapidly as possible, orchestrate a first-class supplier conference and link the supply base into the vision and strategy and what it means to them (more on this later).

Initially, implementation of this approach is challenging. Actually, it has been the most challenging internally. "Old school" buyers have been called "vendor defenders," sometimes for good reason. Old school buyers have to see that they are actually helping long-term faithful suppliers survive by providing the impetus for their improvement programs — the expectation, indeed demand, for continuous competitive sharing of productivity improvements. Good suppliers know that every industry is just coming out of a major transformation, in the middle of one, or just about to go into one.

We have seen the results of this initial fiat be consistently astounding. One example of directly linked actual results, as reported by the finance organization after a year of the changes discussed above, is as follows:

- 5% improvement in operating profit
- 3% improvement in free cash flow
- Another 6% contracted cost improvement for next fiscal year

Step 4. Get the enterprise and the supply chain to play together as a team — internally and externally. In most boardrooms today, the pressure is intense to *continuously shrink* the difference between gross revenue and net operating profit and to *consistently improve* return on invested capital, which means that the interests of the shareholders and other stakeholders are of utmost importance. Many have realized and many more are beginning to realize that a well-integrated, well-managed supply chain is a major driver of continuously improving results.

> *Supply chain is a team sport!*

In many companies, efforts to improve supply chain results have been short lived, incomplete, and suboptimized. Almost always, this is the result of basing the success of supply chain transformation on a singular personality — one who approaches the transformation process as a materials (not supply chain management) technocrat rather than as a senior business executive. Linkage of supply chain process transformation from customers' customers to suppliers' suppliers is one key for supply chain and enterprise engagement and optimized, sustained results — which means that *all* internal organizations, in addition to supply chain, must be engaged.

So, what can really be done to get the enterprise and the supply chain to play together as a team — internally and externally?

Hopefully the supply chain organization will not try to do everything themselves for the sake of expediency. Some Type A personalities have made that error — some more than once. It is much easier to sell a major transformation plan in the beginning than it is in midstream. The transformation journey cannot be made successfully without the entire enterprise team.

Also, do *not* start with reorganization. Reorganization without redesign of the supply chain processes just does not make sense and usually makes a problem worse. Perhaps some people want to reorganize because it makes them feel as though they are doing something — or maybe they are trying to create the impression for others that they are doing something — an approach that is neither new nor rare (often, but "spuriously," according to *Wikipedia*, credited to Gaius Petronius Arbiter, ca. 27—66 A.D.):[5]

> *We trained hard but it seemed that every time we were beginning to form up into teams we would be reorganized. I was to learn later in life that we tend to meet any new situation by reorganizing; and a wonderful method it can be for creating the illusion of progress.*
>
> — Petronius

In fact, reorganization generally is the last thing that should be done. What is the sense of reorganizing around a broken process? Focus on the work and the process. Then analytically decide a course of action from there. Then if reorganization is dictated for the success of a well-thought-out plan based on analysis of the work, reorganize.

Type A personalities are task oriented. They generally are "quick studies," who can rapidly assess the maturity of an enterprise and its processes, sense the urgency of the situation, and see what needs to be done to improve it. Type A personalities have a bent for action and are risk takers, especially if they come from a broader background than just one company, have significant experience, and are full of vigor. Perhaps the most effective personality is a *mellowed* Type A — that is, someone who has made many deployment faux pas (French for screw-ups) on the soft side of the deployment process. Diagnosis and planning are relatively easy compared to successful sustained deployment. Experience has taught, however, that although too much deployment planning is not helpful, not enough is painful and slows down deployment execution and threatens sustainability. Any transformation process needs as careful a job of planning and management of the soft side of deployment planning and execution as it does for the technical elements.

The model shown in Figure 4.8 shows some of the key planning and deployment management elements for a successful transformation no matter how fast the process needs to move:

Create a shared need. Creating a shared need brings the enterprise together to agree on where it is going and on its maturity relative to what *good* looks like

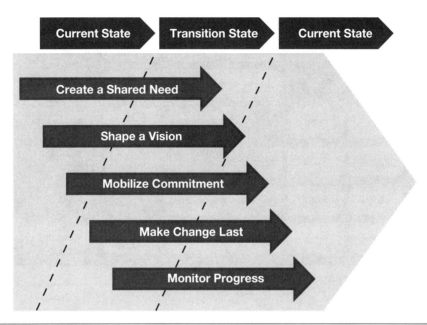

Figure 4.8. Key Planning and Deployment Management Elements to Get a Team Playing Together.

globally. It builds agreement on the need for process improvement and the associated investment for its achievement. It fosters an environment for enterprise-wide engagement in the generation of a process strategic plan and for rolling its essential elements into that of the business. It helps create shared roles and responsibilities for deployment of the plan. It gets a binding commitment of each member of the senior leadership team and key process stakeholders.

Shape a vision. Shaping a vision *together* engages the enterprise in pursuit of its vision. The vision is created in light of the business strategic plan, benchmark results, and process maturity for the supply chain. Do not hesitate to begin shaping the vision while stopping the bleeding — in fact, that may be the best time to begin.

Mobilize commitment. The best planning and orchestration in the world will achieve nothing without mobilizing commitment. The team has to want to start and it has to want the transformation to succeed on a personal basis — so

> *If you don't know where you're going, any road will get you there.*
>
> *But, if you don't know where you **are**, you don't know what path to take, even if you know where you're going.*

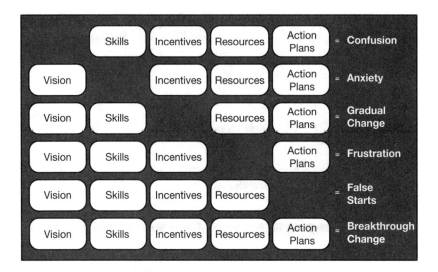

Figure 4.9. A Simple Tool for Quick Sanity Check Analysis.

much that the team forges ahead when the going gets rough. The team balances its achievement with other priorities as they compete for time. This is the leader's job.

Make change last. Sustainability of a change is most important. If a transformation process begins to regress when leadership changes, the people probably never really believed in the vision in the first place. Transformation is incomplete until its key stakeholders have internalized the vision. Commitment must be mobilized, but it must also be sustained. If visioning and mobilizing commitment have been done well, history has shown that sustaining commitment is rarely an issue; but if the transformation was forced too rapidly, sustaining it can be a continual struggle because ownership probably never happened broadly.

Monitor progress. Monitoring the progress and results of the transformation is done differently in different companies. Metrics, review participants, frequency, and levels of reviews need to "fit" and be motivational.

During a review of the transformation, we have found that a useful exercise for the team is to sit down and give itself a short sanity check using the simple tool summarized in Figure 4.9. It is quick, but effective:

- **CONFUSION** results if the linkage of the transformation deployment plan, from CEO to individual contributor, lacks clear, well articulated, and understood *Vision.*

- **ANXIETY** results if *Skills* are lacking to deploy the transformation.
- Only **GRADUAL CHANGE** results if *Incentives* are lacking for individuals, groups, and the organization as a whole.
- **FRUSTRATION** results if *Resources* are lacking to execute the transformation.
- **FALSE STARTS** result if *Action Plans* are missing, incomplete, or unattainable.

Step 5. Do these things as consistently with the long-term strategic direction as possible in the short term. Remember our earlier comment about doing the "right wrong things" today in order to facilitate getting the "right right things" accomplished tomorrow.

This section has discussed pulling people together quickly, explaining the business issues, and then directing near-term supply chain strategies and tactics to stop the bleeding in the financial and customer satisfaction areas. Yet, if policies and actions are directed quickly, with little consensus building, often there is a disconnect in people's minds relative to how all this fits into the picture of the strategic direction.

While the bleeding is being stopped, ensure that the same ground does not have to be covered more than once. To state it succinctly, no matter how much blood exists, be sure that the bleeding is not being made worse. If the company is in a deep downturn, cutting marketing and product development budgets generally is the *wrong* thing to do.

Likewise, in the supply chain, do things that stop the bleeding as rapidly as possible, but not things that will "kill the patient" next year. Do things that free up resources from repetitive tactical transactional work to focus on improving the way the work gets done in the future. This is where experience comes into play. There may not be time to do a lot of analysis before acting when the business is bleeding, but detrimental action does not help either.

Experienced leaders have learned to understand quickly the broad business picture and the process maturity. A saying in the consulting business is that, "We're two hours from being an expert on anything!" This is said as a joke, but it is not really a joke. The point is that when the telephone rings in a consultant's office, he or she does not know who is on the other end or what that person's issues are. Most large consultancies have an internal capability to research the issues quickly and retrieve the answers for the client.

> *Don't stay so busy chopping wood that you don't have time to sharpen the axe.*

Organizations need to ask themselves the right strategic questions and link assessment and improvement planning together at all levels across the organization:

- How does the customer determine value?
- What financial objectives need to be met?
- How is the enterprise doing with meeting financial objectives?
- What needs to be done in the business to achieve financial objectives?
- What does the supply chain need to deliver to support achieving business needs?
- Where is the greatest leverage for improvement in supporting the business plan?
- What relative priority do the levers have in supporting the entire enterprise's achievement needs?
- What processes, tools, and resources will be needed to support the business improvements?
- What should be measured, by whom, and in what combination to achieve the behaviors and results that the business needs?

The process needs to be sure it is not pushing in on the balloon in one spot only to cause it to pop out in another — such as allowing so much inventory to assure customer service that waste, lower return on invested capital, and lower cash flow result.

ENSURE COLLABORATION

At this point, the proposed near-term actions are in alignment with the strategic direction in every sense except one — building a collaborative supply chain. Demanding productivity improvement is good medicine for the long-term health of the total supply chain; but there will be some damage control and rework needed to create the collaborative environment that is essential for the longer-term health of the supply chain. *Real collaboration is the next frontier of full potential supply chain.*

In the 1980s, the competition of lower-cost global competitors drove some early pioneers to successfully explore the full potential of the supply chain process as a competitive differentiator at the enterprise level. An uncoordinated or loosely coordinated group of companies operating as a supply chain, however, cannot possibly compete long term with a group of companies operating in a fully integrated supply chain — integrated in terms of objectives, strategies, processes, and data.

In any given industry, competing end products or services often utilize some of the same suppliers. So, as an end supplier to the ultimate consumer of any given supply chain, to the degree that one company can do a better job of linking and integrating its supply chain than the competitors do, competitive advantage can be created with better results for the end customer and all the stakeholders of the entire chain.

There is a saying that goes: "Relationships are more important than results" — meaning that without relationships, results cannot be sustained. The results of relationships are collaborative supply chains. For years people have talked *collaboration* and *win-win* results. Many thought the walk did not match the talk — and many were right. But today, global competition is making collaboration a competitive imperative. A few are really succeeding at making it a reality in their supply chains. We will explore this in the next chapter.

CONCLUSION

Stop the bleeding! is an expression that has more oomph than "time is of the essence" or something simple like "hurry up!" We wanted an expression that emphasized the importance of making big changes quickly.

The objective of this chapter is to emphasize getting the most glaring supply chain issues and problems solved promptly. We presented some simple ideas, concepts, tools, and techniques that can be used quickly without a lot of education and training of the team and, even, without a lot of data and analyses.

In this chapter, we assume that the problems have been identified (through an assessment such as we illustrated in Chapter 2). We also assume that the organization has been convinced to do something (through an approach such as was presented in Chapter 3). Now, it is imperative that the process be moved along without hesitation (through an approach discussed in Chapter 4).

Next, in Chapter 5, we will begin to tackle some more long-term transformative issues with a collaborative supply chain approach. Developing collaboration simply takes more time and effort than does the *stopping the bleeding* process. Notice that developing collaboration is a progressive, almost step-by-step process.

REFERENCES

1. Rigby, Darrell and David Sweig. *Winning in Turbulence: Model and Manage Cash Flow* 2009. Boston: Harvard Business School Press.
2. See *Wikipedia* article on "Free Cash Flow." Accessed June 2009.

3. Myers, Randy. "Cleaner (Balance) Sheets." *CFO Magazine* 2009 June.

4. Lee, Hau L., V. Padmanabhan, and Seungjin Whang. "The Bullwhip Effect in Supply Chains." *Sloan Management Review* 1997 Spring.

5. See *Wikipedia* article on "Petronius." Accessed June 2009.

5

DEVELOP TRANSFORMATIVE COLLABORATIVE SUPPLY CHAINS

I do detest everything which is not perfectly mutual.
— Lord Byron

The dictionary definition of collaboration is *working together*. Working together is exactly what is meant by a *collaborative supply chain* — that is, a supply chain in which everyone works together in a cooperative fashion to achieve a common set of objectives. As Lord Byron implies, everything is *perfectly mutual* in a collaborative supply chain.

If you have ever watched how a code team responds when a patient in a hospital stops breathing, the response definitely is a collaborative effort. Physicians, nurses, pharmacists, and people from several disciplines come together in a truly cooperative and collaborative effort.

In business, collaboration can be found both within an organization and between organizations. In supply chain organizations, collaboration can range from simple price agreements that pool requirements from multiple businesses to fully integrated global supply chains. Collaboration is a concept that is continuously evolving in business in its definition, scope of application, and reality of success. Much of the 21st century buzz around the term has been of a systems' orientation — facilitating the sharing of real-time data up and down the supply chain. Although this is certainly useful, the scope of collaboration can be so much more, and its successful strategic deployment can be so much more powerful as a competitive advantage.

Ireland and Crum illustrate this point with the following:[1] "Companies are increasingly looking beyond their individual enterprises … [and] are developing a supply chain transformation strategy, with supply chain collaboration as a foundation of the strategy." We see this mentality in any number of companies, even those that are not in a transformation mode. We think it is fair to say that *supply chain collaboration* is one of the hottest topics among supply chain executives.

In previous chapters, considerable time was spent discussing the symptoms of an immature supply chain. Considered also were some initial tactics to stop the customer-satisfaction and financial-performance bleeding due, at least in part, to supply chain performance. The discussion now moves to a discussion of the ongoing race for creating and rapidly improving a full-potential collaborative supply chain as a competitive differentiator. Companies cannot compete in this race if their supply chains have problems with cooperation and collaboration. They have to get these problems under control in order to succeed in this very dynamic race.

So, possibly, the new supply chain leader has been somewhat of a discreet Attila the Hun while leading the team in stopping the bleeding. Progress had to be made very quickly and as such was done without a great deal of consensus building. As some have learned the hard way, a much more flexible leadership style is needed in leading the team to improve the organization's cooperation and collaboration.

A number of years ago, co-author Mike Katzorke was riding down the New Jersey turnpike with his boss, Fred McClintock (who led the supply chain process transformation at Xerox as a part of the overall turnaround of Xerox). They had been discussing the challenges of that transformation process in their current jobs at AlliedSignal and comparing them to challenges in previous environments. Mike asked Fred, "Why does it seem that so many supply chain transformation efforts fail or fail to last?"

Fred thought about the question for a few minutes and gave Mike a profound answer: "Mike, I don't know." Both laughed, gave the question a little more dialog, and came up with the following:

- First, the success and continuation of the transformation process is often based on the personal strength of the individual leading the transformation. As such, the transformation is viewed as his or her initiative. If that individual is a very strong personality and succeeds temporarily, when he or she moves on the process often regresses.

- Second, if the supply chain transformation leader behaves as a process technocrat rather than as a business executive, he or she may devise the correct solution, but be unable to sustain its deployment. If the person is a change agent, but the wrong one, change may happen, but not the change the business needs.
- Third, as was discussed earlier in Chapter 4, when people hear *supply chain* in the earlier stages of transformation — often they think, "click — click — *supply, supplier* — that must have something to do with purchasing — let them address it." Yet experience has taught that supply chain transformation must be a collaborative undertaking by the entire firm and led by a seasoned business executive who really understands the process and its possibilities.

So, we will now begin to address collaborative supply chains with an *integrated* enterprise plan. Transformation works better if led by a supply chain leader who thinks and behaves as a business executive and teaches the team to do likewise. Consider the following sequence of activities to develop an integrated enterprise plan that encourages people to think and behave like business executives:

1. Determine customer and stakeholder objectives.
2. Perform an integrated business and process assessment.
3. Develop an integrated gap-closure plan.
4. Link business objectives, strategies, and priorities.
5. Link collaborative supply chain objectives, strategies, and priorities.
6. Apply an integrated set of improvement tools.
7. Integrate the metrics sets among the supply chain, other organizations, and the enterprise.
8. Integrate the compensation plans to ensure that people have the proper incentives.
9. Finalize the collaborative integrated supply chain.

A prior discussion touched on the importance of a process to ensure continual alignment of supply chain objectives, strategies, goals, and metrics with that of the business imperatives. Questions were posed in Chapter 4 that could provide a quick test of initial tactics for improvement against longer-term strategies needed for business success; but to get the collaborative supply chain working well and have the entire enterprise engaged in its maturation and benefiting adequately from it, using some additional tools is helpful.

SEQUENCE IS IMPORTANT

Consider the applicability of the following story:

> A teacher was presenting the importance of sequencing to his class. He pulled out a 5-gallon jar and began filling it with 2-inch-diameter river rocks. When he could get no more rocks in the jar and still screw the lid on the jar, he asked the class if the jar was full. "Yes," they all replied.
>
> The teacher took the lid off the jar and began putting in pebbles. He added a scoop of pebbles, shook the jar, then added another scoop, and so on. He added scoops of pebbles until he could just barely screw the lid on — 25 scoops. Then he asked the class again if the jar was full. Again, they all replied, "Yes."
>
> The teacher took the lid off once again and began pouring sand into the jar from a bag. He poured and shook and poured and shook until he could just barely screw the lid on. Again he asked the class if the jar was full. This time they were more reserved in their response, but again all said, "Yes."
>
> Now the teacher pulled a large pitcher out from behind the podium and began pouring water into the jar of rocks, pebbles, and sand. He poured and poured and finally the jar was full. Then he asked the class if he could have gotten all the 2-inch rocks in the jar if he had put first the water into the jar, then the sand, then the pebbles, and finally the rocks. They pondered a minute and then all answered, "No." The big rocks had to go in first.

So it is with business priorities, too. We have to approach transformation in a specific order with optimal timing to maximize business impact. We need to apply the always scarce resources of people, time, and capital analytically and in a prioritized approach. Our strategic plan has:

- *Alignment:* A strategic plan keeps us aligned with customer and stakeholder priorities at a high level with key time-phased objectives and goals. The rocks are the alignment.
- *Core/enabling processes:* A process-based business model drills the strategic plan deliverables down to the core and enabling processes. The core/enabling processes are the pebbles.
- *Improvement initiatives:* Core and enabling processes have improvement initiatives. The improvement initiatives are the sand.
- *Metrics:* The processes have metrics that tie to the business objectives and goals. The metrics are the water.

Now, if the *process* objectives, goals, and metrics are set prior to and independent of the *business* objectives, goals, and metrics, there is a pretty good likelihood that the process objectives, goals, and metrics will *not* work on the most important things leading toward achieving the key success factors of the business.

So, let's begin this phase by creating a strategic plan for the supply chain process that links *directly to* and is *integrated into* the enterprise strategic plan (some people shorten strategic plan to STRAP). Sounds simple? Well, the concept may sound simple, but making a strategic plan into an enterprise-owned reality is not so simple — but application of the right tools helps.

Mike Katzorke had his first six sigma training at Motorola in 1986. In industry in those early days of introduction, six sigma was primarily focused on statistical process control. So Mike refreshed his college math, derived the standard deviation again, and added other fun exercises in the training — but he certainly never had an inkling of using six sigma tools to develop a business or process strategic plan. (A large body of literature exists on six sigma, which is beyond the scope of this book.[2] All we will do here is to touch on the subject in a very simplistic manner. Yet, we will use enough specificity to help the reader with some motivation to delve more deeply into a very fascinating and useful subject.)

Today, six sigma has evolved into a business philosophy and set of methodologies that uses data and tools to systematically improve processes and sustain their improvement. People have found that use of the six sigma methodology is a (not always) simple but yet highly effective way to take an enterprise and its key processes through strategic planning and to ensure clear linkage of enterprise and process strategic plans. When developing a strategic plan, it is helpful to bear in mind a paraphrase of a Lord Kelvin quotation, "We don't know what we don't know, and if we can't say it in numbers, we don't know very much."

Creating a business or process strategic plan. Start with the simple six sigma DMAIC model — define, measure, analyze, improve, and control (illustrated in Figure 5.1). Chapter 4 presented a simple planning model for use as a litmus test of short-term tactics and a strategic direction. As shown in Figure 5.1, we can enhance that model with the application of six sigma methodology for a linked and analytical strategic planning process:

- *Define phase:* This phase delineates the overall objectives for the enterprise or process — the things that must be achieved and delivered to customers, shareholders, and other key stakeholders based on their inputs and competitive benchmarking. Business and market data and understanding drive the definition of these key success factors — the *WHAT* we are trying to achieve and *HOW* the planning is to achieve them.

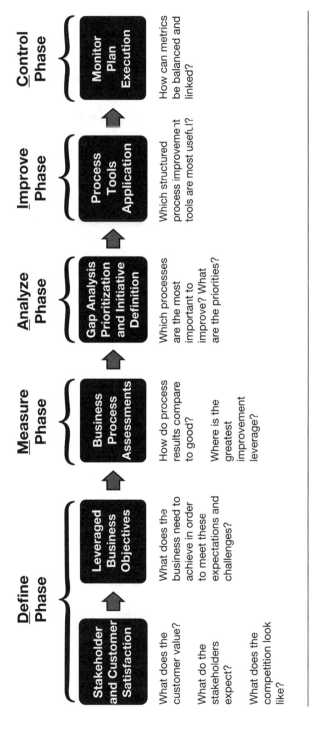

Figure 5.1. Six Sigma DMAIC Model.

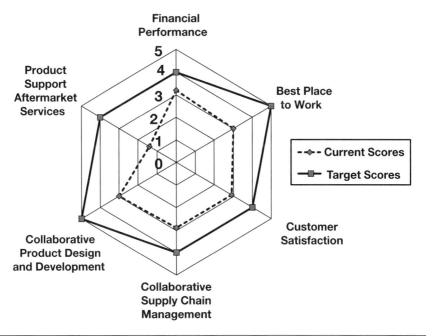

Figure 5.2. Spider Chart: Summary of Key Success Factors.

- *Measure phase:* This phase establishes baselines for the business and processes, defines the input and output variables, and validates measurement systems and processes.
- *Analyze phase:* This phase utilizes data to define key inputs affecting outputs.
- *Improve phase:* Detailed action plans are developed and implemented.
- *Control phase:* This phase monitors and measures progress for plan and performance improvement.

DESIGNING COLLABORATIVE SUPPLY CHAINS

One issue in designing collaborative supply chains is to decide on the key success factors and then to measure performance against each. The key success factors, target scores for each factor, and current scores often can be summarized in what some refer to as a spider chart (depicted in Figure 5.2).

Figure 5.2 shows six key success factors for the business, target scores for each, and current scores for each. The senior leadership team of the business could have jointly decided on these factors from their "voice-of-the-customer" results, internal data, their own personal knowledge, and benchmarking inputs from external consultants:

- *Financial performance:* Benchmarked best-in-class target score is a 4; current score is a 3.2.
- *Best place to work:* Benchmarked best-in-class target score is a 5; current score is a 2.9.
- *Customer satisfaction:* Benchmarked best-in-class target score is a 4; current score is a 2.8.
- *Collaborative supply chain management:* Benchmarked best-in-class target score is a 4; current score is a 2.8.
- *Collaborative product design and development:* Benchmarked best-in-class target score is a 5; current score is a 3.
- *Product support aftermarket services:* Benchmarked best-in-class target score is a 4; current score is a 1.6.

A spider chart is meant to convey a message and thus to be useful as a communications tool. In the example case in Figure 5.2, the business obviously has a journey ahead of it to be competitive in its stated key success factors. Clearly, the business is falling short in each of the stated key success factors. It is doing best in *Financial Performance* and worst in *Product Support Aftermarket Services* — but there is not much difference in several of the scores.

The spider chart in Figure 5.2 shows the key success factors (the *WHAT* the business is trying to achieve) and its relative gaps. The *WHAT* for the enterprise now needs to be linked to specific improvement initiatives and projects to establish their relationships for the total business.

Critical-to analysis. Going forward, then, some six sigma methodologies provide neat tools that do just that. One of the most useful is called *critical-to* analysis, often referred to as *critical-to trees* (illustrated in conceptual format in Figure 5.3). "*Critical-to ...*" are the requirements that are most important to customers and stakeholders. *Critical-to* requirements provide the discipline to go beyond an anecdotal understanding of desires of customers or stakeholders. *Critical-to* requirements facilitate specification of requirements-driven process metrics, which provide a mechanism to change to purpose-driven behavior instead of random firefighting behavior. For the key success factors discussed above, a company can create a *critical-to* customer satisfaction (CTC) tree, a *critical-to* financial performance (CTFP) tree, a *critical-to* collaborative supply chain (CTCSC) tree, and so forth. Ultimately, all of the trees should be linked together and integrated into the enterprise strategic plan.

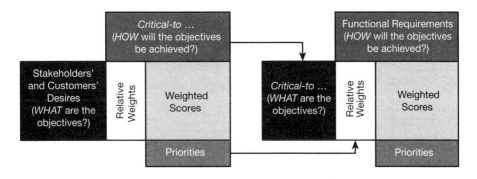

Figure 5.3. *Critical-to* Trees.

In Figures 5.4 and 5.5, a relationship is defined between the *WHAT* and the *HOW*. In Figure 5.4, the stakeholders' and customers' desires specify the ultimate objectives of the enterprise. From the continued drill-downs of *WHAT* to *HOW*, linkage of the key business critical success factors is ensured from senior leadership to every member of the enterprise team.

For supply chains, the discussion is now moving to *WHAT* supply chains need to achieve and *HOW* they can achieve it. They are required to support the enterprise performance with metrics. From the spider chart in Figure 5.2, consider the following as examples:

- Financial performance
- Best place to work
- Customer satisfaction
- Collaborative supply chain
- Collaborative product design and development
- Product support and aftermarket services

With the drill down and linkage at one more level, the focus can now concentrate on the collaborative supply chain — what we call the full-potential collaborative supply chain. Benchmark data and an enterprise assessment (as described in Chapter 2) as well as internal process knowledge and experience can be integrated through some form of a voice-of-the-customer process. This provides the "what are the objectives" (as described above) for the full-potential collaborative supply chain and drilled down to the next level of linkage. This summary usually looks very similar to Figure 5.6.

The picture illustrated in the chart in Figure 5.6 is that the supply chain processes have relatively clear-cut objectives — make customers and stakeholders happy! Success in achieving what customers want and what stakeholders want is impacted by what the supply chains can achieve. When the transformation team

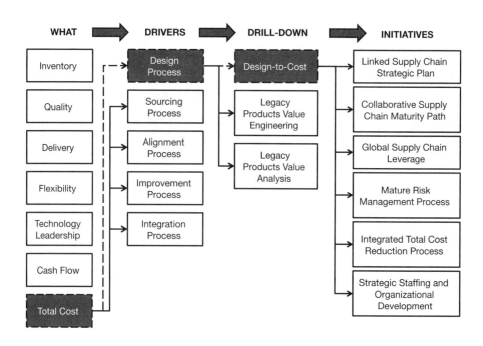

Figure 5.4. *Critical-to*: Total Cost Design Process.

evaluates this in light of the key business levers, it can depict linkage of the key business and supply chain success factors.

"*Critical-to ...*" analyses can establish relationships of performance categories and associated improvement initiatives and projects. For purposes of process understanding, look at only one performance characteristic — cost. The *critical-to* total cost analysis shown as Figure 5.4 depicts the relationships of one of the drivers of cost — the *Design Process*. Figure 5.4 then establishes the relationships of cost improvement through one drill-down of the design cost drivers — the *Design-to-Cost* process(s). Lastly, Figure 5.4 links the design process(s) to specific initiatives.

The transformation team might now look at the sourcing process. Figure 5.5 shows the *Sourcing Process* as another driver of cost. Then it establishes the relationships of cost improvement through one drill-down of the sourcing process — to the *Supply Chain Rationalization Process*. Figure 5.5 links the *Supply Chain Rationalization Process* to specific initiatives or projects.

As the transformation team iterates its way through the *critical-to* trees, the team rather quickly establishes a *critical-to* matrix. The mapping of desired performance improvement in the various performance categories becomes rapidly apparent. Ultimately, as illustrated in Figure 5.7, the team establishes a linkage of

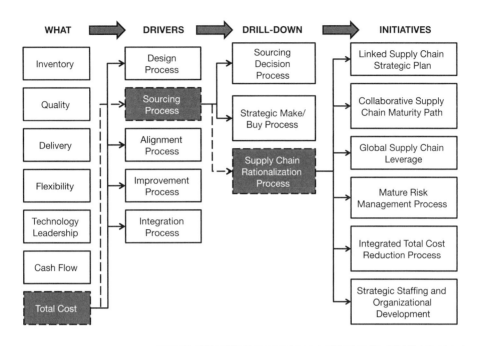

Figure 5.5. *Critical-to*: Total Cost Sourcing Process.

performance categories for improvement and the initiatives or projects that will make the improvement happen.

Once again, the alignment process and the tools have three major objectives:

- Ensure that the supply chain strategic plan will be linked directly to the strategic plan of the business.
- Ensure that supply chain initiatives or project investments are linked directly to achievement of the supply chain strategic plan and that of the enterprise.
- *Most of all* ensure understanding, alignment, and commitment enterprise-wide of the initiatives or projects supporting the supply chain strategic plan.

The strategic plan of a business specifies what it needs for the supply chain to accomplish. Before a good job of weighting and scoring how much investment is needed, and in what sequence the weighting and scoring is needed, however, knowing where the process stands *relative to good* in the world today is important. Management also needs to know how

> *Don't shoot behind the duck!*

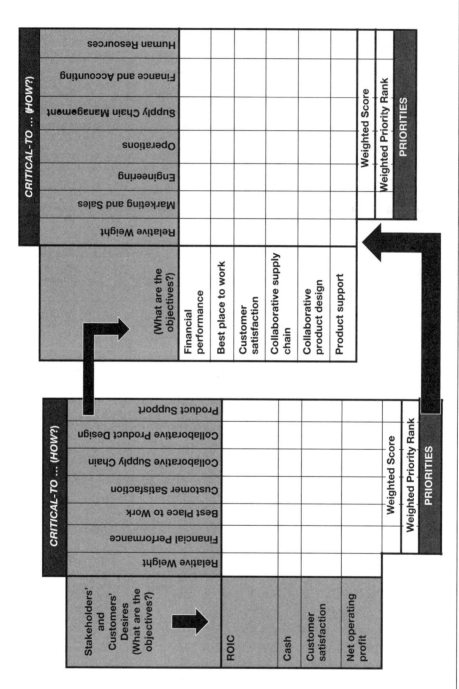

Figure 5.6. Sample *Critical-to* Trees.

Stakeholders' and Customers' Desires (What are the objectives?) ⬇	Relative Weight	CRITICAL-TO ..." (HOW)					
		Linked Supply Chain Strategic Plan	Collaborative Supply Chain Maturity Path	Global Supply Chain Leverage	Mature Risk Management Process	Integrated Total Cost Reduction Process	Strategic Staffing and Organizational Development
Inventory decrease	5	4	4	2	4	4	4
Quality increase	5	4	4	2	2	4	4
Delivery improved	5	4	4	2	5	4	4
Flexibility improved	4	4	4	2	5	4	3
Technology leadership enhanced	4	4	4	2	1	3	4
Cash flow improved	5	4	4	2	4	4	4
Total cost reduced	5	4	5	5	3	5	4
Weighted Score		132	137	81	114	133	128
Weighted Priority Rank		3	1	6	5	2	4
		PRIORITIES					

Figure 5.7. Sample *Critical-to* Full-Potential Collaborative Supply Chain.

much the process will improve over the strategic plan horizon. There is an old saying that implies that a company is aiming at last year's targets: "Don't shoot behind the duck." Consider both the *results* that supply chain processes are delivering and *what* the supply chain is doing to achieve those results — their processes.

A company could spend significant time researching what companies are the best today in various aspects of the supply chain process. Then benchmarking trips could be made to obtain data. And when a company gets their supply chain stabilized in the improvement process, that is exactly what is needed regularly. A company needs to do so to stay on top of their game and to pull the enterprise together around the assessment and strategic plan by doing the benchmarking in a teaming fashion.

In this stage though, rapid movement is key — but be careful to *not* do the wrong things so the situation is made worse. As discussed in Chapter 2, much information is available today relative to process benchmarks and process maturity characteristics — 15 years ago, this was not the case. Improvement planning either took an inordinate amount of time or it was shortcut to the point of being largely inaccurate and ineffective. A relatively accurate assessment is needed in days, not months. Chapter 2 showed how this is done.

CUSTOMERS WANT ...	SUPPLY CHAINS IMPACT BY ...
• Quality	• Designing for robust processes to eliminate variation
• Reliability	• Meeting reliability commitments
• On-time delivery	• Performing to commitments
• Service and flexibility	• Shortening lead times
• Best value	• Optimizing cost per function
• Technology	
STAKEHOLDERS WANT ...	**SUPPLY CHAINS IMPACT BY ...**
• ROIC	• Improving cost
	• Optimizing asset utilization
	• Providing the kind of customer service that enhances revenues

Figure 5.8. The Importance of Supply Chain Linkages: the *WHAT* to the *HOW*.

CONCLUSION

Experience has shown what effective and sustainable deployment of a collaborative supply chain transformation requires. For one thing, effective and sustainable deployment requires an easily understandable, linked, enterprise-owned strategic plan, which the entire organization can accept and agree to implement. The process outlined in this chapter has presented the linkages from the *WHAT* to the *HOW*, beginning with the desires of customers and stakeholders and ending with cross-discipline, cross-function, cross-process, and cross-geography initiatives.

Figure 5.8 provides an easy way to consider these linkages. The linkages are under the headings of what CUSTOMERS WANT and how SUPPLY CHAINS IMPACT BY to achieve these customers' wants. Also shown is what STAKEHOLDERS WANT and how the SUPPLY CHAINS IMPACT BY to achieve these stakeholders' wants.

The chart in Figure 5.8 illustrates what we have been discussing in this book — the importance of linkages. Some people (including us) like to use the term *line-of-sight linkages*, which means that a direct linkage can be drawn from the customers and the stakeholders down to the lowest levels in the organization. The people in the organization, simply put, need to be able to understand how their work links to and is important for the higher-level objectives of the organization. True supply chain transformation requires this.

We expect to see future developments incorporating more and more cross-enterprise initiatives that will truly implement linked supply chains — from the ultimate consumer of products and services back to the ultimate supplier of raw materials.

REFERENCES

1. Ronald K. Ireland with Colleen Crum. *Supply Chain Collaboration: How to Implement CRFR® and Other Best Collaborative Practices* 2005, pp. 1, 7. Ft. Lauderdale: J. Ross Publishing.
2. See Bertels, Thomas, Ed. *Rath & Strong's Six Sigma Leadership Handbook* 2003. New York: John Wiley & Sons; George, Michael L. *Lean Six Sigma: Combining Six Sigma Quality with Lean Speed* 2002. New York: McGraw-Hill.

6

MULTIPLE SUPPLY CHAINS: ROBBING PETER TO PAY PAUL — BUT WHY ARE BOTH UNHAPPY?

When you come to a fork in the road, take it.
— Yogi Berra

Yogi Berra is famous for his "fork in the road" quote. Multiple supply chains are forks in the road. Will you go one way and use a supply chain that really does not exactly fit or will you create a new supply chain that does fit? The answer is not always clear-cut. Creating multiple supply chains adds complexity to an organization and likely will provide a better fit — but at additional cost and managerial complications. We are all in favor of simplicity in the supply chain — and multiple chains do lose some of the simplicity. Supply chain professionals will have to make judgment calls on that. We will try to provide some guidance about multiple supply chains in this chapter.

Until now, we generally have talked about *a* supply chain — singular; but that is not the way it is. Companies rarely have a single supply chain.

Business leaders often have misconceptions and talk as if they have a single supply chain. As such, there is often a tendency to think in terms of designing a *single* supply chain strategy, a *single* group of processes for that single supply chain, and perhaps a *single* supply chain organization. This thinking also applies to incoming supply chains from suppliers as well as outgoing supply chains to customers. But, just as a business often serves multiple markets with different key success factors and associated strategies, the business normally is supported by multiple supply chains requiring differing strategies and processes for optimal results. Sometimes this situation means different supply chain organizations.

As an example, Marshall Fisher published an outstanding article a number of years ago that addressed this question somewhat.[1] Over the years, this article has been a key thought provoker for many supply chain professionals and executives. Succinctly and effectively, the article made the case that the key success factors for a product or service determine the strategies and business processes that must drive the supply chains. Taking that thought to the next level, before a supply chain is defined to support the product or service, the *nature* of the demand in that product or services market needs clear understanding by the designers. Figure 6.1 summarizes Fisher's ground-breaking article which is still valid today.

Figure 6.1 illustrates that by their nature products can be described as *basic* (or commodity or functional) products or *innovative* (or differentiated) products. Basic (functional) products are described as satisfying basic needs, as being highly cost or price competitive, and therefore as requiring highly efficient supply chains to support them in that competitive environment. We sometimes refer to these products as "nuts, bolts, and screws." Additionally, the products from one manufacturer do not differ significantly from the others.

Innovative products, on the other hand, typically have new and differentiated aspects (for example, fast changing technology or fashion goods). Innovative products require a high level of market responsiveness due to somewhat unpredictable demand and relatively short product life cycles. A high level of market responsiveness necessitates a highly flexible supply chain to support the needed responsiveness. Also, their shorter product life cycles need appropriate supply chains.

Fisher makes the general point that different products and services require different supply chains. Although Fisher's point is extremely important, supply chains are more complicated than that. What if a business has products and services with differing key success factors requiring differing supply chain process strategies to support them? Should these requirements be served from a single supply chain process?

For example, a manufacturing business might serve the following markets. All of these markets might fall into either Fisher's functional or differentiated classifications:

- An OEM (original equipment market) for its own products
- A repair business to support products in the field
- A retail aftermarket parts business

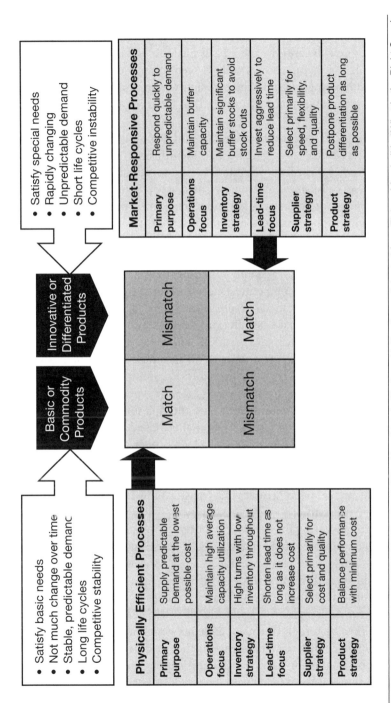

Figure 6.1. Understand the Nature of Demand: Matching Supply Chains with Products. Adapted from Fisher, Marshall L. "What Is the Right Supply Chain for Your Product?" *Harvard Business Review* 1997 March–April.

Basic or Commodity Products
- Satisfy basic needs
- Not much change over time
- Stable, predictable demand
- Long life cycles
- Competitive stability

Innovative or Differentiated Products
- Satisfy special needs
- Rapidly changing
- Unpredictable demand
- Short life cycles
- Competitive instability

Physically Efficient Processes

Primary purpose	Supply predictable Demand at the lowest possible cost
Operations focus	Maintain high average capacity utilization
Inventory strategy	High turns with low inventory throughout
Lead-time focus	Shorten lead time as long as it does not increase cost
Supplier strategy	Select primarily for cost and quality
Product strategy	Balance performance with minimum cost

Market-Responsive Processes

Primary purpose	Respond quickly to unpredictable demand
Operations focus	Maintain buffer capacity
Inventory strategy	Maintain significant buffer stocks to avoid stock outs
Lead-time focus	Invest aggressively to reduce lead time
Supplier strategy	Select primarily for speed, flexibility, and quality
Product strategy	Postpone product differentiation as long as possible

	Basic or Commodity Products	Innovative or Differentiated Products
Physically Efficient Processes	Match	Mismatch
Market-Responsive Processes	Mismatch	Match

Say that the OEM business is focused on technology and price; the repair business is focused on responsiveness due to the need to get products repaired and back in service quickly; and the retail parts business is focused on price and availability. Several times in our careers we have seen companies try to serve these "three masters" with a single supply chain design within a single organization. Although success is possible, many factors need to be overcome to achieve that success.

In previous chapters, the process to develop and deploy a supply chain strategy was discussed. The process begins with an identification of the key success factors for each market served — what does it take to be successful in a given market? It progresses to business and supply chain assessment and gap analysis. The process then moves on to the creation and prioritization of gap closure plans with the application of appropriate tools and structure. Lastly, it drills all this down to the process and individual levels.

In businesses that serve multiple markets, the potential for conflict in priorities is very real, if not a certainty. A conflict in priorities can, of course, be highly detrimental to an enterprise's competitive success in serving each of its markets well. Associated long-term financial results also can be degraded. So, supply chain planning and design for successfully competing in multiple markets needs to be at least equaled by deployment execution. Said simply, although the business wants elements of the enterprise to focus on specific markets, the business also needs these elements to work with the others to optimize overall business performance and success — not just optimizing individual pieces with a resulting suboptimization of the entire enterprise. These multiple-market scenarios are approached with visioning for multiple supply chains that addresses the problem of serving multiple businesses from the supply chain organization(s).

Figure 6.2 depicts a *one-way* flow through the supply chain. The diagram begins with suppliers and ends with customers. Note the connections among suppliers that provide inputs, manufacturers that transform the inputs into products, and distributors that get the products to customers. This illustration does not come even close to presenting the complexity of typical supply chains.

But what about multiple supply chains — both incoming from suppliers and outgoing to customers? There are many models, which only effectively deliver on the strategies when aligned with the way in which the company wants to operate. Most of these actually are networks, not chains.

One thing is true — there is no "one size fits all" when designing supply chain networks. As outlined by Joseph Cavinato, these networks can include many different types of supply chains.[2] Cavinato goes further to describe the complexity of the typical supply chains for a company. These supply chains only effectively deliver on their promise when aligned with the way in which the company wants to go to market. His research indicates that companies have 16 basic forms of

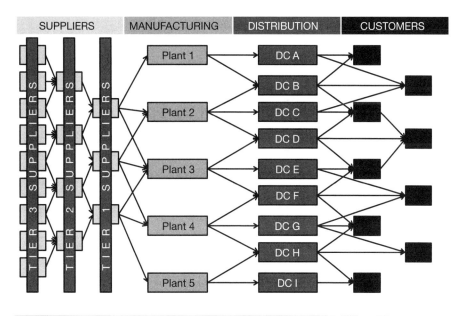

Figure 6.2. Multiple Supply Chains: One-Way Flow through the Chain.

supply chains/networks in use today. Each brings with it relative strengths and weaknesses and varying degrees of complexity. Figures 6.3 and 6.4 illustrate Cavinato's taxonomy. Sixteen types of chains are arrayed on a two-dimensional matrix in Figure 6.3, grouped according to their business impact and complexity. Details about each chain in terms of the characteristics of each are presented in Figure 6.4.

> We recommend Cavinato's taxonomy as a way for supply chain professionals to consider and classify their multiple supply chains. Furthermore, Cavinato provides some good suggestions for managing in the world of multiple, complex, supply chains.

Cavinato suggests (we agree) that Types 1, 2, and 3 are very basic and are dangerous for a company to pursue. He suggests (we also agree) that the middle group containing Types 4 through 9 are the most familiar in today's supply chain world. Toward the high end in terms of competitive advantage and profit impacts are the chains and networks of Types 10 through 16.

Types 1 — 3. We call Types 1 through 3 "heads-in-the-sand" supply chains. Type 1 simply does not understand the whole notion of a supply chain. Type 2 outsources the supply chain and keeps the company's head in the sand relative to

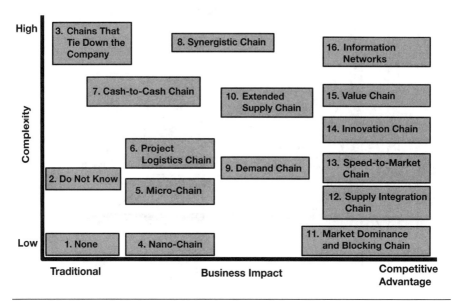

Figure 6.3. Types of Chains and Networks Grouped According to Business Impact and Complexity. Adapted from Cavinato, Joseph L. "What's Your Supply Chain Type?" *Supply Chain Management Review* 2002 May-June.

what is really happening. An example of Type 3 supply chains could be a company that subordinates everything, say, to engineering. Engineering designs the products, specifies the components without regard to procurement or manufacturing issues, and controls product support in the field.

Types 4 — 9. Types 4 through 9 probably are the most common today. Type 4 chains keep manufacturing as the center of the company and subordinate the supply chain accordingly. Type 5 chains may be the most common form — with an emphasis on balancing the various functions in the company. Type 6 chains focus on projects (common in so-called EPC or engineering, procurement, and construction firms such as Bechtel, Fluor, CB&I, and so forth). We also see Type 6 chains operable in large companies which embark on large-scale projects (such as ExxonMobil, Shell, BP, and so forth). Typical Type 7 chains can be found in companies such as Dell, which is justifiably well-known for its emphasis on a supply chain that significantly reduces the cash-to-cash cycle. Type 8 supply chains often are used as justification for mergers and acquisitions that claim synergies from combinations of two or more companies (to us, anecdotal evidence indicates that this usually is hype to get stakeholders to approve the combination). Type 9 chains subordinate everything to the customer, who then frequently demands all the benefits from supply chain improvements.

Type of Chain	Characteristics	Type of Chain	Characteristics
1. None	Current processes function fine as is and provide no competitive advantage	2. Do not know	Third-party logistics handle the supply chain; supply chain outsourced with commodity-like logistics
3. Chains that tie down the firm	Place inordinate emphasis upon an internal aspect of the company to the detriment of the total chain	4. Nano chain	Maximizes manufacturing efficiencies; can divert corporate strategic emphasis/energies toward mostly internal activities
5. Micro chain	Balanced purchasing, production, and distribution; classic logistics model	6. Project logistics chain	Creates supply, flow, and logistics for specific projects
7. Cash-to-cash chain	Maximizes cash flow; can negatively affect suppliers and customers	8. Synergistic chain	Eliminates duplicate costs; gains buying power; provides no competitive advantage
9. Demand chain	Feeds customers in ways that are efficient for them; close collaboration with customers	10. Extended supply chain	Supplier-to-customer efficiencies; good for overall cost and flow analysis of all resources
11. Market dominance and blocking chain	Keeps others out of the market; not legal in most developed countries	12. Supply integration chain	Model supplier-firm linkages; useful for many competitive initiatives; good for cost reduction
13. Speed-to-market chain	Emphasizes product development and launch; flexible supply chain required	14. Innovation chain	Pushes growth opportunities; focuses on creation, launch, and growth phases of product life cycle
15. Value chain	Focuses on competing with chain partners against other chains; emphasizes competing with total chain	16. Information networks	Competitiveness in information flow; emphasize core set of efficient and agile processes

Figure 6.4. Characteristics of the Types of Chains and Networks. Adapted from Cavinato, Joseph L. "What's Your Supply Chain Type?" *Supply Chain Management Review* 2002 May-June.

Type 10. The extended supply chain, Type 10, is one of the most popular desired *to be* states because Type 10 is good for overall cost and flow analysis. With a Type 10 chain, supply chain positions are seen many times as good areas for management development because this chain gives a good view of the entire process.

Type 11. Type 11 is illegal in most countries because it keeps other competitors out of a market.

Type 12. Type 12 chains are highly interdisciplinary because they integrate the entire chain from customers to suppliers.

Type 13. Type 13 supply chains are used primarily in companies that have a continuing flow of new products or services. A company like Zara, a popular-priced fashion manufacturer and retailer, emphasizes speed-to-market for its products to keep a time-based competitive advantage over the competition.

Type 14. Type 14 chains push growth opportunities through innovation and new products. Companies such as Intel have for years emphasized a continuing stream of new, innovative products.

Type 15. Type 15 chains treat their entire supply chain as an integrated competitive weapon — "My chain can beat your chain!" Recall the statement from Chapter 2: "Competition is no longer company to company, but supply chain to supply chain." True supply chain-to-supply chain competition is becoming more common as supply chain integration becomes more of a reality than just an idealistic dream.

Type 16. Type 16 still is mostly a dream of information being a true competitive weapon. As Cavinato says, "Competitiveness is in the information."

Now consider several types of companies that have different business examples and different supply chain requirements:

- Companies selling compressors:
  - Selling compressors for large projects, such as offshore oil and gas drilling ships or natural gas pipelines
  - Selling the same type of compressors to factories
  - Selling spare parts for those compressors
  - Selling product service for those compressors

- Companies selling business jets:
  - Selling business jets to fleet operators, such as fractional owner-ship companies
  - Selling business jets to government agencies, such as the Department of Defense, Department of the Interior, and so forth
  - Selling business jets to large companies that operate a fleet of the same business jets
  - Selling business jets to wealthy individuals
  - Selling spare parts for business jets to service facilities
  - Selling spare parts to company-owned service facilities
- Companies selling automobiles:
  - Selling automobiles directly to rental fleet operators, such as Avis or Hertz
  - Selling automobiles through dealers to individual consumers (people like us)
  - Selling spare parts to dealers for their service departments
  - Selling spare parts to independent aftermarket channels
- Companies selling tires:
  - Selling tires to automobile assembly plants for installation on new cars
  - Selling the same type of tires through a distribution network to repair shops
  - Selling the same type of tires to individual consumers through independent tire dealers

The list goes on and on and on, one product after another and one supply/demand chain after another.

CUSTOMER SATISFACTION WITH THE BUYING EXPERIENCE

The key decisions affecting all types of supply chains are how to integrate the supply chains in ways that enhance the customer's experience. Companies such as J.D. Power and Associates regularly measure customer satisfaction for a number of industries. These measurements and rankings can indicate the level of satisfaction with the supply chains.

In their book, *Satisfaction: How Every Great Company Listens to the Voice of the Customer*, Denove and Power state: "One of the first things we do when we engage a new client is try to understand how customer satisfaction affects their particular business."[3] This approach is not a bad way to begin a relationship — we have often used it in our consulting and education experiences. Although Denove and Power do not say so in their book, *understanding the business* includes understanding the supply chains of the business.

Clearly, the supply chain has a significant impact on customer satisfaction. Understanding the linkages between customer satisfaction and appropriately designed and operated supply chains is incumbent upon supply chain professionals. Even more important is that a company's multiple supply chains be appropriate to the demand characteristics of its customers. According to Denove and Power, for most companies this link is manifested in several ways. All of the following are impacted by a company's supply chains and the supply chains impact each of these satisfaction indicators:

- *Loyalty:* Satisfied customers are significantly more likely to come back to do business in the future.
- *Word of mouth:* Satisfied customers not only solicit others to do business with you, but their opinions also carry more weight than all the company's advertising combined.
- *Price premiums:* Satisfied customers will pay a hefty premium to do business with companies that have a reputation for high quality and great customer service.
- *Reduced operating costs:* High-satisfaction companies have lower warranty expenses and spend less on service recovery.
- *Customer close rates:* High-satisfaction companies make a sale to a higher percentage of potential customers.

Denove and Power report further on the relationship between customer satisfaction and shareholder value in companies. For companies whose J.D. Power ranking improved in their industry, there was a median increase in shareholder value of +52%. For companies whose ranking declined, there was a median decrease of –28%. These results are pretty powerful arguments. Denove and Power also report that sales of high-satisfaction companies increased by more than 40% in the 5-year period of 1998 to 2003, while low-satisfaction companies actually lost sales.[3]

A close friend of Mike Katzorke, Warren Brower, worked in John Deere dealer network leadership for several decades. Brower's commentary on his experience demonstrates that John Deere really "gets it" relative to the importance of the parts and service business in delivering a completely satisfying total customer experience. When customers in a construction business or the agricultural industry cannot operate their equipment, even for a brief time, the financial impact can be substantial and often cannot be recovered — and their customers do not appreciate schedule impacts.

John Deere. The Deere organization has a dealer network that it tightly integrates for customer support in the field. The degree of investment by Deere in dealer linkage and training demonstrates the maturity of the understanding of supply chain linkage in the organization. Deere dealers receive training and understand the Deere systems; they are integrated in the forecasting processes and support inventory planning processes; and they receive education and training in both the parts and service businesses from the OEM in an exemplary and highly effective fashion. Keeping equipment continuously operational with minimal downtime is a key priority for everyone in the supply chain and a critical purchasing decision factor for operators. Deere shareholders, of course, want to see this service level accomplished in the most cost-effective manner. According to our understanding, Deere is good at that too. Their linked inventory planning and production scheduling are based on data, are strategic, and are integrated up and down the supply chain — integrated in terms of objectives, strategies, processes, and data — which results in excellent parts and service support for Deere owners with near-optimal inventory investment.

Aviation. The aviation OEM industry is largely a build-to-order business. Although much effort is put into forecast linkage up and down the supply chain, the effectiveness and maturity of that effort generally are relatively low as compared with other commercial industries. This industry was highly vertically integrated 25 years ago and could control its own destiny in manufacturing. Today it relies heavily on external supply chains which support many customers, who are themselves competitors of each other, which exacerbates the impact of the relative immaturity of integration. Parts and service businesses in the aviation industry also operate relatively independently of the original manufacturing business. Parts and service businesses often compete in their own factories and at suppliers for field support requirements and do so with relative autonomy. Often their detail requirements forecasting (if done it at all) is done in isolation from the OEM requirements and vice versa. Forecasting is also largely developed from backward-looking models and often includes retrofits and engineering configuration changes very late in the process.

A reader might now say, "Hey, wait just a minute. Because of the very nature of operating heavy construction equipment in the field, major failures are experienced earlier in the product life cycle than in aviation. The certification process for aviation products requires extensive reliability testing, unlike heavy equipment. Plus, digging boulders out of the ground is difficult work."

Experience has demonstrated, however, that when aftermarket support is governed by past history alone, customer satisfaction is impacted negatively in the OEM's field support. Yet, if reliability design information is utilized in a data-driven, statistical, and forward-looking forecast model, and it is effectively

Key Success Factor	OEM Manufacturing Business Weighting	Service and Retrofit Business Weighting	Retail Parts Business Weighting
Product Quality	5	4	4
Product Reliability	5	4	3
Promised Delivery	3	5	5
Lead Time	3	5	5
Stock Availability	2	5	5
Schedule Flexibility	4	5	5
Ease of Doing Business	4	5	5
Cost or Price	4	2	2
Technology Leadership	4	3	3

Figure 6.5. Supply Chain Key Success Factors: Sample Weighting.

integrated with historical data, then the level of customer satisfaction with field support in companies such as Deere can be accomplished in any industry.

Other contributors to enterprise supply chain optimization are the measures of success and associated rewards systems. Figure 6.5 shows an illustrative sample weighting of key success factors for OEM, service, and retail parts businesses in a given enterprise. Notice the differences. Key success factors for service and retail parts businesses tend to be more heavily weighted in availability and turn-around time, while OEM businesses tend to have a more balanced weighting across quality, cost, delivery, service, and technology leadership — which simply reflects the difference of what is important to the customer before taking delivery of a product and after it is functioning to generate revenue and profit in the business. But, how does this difference manifest itself with the people in the supply chain (both internal and external) trying to do a great job for the customer in a total sense?

Many disruptions can occur along supply chains. One is unplanned demand with shorter-than-normal lead time — it happens all the time in all industries:

The factory. So, how does a factory see unplanned demand that is needed immediately?

Q: As an opportunity to excel?

A: One can hope, but not so much.

Q: As a headache?

A: Closer to reality.

Q: As a pain in the proverbial posterior?

A: Pretty much — because factories typically are judged on on-time delivery, output, and efficiency and/or utilization, all of which tend to suffer with unplanned demand.

Parts and service. How do retail parts people and service people see the factory as part of their supply chains? Too often, they hear the following from the factory:

- *If you can't live with that delivery, well then die with it!*
- *It's not in the production plan.*
- *It isn't due for 3 weeks.*
- *Take your stupid customer problem and get lost!*
- *If you would get off your backside and plan better, you wouldn't have all these surprises!*
- *You know my lead time.*

Well, something like that anyway! Perhaps we are exaggerating, but not much.

Finance. How do people in financial areas of the company see these same kinds of unplanned-for requirements? On the plus side, unplanned-for demand is seen as producing more revenue because service and spare parts generally carry significantly higher margins than original equipment. On the negative side, in immature supply chains, unplanned-for demand disruptions are costly. They tend to increase inventory, decrease manufacturing efficiency, and increase the excess overhead as more expeditors are required to move these surprises through the supply chains.

The suppliers. What about suppliers? Like the financial people, suppliers see more revenue and the potential for more profit; but they also see the same things as the manufacturing people. Suppliers are not going to get any schedule relief from other customers (either the one causing the problem or any of its other customers) for the disruption of handling these unplanned requirements. Do not forget: in immature supply chains, service and parts businesses sometimes operate off their own orders with suppliers and occasionally are the referee between a customer's OEM and service- and parts-buying entities (but suppliers do sometimes enjoy playing "divide and conquer").

The customers. What about the customers? Customers want three things:

- To get new OEM products delivered
- To service and support the ones they have in order to avoid expensive down-time and unhappy customers
- To obtain parts for immediate field repairs

Do customers really understand or appreciate a less-than-stellar performance from any or all three of a supplier's businesses because these businesses operate in isolation and in competition with one another? Frequently, customers begin to look for a more mature supply chain partner.

The CEO. Then the CEO frequently asks, "Why can't you guys all just get along and work together — we're all part of the same team, aren't we?" (The amazing thing is that a CEO can ask this question with a straight face because he or she sets and enforces conflicting metrics and compensation schemes for the various business units.)

So, how can an enterprise best support its multiple businesses that are linked to its multiple markets? What kind of process and structural changes are needed to bring relatively immature processes that the prior discussion describes to a world-class level of competitiveness and financial results?

DESIGN OF MULTIPLE SUPPLY CHAINS

If the current state of support for the enterprise supply chain processes looks anything like what we have described (and probably most still do today), the enterprise needs to begin improvement at the beginning. Companies need to follow a proven path for effective process change. There really is no shortcut. Intuition sometimes works (when no useful data are available); but usually intuition fails miserably because it is often technically wrong, only fixes part of the problem, or has no ownership by the organization. So, supply chains eventually revert to their original states. A proven path would dictate something similar to the following approach:

- Paint a picture of how existing processes and results look to customers and shareholders.
- Map the total supply chain process in each business and then meld them to understand how the situation really looks. This usually provides some of those "ah ha" moments: "This thing really doesn't work like we thought it did — no wonder we've got such poor performance, so much cost, and so much conflict."

- Benchmark both processes and results against best-in-class companies in a careful and focused manner.
- Lay out desired operating characteristics and associated results for the *to be* situation.
- Create a contrasting *could be/should be* map.
- Plan the *to be* deployment.

Many of us have seen something similar to this approach before. The issue lies in how well the flow is planned and executed. Having experienced people available for utilization and consultation to the transformation teams has proven extremely valuable in getting solid, objective, holistically correct results the first time through. For purposes of this discussion, the writers are going to make the assumption that the wealth of information available on process mapping techniques and benchmarking is sufficient to guide the reader through design and effective execution of those activities. Our experience is that the more difficult areas in this process tend to lie in the last three steps:

- Lay out desired operating characteristics and associated results for the *to be* situation.
- Create a contrasting *could be/should be* map.
- Plan the *to be* deployment.

THE HARD STUFF IS THE SOFT STUFF

Earlier in this chapter, Figure 6.5 pointed out the differing priorities of the three business markets of OEM, service, and retail parts of a hypothetical enterprise. We have also discussed human perceptions of the importance and impact on their lives of the business elements serving other than "my" business market which pointed to a variety of human behavior and misbehavior realities. To a very large extent, these behaviors are caused by perceived expectations, such as: "What defines success for *my* business, *my* process, and *my* career? When have we done a good job? And how do we know it?"

The Soft Side

Wanting to be part of a winning team is completely natural and desirable. Yet the definitions of a team's charter and objectives often get lost in the desire to break the work down into little pieces of clear accountability and definitive measurement. Sometimes this situation is like looking at a forest fire — some of the trees are still very healthy, but the forest is still on fire. Breaking down the work into individual accountabilities and metrics is perfectly fine as long as a "no one is successful unless everyone is successful" culture is in place. This culture includes everyone meeting their own objectives as well as meeting customers' and share-holders' objectives on an enterprise level.

Some companies express this lovely *no one is successful unless everyone is successful* platitude, but they fail to make it pragmatic. Pragmatism occurs with shared metric ownership and effectively linked compensation for both individual and enterprise-level performance. The reasons for shortcomings are many, but they all boil down to the fact that it is very difficult to create a system that is perceived as fairly rewarding enterprise-focused behavior equally. Those who have succeeded have done it with very careful analysis and planning and the involvement of the enterprise's extended leadership team. Those who fail generally have chartered the human resources organization to come up with the program or the senior leadership team tried to do it themselves without sufficient participation of the broader team.

With the supposition that the enterprise has undertaken the creation of metrics, a compensation system, and a culture following the models of engagement of companies who have succeeded at this culture-shift process, the people still need to see the bigger picture. The people are probably asking questions such as the following:

> *What is the business trying to do? How does it relate to each business unit serving each market? How does it relate to the supply chain processes? How does it relate to me personally? I can no longer focus only on getting supplier X to 99.5% on-time delivery to my OEM business consistently. I need to work with my counterparts in retail parts and the service business. I need to leverage my business with supplier X to effect a lead-time reduction of 50% for the retail parts business and an improvement in MTBF* [mean time between failures] *performance and improved warranty coverage in support of the service business.*

Virtually every aspect of the supply chain management process needs to be melded together — both structurally and operationally — to ensure success of the enterprise, while not losing market specialization and focus. Essentially, the people in the supply chain processes become representatives of their businesses *to* the enterprise-level processes and *of* the enterprise processes back to their businesses. This is not a pipe dream — it really works, and works well, if the metrics are balanced for each team and individual and if the culture is one of both enterprise success and each business unit's success — everyone makes their objectives or no one has fully succeeded.

The Hard Side

On the hard side of process change, in both the Deere case and particularly in the aviation industry case, product life cycles are fairly long. Service procedures are fairly easily updated; but material and parts availability is another issue. An airplane has a life cycle of over 20 years, while electronics can have a life cycle as short as 6 or 7 months depending on the technology. In addition, with model upgrades and configuration changes, parts and assemblies needed in the field for routine service and planned maintenance are often no longer being produced currently. To interject these legacy requirements into current production, externally or internally, often wreaks havoc with on-going work flow across the supply chain; but quick and efficient fulfillment of these field requirements has been shown to be a key success factor to future OEM purchases, overall reputation, and both short-term and long-term financial performance for the entire supply chain.

Long life cycle. In products with long product life cycles, it seems that OEMs could forecast, plan surge production capacity and inventory, and supply parts and assemblies in demand for current production from their existing manufacturing processes and those of their external supply chain. For field requirements no longer being stocked or produced for current production, a separate "short-order shop" capability and associated inventory could be forecast and maintained across the supply chain to satisfy these requirements rapidly without disruption to existing OEM-related production. The additional cost for this legacy production and stock can be passed along to the ultimate customer without significant difficulties because the tradeoff is to be able to operate with minimal downtime and inventory protection on their own books. OEM factory efficiencies resulting from less unplanned demand and associated excess surge capacity and inventory waste can be shared with the customer in their next equipment purchase.

Short life cycle. For shorter product life cycles, a smaller proportion of the requirements would be for out-of-production products because the products are no longer in use due to operating life. These products usually have been replaced by newer and better products. Furthermore, sometimes there is an OEM policy of notifying customers of a production end date and providing them with the opportunity to make a final lifetime buy. In any case (including the licensing or sale of the rights to produce these legacy requirements), the shorter the effective life cycle of a product, the more the supply chain impact of these short life cycle products can be mitigated with much more simple solutions.

How about service businesses and raw material suppliers? They do not have to deal with OEM production, retail parts, and repair and overhaul market segments. Really? When consideration is given to the plethora of service and raw material businesses, thinking of which ones *do not* buy supplies, equipment, software, and so forth is difficult. Service businesses and raw material suppliers are affected by the same types of issues discussed previously for long and short product life cycle manufacturing.

From an oil company, to an automobile company, or to a distribution company, if analytical thought is applied to them, none are exempt from some level of the complexities of multiple supply chains. If companies do not think they have this challenge, chances are pretty high that they are not doing very well with their supply chains.

Nonproduct procurement. When one considers nonproduct procurement in any major corporation, it is often not done with the same strategy, precision, and discipline as is product-related procurement because the challenge is somewhat ill-structured, or so it seems. Yet nonproduct procurement is often 25 to 40% of a company's external expenditures. Nonproduct procurement can be done with the very same strategy, precision, and discipline as the rest of the expenditures, albeit with a modified process, with recognition of the challenges and with adequate analytical thought and process discipline.

Soft-Sided Issues in Transitioning to Effective Supply Chain Process Design

Our discussion now returns to final consideration of the soft-sided issues in transitioning to a supply chain process design that effectively serves multiple markets in a given portfolio of a business. How might a melded supply chain operating characteristics transition summary look like for the enterprise?

Current state. The supply chain operating characteristics of the current-state model are represented by a fragmented process that is internally competitive for requirements and resources. The current process is one that reflects many and often conflicting faces and requirements to both the internal and external supply chains operating in a tactical, reactive, transactional mode with constant firefighting and a firefighting hero mentality. The current state yields suboptimal enterprise performance with less-than-delighted customers in all three markets and nervous if not displeased shareholders as well. Results in the current-state model reflect delivery performance and flexibility that is subpar in all the businesses. They exhibit an inefficient and noncompetitive cost with too much and ineffective inventory, occasional quality lapses due to process disruption, and many frustrated hard-working people.

Future state. The future-state model is one of an integrated, collaborative, enterprise process that works for optimization of results while still ensuring significantly improved results and focus at the individual business unit level. The future-state model matures to one of strategic tactical balance with a proactive mentality of avoiding problems rather than one that puts out fires in some nonsensical fashion. The future-state model becomes highly flexible, partially due to fully linked real-time information flow and partially due to manufacturing process redesign around market flexibility needs. Firefighting becomes the exception and the mindset shifts to one of constantly improving the process rather than expediting around its deficiencies. In the future, culture and process change bring about enterprise optimized results and solid business market competitive performance on an on-going basis, which, of course, is reflected in delighted repeat customers and satisfied shareholders. In the future-state model, the supply chain processes have been redesigned and provide superior delivery and flexible performance for all the businesses with a competitive cost structure. The process yields results with minimal firefighting. Quick-turn capability has been designed into the manufacturing process for legacy or rare requirements for the aftermarket. Inventory levels are competitive and strategically effective while quality processes are designed with enough robustness that they can effectively handle the real-world operating environment of different markets drawing from the same supply chain. Most importantly, the culture and compensation systems reflect and reward enterprise team operational behavior.

CONCLUSION

Supply chains are integral parts of almost all organizations. Companies typically have multiple supply chains, both on the incoming side from suppliers and on the outgoing side to customers. Multiple supply chains are designed to satisfy different requirements both for purchased goods and services and for goods and services being sold. The purpose of supply chain management is to design the supply chain and to synchronize its key processes so they match the flow of goods and services which match the requirements.

This chapter has described the multiple supply chains that likely are faced by many, if not most, companies. These supply chains can be very complex and can consist of many firms, which are linked to other firms. As a result, the supply chains are prone to disruptions. The robustness of the design and synchronization is one means by which companies mitigate these disruptions. This book has built an approach to transforming the supply chains in a systematic and logical manner.

REFERENCES

1. Fisher, Marshall L. "What Is the Right Supply Chain for Your Product?" *Harvard Business Review* 1997 March-April.

2. Cavinato, Joseph L. "What's Your Supply Chain Type?" *Supply Chain Management Review* 2002 May-June.

3. Denove, Chris and James D. Power, IV. *Satisfaction: How Every Great Company Listens to the Voice of the Customer* 2006. New York: Penguin/ Portfolio.

7

NINE KEY INITIATIVES FOR TRANSFORMATION

Strategy is the art of making use of time and space.
I am less concerned about the latter than the former.
Lost time we can never recover.
— Napoleon

Be careful that victories do not carry
the seeds of future defeats.
— Bits and Pieces

The quote from Napoleon says a lot about supply chain transformations — be wary of how much time transformation takes. Taking more time than is necessary helps to ensure defeat of the entire effort. The second quote also has relevance because we do not want supply chain transformations to put in place changes that turn out not to be correct and become difficult to undo. These two quotes in some respects are two sides of the same coin — hasty transformations can mean doing the wrong things. Beware!

Previous chapters have a good deal of discussion on a linked strategic plan — the foundation for a supply chain transformation process. Now the discussion will focus on key initiatives and projects for a full-potential collaborative supply chain in support of the supply chain transformation effort and the strategic plan of the business. The initiatives which will be discussed are (for any given company, some or all of these likely will be appropriate in a supply chain transformation effort):

1. Linked supply chain strategic plan
2. Collaborative supply chain maturity path
3. Global supply chain leverage
4. Collaborative e-business
5. Third-party logistics
6. Total supply chain aggregation
7. Risk management process
8. Integrated total cost reduction process
9. Strategic staffing and organizational development

The discussion in this chapter is structured around these key initiatives. Do not assume that these are the only initiatives — just that they are typical for companies in supply chain transformation efforts.

LINKED SUPPLY CHAIN STRATEGIC PLAN

Companies that succeed with supply chain transformations view the supply chain as a strategic asset. Companies such as Wal-Mart, Amazon, and Dell are rightfully known for their supply chain strategies.

Co-author Bill Lee, during a consulting engagement, once was part of a conversation with two key executives in a client company. One asked, "We've always focused our supply chain on cost, but can there be more to it?" The other replied with a question that captured the essence of transformations: "How can the supply chain contribute to profit and growth?"

Of course, a supply chain should not be focused *just* on cost — a supply chain should contribute to profit and growth — that, as the saying goes, is a "no brainer!" One might argue that these two comments are very naïve; but unfortunately they represent the level of understanding that many people have about the notion of supply chain strategy. Picking up on the second comment for a moment, consider the clear supply chain linkages to some key measures of company health:

- Profitability and growth: revenue, cost of goods sold, profit margins, and ultimately earnings per share
- Asset and capital utilization: return on assets, return on investment, return on capital, and return on equity
- Purchasing efficiency: cost savings of purchased goods and services, administrative expense savings, and operating expense savings
- Cash flow efficiency: cash generation and cash cycle time reduction

Before this discussion goes much further, here are some relevant questions for you, the reader, to ponder for your company:

1. What is strategy, how do we think strategically, and what does strategic thinking mean?
    *   What is strategic thinking and how do we know it when we see it?
    *   What about your company and its approach to supply chain strategy?
2. What might be an approach to strategy deployment in a company such as yours?
    *   What are some strategic objectives of your company?
    *   What is the company's strategic link to the supply chain organization and vice versa?
    *   What are some corporate-level initiatives to achieve the objectives?
    *   What are some supply chain initiatives to achieve the objectives?
    *   What are some measures of success with both the corporate strategy and the supply chain strategy?
    *   What resources are focused on the objectives?
    *   How is strategy deployed to the region, district, and site levels?
    *   What does all this mean to the company and what are the "learnings?"

A number of strategic operating models have been put forth in the literature. The authors have worked in, consulted to, and performed research on a number of companies. Rarely have we seen a company fail when it has a clear definition of its strategic operating model(s) and the applicability of that (those) model(s) to the company's supply chains. Several of these models have direct applicability to supply chain transformation:[1,2]

Operational excellence. Deliver a combination of quality, price, and ease of purchase that no one else in the market can match:

*   Treacy and Wiersema cite the early Ford Motor Company (p. 37):[1]

    Ford ... [was] a paragon of operational excellence, because the founder's business model was tuned to a single purpose: delivering an acceptable product at the lowest possible price. As Ford's costs fell, the retail price of the Model T car fell too, from $850 to $290.

    Ford's supply chain essentially was something not seen too much today — fully integrated from the raw materials (ore for steel, rubber for tires, and so forth), through all stages of manufacturing and logistics, to the ultimate finished drive-away automobile.

- Meeting this strategic objective requires collaboration among the supply chain, product development, operations, and sales and marketing.

Overall cost leadership. Aggressive pursuit of efficient-scale facilities and equipment, vigorous pursuit of cost reductions, tight cost and overhead controls, and avoidance of marginal customer accounts:

- Porter discusses the advantages of overall cost leadership (p. 35):[2]

> *Having a low-cost position yields the firm above-average returns in its industry despite the presence of strong competitive forces. Its cost position gives the firm a defense against rivalry from competitors because it can still earn returns after its competitors have competed away their profits through rivalry.*

- Meeting this strategic objective is mostly the responsibility of the supply chain organization, but also requires collaboration with sales and marketing.

Product leadership. Consistently strive to provide the market with leading-edge products or useful new applications of existing products or services:

- Treacy and Wiersema cite Thomas Alva Edison (p. 83):[1]

> *What few people realize is that he bestowed on mankind a gift far greater than any single invention: the process that underpins product leadership. In 1879, Edison pioneered what was probably the industrial world's first effective product development process, [which] became the model for the labs of today's product leaders.*

- Meeting this strategic objective is mostly the responsibility of product development, but also requires collaboration with the supply chain organization.

Differentiation. Differentiate the product or service offering, creating something that is perceived *industrywide* as being unique, such as a design or brand image, technology, features, customer service, and location:

- Porter discusses what makes differentiation such a powerful strategy:[2]

> *Approaches to differentiating can take many forms. Caterpillar, for example, is known not only for its dealer network and excellent spare parts availability but also for its extremely*

*high-quality durable products, all of which are crucial in heavy
equipment where downtime is very expensive.*

- Meeting this strategic objective requires the collaboration of almost
  the entire enterprise.

Customer intimacy. Do not deliver what the market wants; deliver what a
specific customer wants:

- Many people cite the IBM of the 1970s and 1980s. Computer sales-
  men often gave only one reason to buy from IBM: "Nobody ever got
  fired for buying from IBM." Corporate America, it seems, was so convinced of IBM's technological mastery that computer chiefs dared not
  buy from any company with a less formidable reputation than IBM.
- Meeting this strategic objective requires the collaboration of sales
  and marketing, product development, operations, and supply chain
  organizations.

Focus. Serve a particular target very well — and *better* than others who are
competing more broadly:

- This strategy focuses on a particular buyer group, segment of the
  product line, or geographic market.
- Meeting this strategic objective requires the collaboration of the
  entire organization, depending on the target definition and the needs
  of that particular set of customers.

Clearly, companies cannot serve all of these masters at the same time. In
fact, serving more than one is difficult because all of them require trade-offs that
balance important factors — all of which are not attainable at the same time. To
express this, people often say, "You cannot have it both ways." Trade-offs require
choices. Each strategic operating model also requires choices — both in terms of
what to do and what not to do.

Figure 7.1 illustrates a supply chain strategic plan that is linked upward to the
corporate strategic plan and downward to the supply chain organization — all the
way down to an individual contributor. Let us explain how this works.

Level 1 is the top company level (corporate). Level 2 is the supply chain
organization. The supply chain processes are in Level 3. Level 4 is the individual
contributor level. Notice the cascading level-by-level structure of this model.

Level 1. At Level 1, the following actions occur:

- Company senior management establishes the *vital few strategic objectives*. These vital strategic objectives are the essential elements of the
  corporate strategic plan.

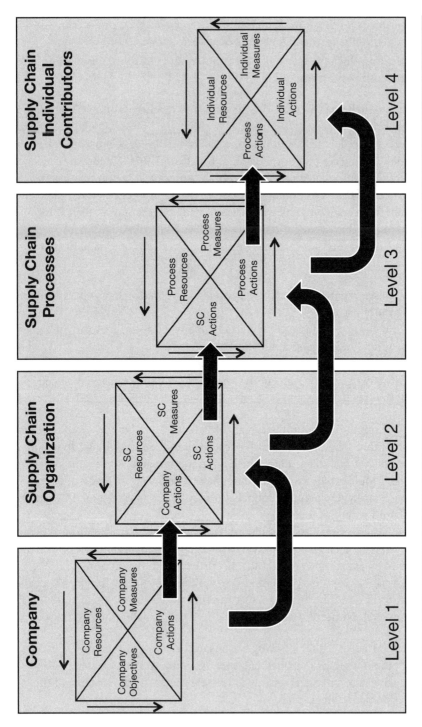

Figure 7.1. Strategic Linkage: Supply Chain Strategic Plan Linked Upward to Corporate Level and Downward to Supply Chain Processes and Individual Contributors Using Hoshin Planning.

- *Current and new actions* are specified in ways that support and implement the strategic objectives from the corporate strategic plan. Actions are checked to ensure their ability to support the plan and the objectives. (Some companies choose to use the term *initiatives* instead of actions.)
- *Measures* are chosen which specify how the actions (or initiatives) will be evaluated for each. These measures map the corporate objectives together with the actions, which allows progress toward the objectives to be monitored and appraised.
- *Resources* are specified that are required to implement the actions to support the plans and objectives. Resources are people who can take ownership of the actions and measures along with the time and money required.

Level 1 (company/corporate) actions become the links to Level 2, the supply chain organization. The company actions or initiatives set the requirements for the supply chain actions or initiatives, which in turn drive the supply chain measures and the resource requirements for the supply chain organization.

Level 2. Level 2 (supply chain organization) actions become the links to Level 3, the process level, that make up the supply chain in its entirety. Please recognize that the supply chain processes are not necessarily (and almost certainly *are not*) contained wholly within the supply chain organization. For example, a supply chain process may be defined as something like the quote-to-cash or order fulfillment processes — which almost certainly cross multiple organizational units.

Level 3. Level 3 (supply chain processes) actions become the links to Level 4, the individual supply chain contributors. Each person, then, has his or her actions, measures, and resources.

In this manner (Level 1 to Level 2 to Level 3 to Level 4), the corporate strategic plan is implemented with objectives, actions, measures, and resources. Notice also the circular arrows in Figure 7.1, which indicate the iterative nature of this process — go around the boxes enough times to get it right. This process:

- Sets strategic *direction* for the business
- Establishes the *objectives* to deliver results
- Identifies the *initiatives* required to meet those objectives and deploys them down through the organization
- Creates *measures* to track progress of the initiatives and to link them back to higher-level objectives and actions
- Identifies *resources* required to complete the initiatives and aligns responsibility
- Specifies *behaviors* that are required to implement the strategy

This approach generally is known as Hoshin planning.[3] Hoshin is a system that was developed in Japan in the 1960s and is a derivative of management by objectives (MBO). The Hoshin system is more than just *planning*. It also includes the *implementation*, or the *doing*, of what is planned, as well as the *review* and *evaluation* of *what* is done. Hoshin has been described as being a *closed loop* system. The Hoshin planning system is the basis for how we like to look at a linked supply chain strategic plan.

COLLABORATIVE SUPPLY CHAIN MATURITY PATH

The Arizona Cardinals football team moved from St. Louis to Phoenix in 1988. The team struggled for the right combination and finally competed in the 2009 Super Bowl, giving a very respectable performance. When speaking on supply chain transformations, Mike Katzorke often jokes with audiences that leading a business in creating a collaborative full-potential supply chain is a lot like the job of a new Arizona Cardinals' coach. Where do you start?

When Mike poses this "where to start" question to audiences, the dialog ultimately arrives at the same conclusion. First, the coach has to get the right players. Second, once what the team should "look like" is defined, an excellent playbook is needed. Third, the coach then has to get the team to be consistently excellent at running the plays. Finally, the players need to play as a team — no grandstanding, thank you.

For the supply side of the supply chain, the process begins with defining the preferred supplier base analytically. Align it contractually with the business and associated supply chain strategic plans. Help it improve its performance and consistency levels. Integrate its objectives, strategies, processes, and data — from its supply base to its customers.

There is no need to elaborate in any depth on the individual steps of the maturity path process summarized in Figure 7.2. However, touching on the key elements that have yielded a successful result is useful:

Collaborative partner analytical selection process. At the base of Figure 7.2, the collaborative partner analytical selection process has some key success factors. First, there is no sense attempting to align, improve, and integrate with suppliers that are philosophically at odds with the objectives and strategies of their customers and those of their customers' customers and shareholders. Collaboration presumes the selection and alignment process establishes this essential requirement. For example, if a potential supplier intends to sustain margins simply by raising prices annually while customers expect and need improved value to remain competitive, there is a disconnect. If a potential supplier is focused solely on their own

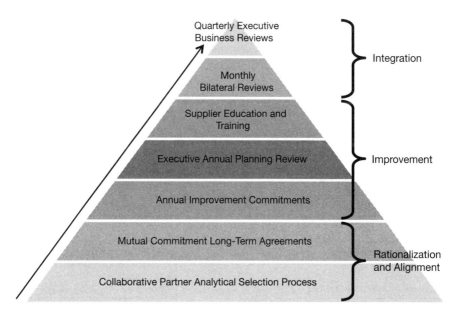

Figure 7.2. Steps in Collaborative Supply Chain Maturity Path.

returns, irrespective of the rest of the supply chain, disconnections are present. These disconnects must be resolved and documented contractually before any further progress is made down the collaborative partner path.

Companies do not, however, need partnership relationships with all their suppliers. Figure 7.3 illustrates how suppliers fit into multiple segments. Beginning the maturity path process requires that companies create categories with different approaches to supplier management, as shown.

Rationalization needs to be a data-driven, analytical process with definitive criteria. Consider a supplier's historical performance in terms of technology, quality, cost, delivery, service, flexibility, lead-time, and so forth. Also look definitively and objectively at what the supplier is doing to be the best tomorrow. It does not make sense to align with a supplier who has good performance today only to discover 2 years into the future that the supplier has invested little or nothing to improve and thus has fallen behind. Because a company is only as good as the weakest link in its supply chain, a company simply cannot align with a poorly performing supplier. A Baldrige-type self-assessment with key improvement level milestones bilaterally verified and rewarded with additional business share has worked wonderfully to avoid this peril.

With a bilateral assessment in place, collaborative improvement plans can be developed jointly with key partners. The joint effort is collaborative because

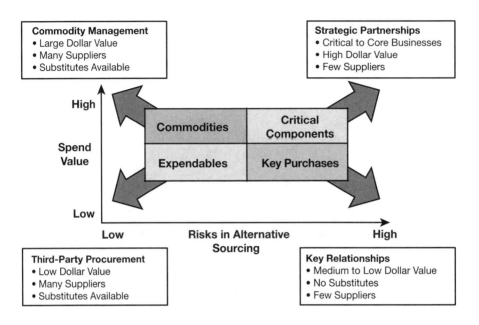

Figure 7.3. Supplier Segmentation: How Suppliers Fit into Multiple Segments.

often for a supplier to improve a specific parameter, the customer has to improve its processes. For example, if a supplier submits a significant cost-reduction idea, the customer needs to have a responsive process in place for analysis and decision making.

The upper-right quadrant on the segmentation chart shown in Figure 7.3 would typically be the group of suppliers with which a transformative company would normally begin its collaborative partner relationships efforts.

Continuing with the key elements in Figure 7.2:

Mutual-commitment long-term agreements. Next, mutual commitment long-term agreements are documented — not merely in terms of price, but in terms of what each party is committed to in terms of specific business, good-faith volume estimates, and maturity path progress. Long-term agreements should reflect a collaborative environment committed to mutual objectives and goals and be unending (or evergreen), contingent upon mutual performance to the requirements and progress to improvement objectives.

Annual improvement commitments. The annual improvement commitments are developed in a collaborative fashion and are documented in an annual maturity path plan with each key supplier partner. Improvement commitments are not just flowery verbiage that speaks of nebulous, touchy-feely, work-together "isms." They are specific quantitative deliverables from both parties who are mutually committed and tied to specific action plans — agreed to at both the individual contributor level and the senior leadership level. Improvement commitments are supported with rolling action item lists on-line and frequent collaborative mirror team reviews. (Mirror teams are cross-functional teams that mirror one another at both customer and supplier and are jointly accountable for the action items.)

Executive annual planning review. Annual executive planning reviews ensure that once the teams have drafted the collaborative annual improvement plan, it is agreed to by both senior leadership teams in terms of scope, timing, and resources.

Supplier education and training. Education and training of suppliers have a threefold purpose:

- To develop a common language of improvement in the cross-enterprise supply chain in terms of objectives, processes, and tools
- To develop an understanding of the velocity and mutual impact of cross-enterprise improvement programs
- To develop a collaborative environment that facilitates cross-enterprise improvements.

Companies sometimes talk as if it is their *suppliers* who need education and training. Oftentimes, however, both suppliers *and* customers need it — sometimes customers more so than suppliers. We believe strongly that one of the most effective questions a company can ask its suppliers is, "What can *we* do, as your customer, to make your job easier and more effective?" Build a joint education and training program at least partially around the answers to that question.

> We suggest that education and training sessions be facilitated by a qualified, experienced outsider. This approach prevents any implication that the customer is educating and training the supplier, when it is actually the customer who may need the most help. A facilitator can ensure that the program is fair and balanced and that it is focused on joint improvement opportunities. (Bill Lee and Mike Katzorke have worked together to facilitate education and training sessions in three companies. Also each has worked independently in many more.)

Supplier education and training can be one of the most helpful approaches to supply chain improvement — as well as one of the most damaging to a collaborative environment. Why? The answers are simple:

- Everyone does not need the same help (or at least does not think they do).
- Everyone has multiple customers with their own brand of improvement process and tools, which have been improved greatly in recent years.
- For most suppliers today (as we say in Texas and Arizona), "This ain't their first rodeo." Some suppliers may be well ahead of their customers in process maturity.

For these reasons, it is far better to make education and training available and to have it collaboratively decided to prescribe specific content for specific partners in the annual bilateral improvement planning process. Also, including joint supplier/customer education and training programs so both sides can learn from each other is far better.

On-site supplier development is both an extremely powerful improvement process and a very costly one. As illustrated in Figure 7.4, on-site supplier development should be a multistep process, which dedicates both customer and supplier resources to a specific joint relationship for about 3 months or so. The teams should jointly evaluate, redesign, and deploy the redesign of specific processes. Redesign of specific processes should be specified in the annual improvement plan only after careful study and agreement along with a top-level commitment of resources.

Our approach is unlike that which some businesses employ with their suppliers — a quick-hit project with the attitude: "We're here to fix you and we'll collect a price reduction on our way out the door."

For smaller businesses, when resources and improvement capital can be an impediment to improvement projects, sometimes subsidized alternatives exist. One program is the Manufacturing Extension Partnership (MEP) by the National Institute of Standards and Technology. The MEP mission statement is as follows:

To strengthen the global competitiveness of US-based manufacturing by providing information, decision support, and implementation of innovative approaches focused on leveraging technologies, techniques, and business best practices.

The MEP program is funded one-third federal, one-third state, and one-third industry. MEP focuses on meeting the short-term needs of a business, but in the context of an overall company strategic plan. MEP provides on-site guidance with engineering services, growth opportunities, application of lean techniques and tools, quality programs, environmental issues, and workforce development. On-site resources are primarily highly experienced hands-on professionals

Step	Pre	1	2	3	4	5	6	7	8	9	10	11	12	13
							WEEKS							
Select supplier(s) to participate	X													
Meet with supplier management	X													
1. Perform situation assessment		X												
2. Conduct orientation			X											
3. Determine project scope			X	X										
4. Obtain baseline data			X	X										
5. Analyze baseline data					X	X								
6. Develop vision and establish goals						X								
7. Develop improvement ideas						X	X							
8. Develop implementation plan						X	X							
9. Implement improvement initiatives							X	X	X	X				
10. Collect and evaluate new data										X	X	X	X	
11. Determine follow-up plans													X	
12. Prepare for and conduct management review													X	X

Figure 7.4. Joint Customer and Supplier Development: Steps in Sample Plan.

from the private sector. MEP coordinates their assignments to businesses. (The National Institute of Standards and Technology may be reached via www.mep. nist.gov or 1-800-MEP-4MFG.)

Returning to the key elements in Figure 7.2:

Monthly bilateral reviews. Monthly bilateral reviews summarize and elevate the weekly team reviews to the director levels in mirrored fashion and keep the momentum moving forward in accordance with the schedule, often by addressing resource and policy issues.

Quarterly executive business reviews. Executive business reviews have three objectives:

- To conduct a summary review of progress to the annual improvement plan
- To conduct a collaborative discussion of progress to plan and identify any intervention needed
- If warranted by results of the above, to conduct a discussion of new business opportunities, new product developments, and new technology developments and requirements

We have seen application of the maturity path process to the external supply chain yield actual results such as these:

- 2% cost improvement
- 86% improvement in supplier quality
- 28% improvement in partner delivery
- 42% improvement in factory delivery
- 52% improvement in purchased material inventory turns

GLOBAL SUPPLY CHAIN LEVERAGE

A global supply chain leverage initiative simply means that a supply chain transformation will include the best partners anywhere in the world. Good companies do not select partners passively, but rather they actively and aggressively research and seek out global sources that improve their competitive posture both today and in the long run.

In the early days of deployment, this approach was called *global sourcing*. It also has been called *outsourcing*. Over time, global sourcing evolved to *low-cost-country sourcing*. Today, the term is most commonly referred to as *off-shoring*.

Off-shoring. Early on, off-shoring typically began first as a research process to find desired potential capabilities in low-cost countries. Then off-shoring became an enabling process to help potential suppliers in those countries develop their processes, people, facilities, and leadership. This evolution was needed to ensure consistent quality, delivery, and cost to meet the supply chain's needs.

Risk identification and management along with cultural and language barriers were all key elements to be addressed. Companies found that transition of work from their internal processes to low-cost countries required internal resources to be co-located with new suppliers for extended periods of time — as well as the development of in-country resources hired by the customer to ultimately replace the internal resources. The process was slow, tedious, costly, and risky.

Having commercial arrangements at the outset to govern the relationship and its evolution as well as to control the progression of pricing was also important. Tying down commercial arrangements on the front end of the relationship was very important — so that as the off-shoring company helped develop the capability of the low-cost-country source, the low-cost-country source did not simply market those capabilities to a competitor of the off-shoring company for a higher return. Exclusivity agreements and long-term pricing were crucial in commercial agreements.

Some pioneers who wanted to move more rapidly simply acquired companies in the low-cost countries where they could strike long-term arrangements with the governments there. For example, Pratt and Whitney did this exceptionally well in Central Europe.

Clearly, globalization is here to stay, regardless of the pontificating of politicians. Although there is much debate today about the macroeconomic impacts to national economies, both short- and long-term, off-shoring has moved well beyond outsourcing manufacturing. The focus has shifted to service processes, with general and administrative costs also being opportunity areas. There is no longer anywhere near the levels of research or risk previously involved in off-shore activity. A myriad of companies have well-developed databases on low-cost country capabilities and in country resources to help move and manage the work rapidly.

We often worry that possibly companies are chasing next quarter's numbers so hard that they may not be doing a really thorough, objective job of core/context decision making and might live to regret some of what is being off-shored. The transition process is still important today, but a great deal of focused and experienced capability exists to help smooth and speed the process to results. The authors recommend engaging external help initially to greatly increase speed to results and to avoid experiencing the same pain, cost, and potential land mines suffered by earlier companies. External help can greatly help with source selection specific to a company's needs and with smoothing the actual transition of business. Figure 7.5 summarizes the key elements of an off-shoring transition process.

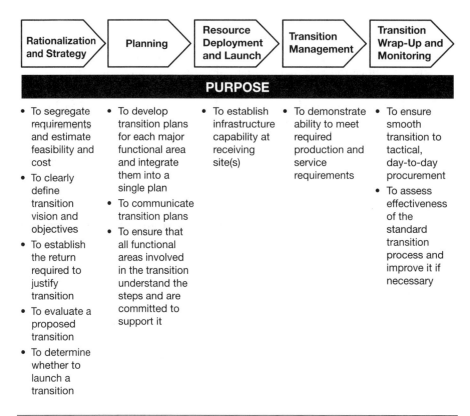

Figure 7.5. Key Elements of an Off-Shoring Transition Process.

COLLABORATIVE e-BUSINESS

Collaborative e-business sounds like a buzzword term before we even write the first sentence of this section! But, the term really describes this strategy. Transformative supply chains should optimize, to the extent possible, integration in terms of objectives, strategies, processes, and data.

> Bill Lee dislikes using the term *optimal* except in the sense of mathematical optimization. He thinks it degrades the true meaning of the term. Nevertheless, because *optimal* is in such common use, Bill swallows his academic snobbery and acquiesces! His request to the reader is as follows: "Please use the word *optimal* sparingly because you may be embarrassed when some mathematical snob calls you out by asking you to prove that optimization really has occurred and what optimization algorithm you used." (But if you, the reader, really wants to act

snobbish, just do the same thing to someone else when they talk about *optimizing* the business. That guarantees you will be viewed as the snob! Sometimes it is just fun to act that way!)

Optimal means adding value to customers and stakeholders of the chain, keeping the two in balance. Speed, accuracy, and associated integrated responsiveness are the key values to the chain. Human beings need to think and make solid judgments and decisions from dynamic current data and to respond rapidly. They should not execute repetitive transactional work. (Figuratively speaking, of course, the integration should be so tight and instantaneous across the chain that when a customer selects leather seats for a new truck, a cow in the field winces.)

The scope and speed of the evolution of e-business supply chain integration and the associated applications have been somewhat dizzying over the last 10 years. Just 5 years ago many viewed e-business as a toolkit — from which to pick and choose; but this is true no more.

Direct e-business results are difficult to accurately detail. The IT director may feel that he or she has driven every improvement and savings in the business in the last 10 years. The CEO knows there is goodness there, but he or she is not so sure what the cost versus return actually is. Why? Because the CEO knows that costs actually taken out of the business are difficult to track. Furthermore, the returns to the business are also frequently difficult to identify. Yet, the supply chain leader should have no doubt that the e-business revolution has contributed immensely to process improvements that have yielded results in the following areas and magnitudes:

- Consistency of on-time deliveries to customers: improved by at least 50%
- Reduced material lead times: improved by at least 50%
- Reduced inventories: improved by at least 30%
- Reduced shortages: improved by at least 40%
- Reduced supply chain overhead costs: improved by at least 30%
- Improved product quality: by at least ten times
- Enabled reduced actual material cost by lowering partner costs (schedule, overhead, compliance, etc.): resulted in annual productivity gains
- Enabled concurrent design at multiple locations: shortened design time and reduced costly rework and changes

Although the numbers may be debatable, there should be little debate on their relative magnitude. e-Business has enabled step-function improvements in the vision of what is possible in supply chain integration. Yet, an integrated collaborative supply chain is so much more than e-collaboration of data. And if *optimal* e-business results improvement is desired, executives need to remind themselves regularly that the e-business strategy was and is an *enabler* of the process improvements that yield the business results improvement — not the other way around. The e-business strategy removed barriers and transactional work, increased speed, and fostered immensely improved linkage — needed, however, is to start with the customer and the stakeholder, link competitive performance levels to their desires, and then link these to process capabilities. Then, look at the associated work, the way it gets done, and the way it might be done and develop strategies and tools that move the process to new levels of what is possible.

THIRD-PARTY LOGISTICS

Third-party logistics is neither a new idea nor a revolutionary one. It has, however, become a feasible strategy that yields positive business results rapidly when employed well. Third-party logistics is not a viable strategy if employed as: "I have problems with parts flow — I think I'll outsource procurement." Third-party logistics is a very powerful approach if utilized for *context* procurement. Several more progressive *Fortune 100* companies and their peers worldwide are deeply engaged in third-party logistics with very satisfactory improvement results in quality, cost, delivery, service, overhead, and inventory.

Many starts at this concept of third-party logistics have been made over the years; but they were mostly made by distributors, who, although well intentioned, really only marked up material and then added their overhead costs of materials management. These distributors never really built a viable business model around third-party logistics from the ground up — just mostly as a "bolt-on" to their distribution businesses. For the successful third-party logistics companies of today, third-party logistics is their core business — they invest in its process design, development, improvement, and innovation as key success factors to their business. They ensure that assets are taken off their clients' balance sheets and at the same time save money on the actual cost of the material they supply and the overhead to manage it. These companies are committed to be better at it than their customers. They are profitable because their processes are better and more focused on those items they handle and because these processes combine their requirements with those of other clients for cost-effective procurement and economies of scale in overhead.

Materials overhead. In many companies, materials overhead is a significant cost — sometimes as high as 8 to 9% of direct material cost. Benchmark levels today are probably in the range of 0.5 to 0.75%, but that is certainly not typical of business as a whole. Many companies are at 4 to 6 %. Material overhead often includes purchasing, incoming inspection, materials quality, production and materials planning, and shipping and receiving. As discussed in Chapter 4, supply chain people in immature supply chain processes often spend two-thirds of their time on so-called C items — 80% of the items and 5% of the money. Visionary third-party logistics companies have made those C items their A items and have developed a core competence for their quality, delivery, and cost-effective supply. Corbus, one of these companies, is so confident in their process, its performance, and their people that they contractually commit up-front to double-digit, first-year material overhead savings with customers. They also make the transition relatively painless by incorporating client resources into their business with minimal human resource impact being part of their business model.

Leading third-party logistics companies perform and execute an in-depth supply management process for C items the way other excellent companies do for their A items because those C items are their A items. They deliver:

- In-depth assessments and reporting to continuously identify opportunities for savings and business process efficiencies
- Co-developed multiyear deflation targets, specific service-level agreements, and key performance indicators (KPIs)
- Shared productivity gains year over year
- Seamless migration of processes with mature detailed transition methodology

Typical actual results from the deployment of this strategy have been outstanding:

- Process cost: average reduction realized of 25 to 30%
- Global sourcing: average cost reduction realized of 15 to 30%
- Increased operational efficiency: ~20%
- Resource optimization: ~30% of client material resources freed up
- Service level: ~10 to 20% distribution centers, 20% spares
- Line-item fill rate: ~50% improvement
- Delinquency: ~25% first-year improvement

Third-party logistics can be an excellent approach to free up resources (people and capital) to improve the core processes and capabilities of an enterprise.

Indirect material management. A second major factor in the third-party logistics approach is indirect material management. Indirect material often accounts for 15 to 40% of external expenditures — and historically indirect material has not been very effectively managed. Too often, the weakest quartile of the supply chain talent pool was assigned to the indirect material area because it was viewed as tactical procurement, unidentifiable for forecasting and unmanageable strategically. Today, that has changed — companies began to look at their total cost pictures in more depth and it became apparent that they needed to find a way to do a better job of managing indirect expenditures.

As the process of indirect material management evolved, more and more expenditures fell under increased analytical scrutiny, including previously sacrosanct areas such as advertising, health benefits, and so forth; but a process and a tool were needed to understand future spend so it could be categorized, analyzed, and contracted. Although the process could be developed internally, at least one well-known company (Ariba Inc.) had a relatively easily deployable, highly integrated process and system for data capture and management of indirect spending.

> Procurement traditionally was a paper-based, labor-intensive, inefficient process. Ariba, a provider of spend management solutions, was established on the premise that the Internet could be used to enable companies to facilitate and improve their procurement processes (see www.ariba.com/about/).

Mike Katzorke and his teams worked with Ariba in two different venues to address the opportunity of indirect spend data capture and management. It was almost as simple as directing that every indirect dollar spent must be processed through Ariba, with supplier catalogs added as spend profiles dictated over time. Within 1 year, his teams were able to manage indirect spend with almost the same process and precision as direct spend, which was forecast from the master schedule and bills of material extrapolations. Ariba's people and systems did the rest in conjunction with Mike's teams and their IT partners. Ariba spend visibility delivered a structured view into indirect spending and compliance, empowering process stakeholders to identify quick-hit savings opportunities, implement appropriate sourcing strategies, and improve compliance with existing contract terms to sustain long-term savings. Keys to this success were:

- *Speed*: Rapid implementation and integration with existing systems ensured that all spend data were captured and accurately classified. Dashboards, reporting, and analytical features enabled fast, accurate, and personalized analysis.
- *Sustainability*: Automated classification to both industry (UNSPSC) and company-specific standards provided consistent, highly repeatable spend analysis.
- *Coverage*: Commodity-specific detail derived from all data systems yielded comprehensive, *clean* data.
- *Flexibility*: Tailored solutions were delivered that helped easily integrate into the overall spend management process.

No matter the business or industry, a lot of improvements are possible in indirect spend. Many good companies are reaping the rewards of approaching indirect spend with data and a process that parallels the process most used on the direct spend side.

TOTAL SUPPLY CHAIN AGGREGATION

Total supply chain aggregation is a strategy that can be beneficial to any manufacturing company and many service companies. Trevor Stansbury and his team at O'Neal's Supply Dynamics were visionary in their design and development of the process and an associated toolset and have been successfully pioneering its deployment with some of industry's most progressive companies. With all the outsourcing and off-shoring today, this is a strategy in the right place at the right time that really yields near-term results.

Supply chain aggregation is a concept that has existed for many years in the minds of supply chain leaders, but the high degree of outsourcing over the last decades have made supply chain aggregation a vital and extremely powerful strategy. Until recently, the ability to facilitate realization of supply chain aggregation on a broad scale did not exist. It was simply too labor intensive. Many supply chain people moved on what some called *draw down* agreements that allowed lower-tier suppliers to buy common requirements off higher-tier customers' agreements. For this discussion, however, the authors are talking about a very different concept.

Total supply chain aggregation is defined as a process and operational toolset. They specifically and analytically identify, combine, and contract the material requirements of the internal operations of a business and those of all subtier partners in the chain by utilizing a defined process and focused technology for speed, accuracy, and timeliness. The process consolidates multiple bills of materials across the supply chain and organizes them into generic categories for contracting and management, both tactically and strategically. This structure is not simply a consortium buying solution or a right-to-buy contract in which subtier suppliers simply buy off a customer negotiated agreement. It also is not a Trojan horse that extracts benefits from one player in the supply chain at the expense of another. What the structure does is create visibility — for the entire supply chain — and enormous leverage, not only for price, but also for all the elements of total cost, including quality, delivery, service, flexibility, and material availability. In addition, instead of each of the companies at various tiers in the supply chain competing for materials, the demand for these materials can be managed in a concerted fashion, improving results and minimizing cost for the entire supply chain. Additionally, a supplier has less risk because of better visibility into all their customers, thereby reducing buffer inventory and process disruption costs. It also provides the information for:

- New source development
- Material standardization
- Spares requirements planning
- Surplus management
- Mill-to-manufacturer-to-distributor supply chain improvement

Requirements are aggregated first at a supply chain level. If an enterprise is using a third-party aggregator, however, the enterprise can aggregate across multiple supply chains, which can greatly enhance collaborative relationship possibilities and the associated benefits of risk management through visibility and control. In times of material allocations and the associated upward cost pressure, the added visibility and control through collaborative relationships have proven a distinct competitive advantage.

A number of companies are successfully employing this common sense supply chain integrating approach. Results of deployment are as follows:

- Total supply material aggregation has typically yielded a first-pass improvement of 15 to 40% on the commodities aggregated.
- Of that savings, 75% usually has come from incumbent suppliers so:
  - Savings were realized sooner.
  - Risk and cost of supplier change were avoided.
- Follow-on improvement typically has been 2 to 3% per year in productivity gains.
- Subtier suppliers saved typically about 25% on materials as a result of the process facilitating further savings for the end supply chain product.
- The collaborative supply chain benefits to both customers and suppliers in terms of visibility, control, and risk management afforded significant improvements in overhead costs.

Total supply chain aggregation is a strategy that can be beneficial for any manufacturing company and many service companies. Trevor Stansbury (President, Supply Dynamics) and his team were visionary in their design and development of the process and an associated toolset. Supply Dynamics (acquired by O'Neal Steel in November 2006) has been successfully pioneering its deployment with some of industry's most progressive companies.

THE RISK MANAGEMENT PROCESS

In the early stages of an earlier recession (from about July 1990 until March 1991), many supply chain executives began to think about risk management.

Businesses had not only moved more activity outside their four walls, but they had also moved it off shore — thousands of miles away, with new logistics challenges, cultural challenges, and financial challenges. Risk management started with worry over the financial failure of niche suppliers of very long lead-time and very long-development items with unique processes.

Dun & Bradstreet®, an enterprising company with access to enormous amounts of financial data and expertise, began to offer a service to provide a regular financial health analysis of a company's suppliers' businesses.[4] D&B also provided early warning reports if an analysis projected a potential problem. Mike Katzorke and his team decided to employ the service and found it useful for sleeping better at night. The D&B service was utilized surgically with an analytical selection of those key niche suppliers selected for monitoring. It was also actually useful in avoiding severe production interruption issues when some key niche suppliers got into cash-flow problems during the recession.

Over time, risk management has expanded in scope well beyond supplier financial health monitoring. Today, risk management is part of the annual strategic planning process and is based on much more comprehensive analysis, including:

- What can go wrong?
- What is likely to go wrong?
- How can we avoid these things?
- What can we do about them if they do go wrong?

More terms for this process, of course, are risk assessment, risk analysis, and risk mitigation planning — all of which have different meanings.

Risk management is arduous, data-centric, and analytical thinking — but necessary. Supply chain risks can include all sorts of things: natural events (hurricanes, tornados, floods, etc.), political crises, terrorism, data security, raw material supply shortfalls, strikes, mergers and acquisition stumbles, financial failures, and many others.

Interestingly, but not surprisingly, some of the best information on risk management comes out of the project management profession and literature. Specifically, the Project Management Institute (PMI) has been at the forefront of developments in this area. PMI published a seminal work: *A Guide to the Project Management Body of Knowledge (PMBOK®)*.[5] According to PMI, the project risk management processes are as follows:

1. Risk management planning
2. Risk identification
3. Qualitative risk analysis
4. Quantitative risk analysis

5. Risk response planning
6. Risk monitoring and control

These processes interact with each other. The PMBOK shows these in an input-process-output format that is very useful. We have used the PMI methodology in our consulting engagements. (A risk management plan clearly is one of the most important and useful documents, as one might suppose. However, we also have found two additional documents to be highly useful: a *risk register* and an *assumptions register*.)

A maturity path for risk management is developed like other maturity paths, which we have discussed in this work: beginning — transition — advanced.

Risk management has its origins in the uncertainty that is present in all supply chain activities. There are *known* risks, which have been identified, analyzed, and quantified and for which plans can be developed. There are *unknown* risks that cannot be identified and analyzed, but for which some general contingency planning can be accomplished.

A few years ago during the height of the U.S. space program, Bill Lee did some consulting with NASA on planning processes for the Space Shuttle. Although the process was not called supply chain, it nevertheless had a lot of similarity. While spending time at the Johnson Space Center, just south of Houston, Bill was introduced to a new term — *unk-unks* — or unknown-unknowns. *Unk-unks* were the unknown risks, about which NASA did not know enough to even know that they were risks! We suspect that many companies have supply chains with lots of *unk-unks*. The unknown-unknowns make it all the more imperative that risk planning be an integral part of a company's key initiatives for supply chain transformation.

THE INTEGRATED TOTAL COST REDUCTION PROCESS

If management desires to maximize reduction of costs in the supply chain, the process should start with the people who normally best understand all of the costs in the business — the chief financial officer (CFO) and the team in the finance organization. Historically, supply chain people have analyzed spending and budgets. When supply chain people focus on cost reductions, however, the team often jumps first to external spending because typically external spending represents about 65 to 90% of the costs of a business. This approach, however, often leads to a misallocation of resources and relatively slow progress toward objectives — which occurs because the greatest cost-reduction opportunities for the business, that the supply chain team could help improve, are not necessarily addressed.

Other opportunities. There are other expenditures in the *total cost* opportunity set: marketing and advertising expenditures (often with control by marketing), health and other benefits (often with control by the human resources organization), travel (often with control diffused throughout the organization), technical consulting (often with control by engineering), information technology consulting (often with control by the IT organization), and so forth. The relative magnitude of these and other possible cost-reduction opportunities usually cannot be seen without the assistance of the finance organization and without going through all of the costs in the enterprise. A top-level view from the CFO might look something Figure 7.6.

Direct and indirect expense. Direct material (procured material actually used in production) usually accounts for 50 to 90% of cost in most manufacturing businesses today. Analysis and experience, however, have shown that indirect purchases (products and services not directly used in production) can account for about 15 to 40% of all external expenditures in these same businesses (capital equipment purchases excluded). A discussed earlier in this chapter, Ariba has created some very useful software to help companies find and categorize indirect expenditures;[6] but about a year of running all the indirect business through the software is required before the captured information provides a clear picture of the expenditures. At that point, companies can begin to apply the supply management processes and tools that they use on direct materials. So, while Ariba-type tools are being implemented, process or functional budget reviews with finance and the process leaders have proven very effective at finding opportunities and harvesting improvements in indirect and new product development external spend.

The human element. What about human nature in the cost-reduction process? A cost-reduction initiative identifies opportunities and helps process owners reduce their costs. The business, however, needs a policy on whether it allows the process owners to spend the savings or whether the money goes back to the CEO and into a pool that can be used for the overall best impact in the business. Now, process owners generally are very creative people. So, any policy on this topic really needs to be designed to take human nature into consideration. The dilemma here, of course, is twofold: if the process owner gets to keep the savings and reinvest it in other parts of his/her process, there is added incentive to achieve savings; on the other hand, if the savings go back for reallocation to other parts of the business, there is less incentive to identify savings. Nevertheless, in the second case, the entire business benefits from the improvement.

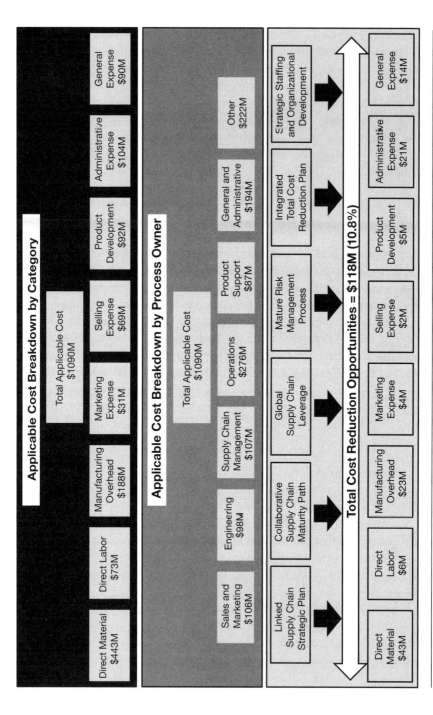

Figure 7.6. An Integrated Total Cost Reduction Plan: An Enterprise Top-Level View.

The teams. With the cost-reduction objectives quantified with time lines specified by the CEO, each process leader can charter a team to work cross-functionally to put projects in place to achieve these objectives. A vital responsibility for the CEO is to establish a culture of *team success.* Every process leader has the responsibility to champion specific initiatives and projects to achieve specific cost objectives. The CEO absolutely must foster a climate that says no process leader is a success unless all process leaders are successful. This mentality must be reinforced in compensation plans for the CEO and the process leaders (usually the enterprise vice presidents) and drilled down through the organization to the individual contributor level. Otherwise, competing interests will prevail. The most important progress likely will be subjugated to lesser priorities and improvement likely will be suboptimized.

Scorekeeping. Finance needs to be the scorekeeper in a total cost-reduction initiative. In any cost-reduction initiative, when process leaders report their own financial progress, their accuracy is in doubt. Then their integrity comes under suspicion. In one company, when so much money was taken out of cost by Fred's materials organization (we just call him *Fred*), the savings were calculated and reported monthly by Fred's finance director to senior leadership. Although cost reductions were real and Fred could demonstrate them, because the enterprise's finance people were not involved in creation and reporting of the numbers, the savings were often called "Fred dollars" in the business units. The other business units did not know whether to believe the numbers or not. As a result, some support was forfeited for the team generating the improvements — which goes to show that the enterprise finance organization needs to be the scorekeeper.

Plan execution. How should a cost-reduction plan be executed? Mike was employed by two businessmen while working his way through college. These men kept a little sign by the cash register that said, "Nothing happens until someone sells something." (Mike thinks he learned far more about practical business principles from these men than he did in business school. Bill, as a business school professor, agrees that that easily could have been the case!) With linked business and process strategic plans in place, and accountability and an acceptable culture clear, it is still true that nothing improves until the plan is executed (no, not the people, the plan!). So how can execution get moving? That is easy. Initially have monthly reviews with the CEO to get things moving. Then make the reviews quarterly once some momentum is built. A great deal of latitude typically is given in the reporting sessions because reporting sessions primarily are designed to facilitate discussion and coaching. At the same time, reporting sessions often degenerate into "dog and pony" show competition and probably miss the mark a bit in keeping the focus on the important actions. As the reporting mentality becomes more and more a cultural norm, reviews typically become more directly linked to the actual progress against specific projects that would yield the required deliverables. In one environment, each initiative or project was synthesized for executive reviews and monthly reports into what is known as a four-up chart (shown in Figure 7.7).

Progress reviews. The four-up chart in Figure 7.7 is very straightforward and simple. It contains a great deal of information and serves as an easily used but effective tool to facilitate discussions of initiatives. Verifying plan linkage and completeness is uncomplicated. For example, there should be direct linkage of the actions, their impact, and the completion date with the plan. If the contract renegotiations, for example, are scheduled to complete on August 8 and have a 10% impact in total cost reductions, one would expect to see that impact in the plan by that date. If the chart shows the project to be ahead of or behind plan, obvious questions and explanations are called for. Risks, mitigations, barriers and issues, and completion dates all provide information for understanding, interaction, and dialog. Monthly process owner reviews and quarterly senior leadership reviews are very effective in keeping a team focused and the plans on track in most organizations.

Scope. Because external purchases account for a majority of the cost in most businesses today, supply management has become a competitive differentiator for almost all supply chains; but before a discussion begins on the alignment, integration, and improvement of the external supply chain, first consider its scope. Far too many supply chain leaders launch their transformations with little work done on core/context decision making and the associated implications for both internal and external planning. The definition of core and context can be summarized: *any activity that can raise the company's stock price is core … everything else is context.*

Core versus context. Core/context transformation policy needs to be established and agreed upon by the senior leadership team of the business. Anything less has traditionally led to a three-way contest among manufacturing (wants to outsource very little), supply management (wants to outsource as much as possible), and engineering (is conflicted between wanting the latest technology immediately while at the same time having the ability to do spur-of-the-moment changes on the operations floor). Clear decision parameters need to be given to the transformation team in order for the business to minimize rework in the process. Companies can use a core versus context analysis to focus resources to achieve and sustain market leadership.

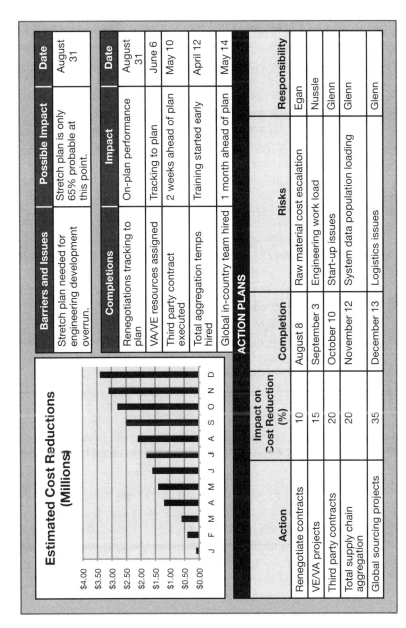

Estimated Cost Reductions (Millions)

Barriers and Issues	Possible Impact	Date
Stretch plan needed for engineering development overrun.	Stretch plan is only 65% probable at this point.	August 31

Completions	Impact	Date
Renegotiations tracking to plan	On-plan performance	August 31
VA/VE resources assigned	Tracking to plan	June 6
Third party contract executed	2 weeks ahead of plan	May 10
Total aggregation temps hired	Training started early	April 12
Global in-country team hired	1 month ahead of plan	May 14

ACTION PLANS

Action	Impact on Cost Reduction (%)	Completion	Risks	Responsibility
Renegotiate contracts	10	August 8	Raw material cost escalation	Egan
VE/VA projects	15	September 3	Engineering work load	Nussle
Third party contracts	20	October 10	Start-up issues	Glenn
Total supply chain aggregation	20	November 12	System data population loading	Glenn
Global sourcing projects	35	December 13	Logistics issues	Glenn

Figure 7.7. Four-Up Chart: Sample Synthesis of Information to Facilitate Process Review (VA/VE, value analysis/value engineering).

Core activities. Core activities set an enterprise apart from its competition. Leadership in core activities directly advances the mission and, ultimately, the stock price. This means that, when improved, core activities bring about direct recognition from the marketplace. Core is what an institution must continually innovate in to achieve and maintain leadership. Core activities are those in which a business should focus its own key talent, leadership, management, and internal resources. The core activities are key success factors of the enterprise strategy.

Context activities. In contrast, context activities are those that, although they may be critical, do not in themselves distinguish the organization from others in its market segment. Context activities are activities that could economically be provided to the business by partners for whom these context activities are core. Context is critical, but not strategic.

A core versus context policy summary might look something like the following:

- Activities are performed for the purpose of producing products and/or services for customers that create value to the stakeholders of the business. Core activities directly impact value creation. Core activities often are described as *strategic* or *high-value* activities.
- All business resources are by definition costly and therefore scarce, so they must be employed first in core activities.
- Core activities are to be focused on creating competitive advantage.
- Activities that do not directly contribute to the creation and/or maintenance of competitive advantage for the business are defined as not essential to the enterprise and should be categorized as context.
- Context activities typically are low value and necessary activities.

With the transformation team core/context decisions made through applications of this policy, the team and the leadership reviewing the team's decisions should give the decisions a final check before their implementation is planned and executed:

- Do the activities being categorized as *core* create value from the perspective of the customers and the stakeholders such that the customer is willing pay a premium for them?
- If expertise for the items defined as *context* became available to competitors:
  - Would the competitive advantage of the business be impacted significantly or would a key entry barrier be removed?
  - Would an opportunity be provided for synergy that would be unavailable any other way?

- Would a channel of entry into new product or service markets area potentially be created?

With core/context decisions addressed, a clearer picture emerges of the scope of work that needs to be addressed.

STRATEGIC STAFFING AND ORGANIZATIONAL DEVELOPMENT

Staffing is the most important of the initiatives addressed in this chapter. We have heard the adage, "Good people in a poor process will do better than weak people in a good process." Why don't we go for good people in good processes — isn't that best? We have observed, and research has seemed to bear out our observation, that one thing which makes outstanding leaders outstanding is their ability to surround themselves with good people and to grow these people into great teams.

> *Supply chain is much easier to learn than leadership.*

Mike Katzorke has taken on three supply chain transformations in his career. When he was recruited to these jobs from the outside, Mike knew that companies do not generally go outside for senior leaders unless they have something they want to significantly change and think that only an outside perspective will get it done. In other words, Mike knew he was not being invited to a tea party. After an analysis of the business and the supply chain process and results, invariably, an infusion of experienced leadership talent was needed. There were always supply chain leaders in place at various levels of maturity in both leadership and supply chain vision, and the vast majority of them could be grown into both strong leaders and world-class supply chain professionals, but supply chain is much easier to learn than leadership. A new supply chain process leader, therefore, needs experienced, developed leadership talent that he or she can tap and put to work early on tough transformational issues.

Four-part approach. We suggest a four-part approach to supply chain staffing at the outset of a transformation project:

- Consider recruiting junior officers who are leaving military service. The military does a superb job of developing leadership capabilities in their junior officers, who usually are the best and the brightest college graduates. These individuals can provide experienced and developed leadership skills and exceptional analytical brainpower.

- Establish a policy of hiring only degreed people for supply chain professional jobs. Hiring degreed people helps establish an atmosphere of professionalism in supply chain organizations. (All too often, we have seen that some companies seem to place individuals in supply chain positions who have flunked out of their previous jobs. This practice transmits a very clear, but highly incorrect view of supply chain: "If you cannot cut it elsewhere, you always can get a supply chain job!")
- Develop relationships with targeted universities that have a strong reputation for their supply chain programs. Recruit recent graduates from the undergraduate and MBA programs at these schools. Integrate them into the individual contributor ranks for more gradual development into supply chain leadership positions while they provide immediate analytical brainpower.
- Establish a policy for supply chain professional jobs that requires nondegreed incumbents to become ISM- and/or APICS-certified within 18 months. Companies often have good people, who for whatever reasons do not have college degrees; yet these people should be encouraged to develop to the limits of their capabilities. Also encourage these individuals to return to college and complete their education. The most progressive companies have education-assistance programs for their employees. Employees should be encouraged to take advantage of these programs.

This four-part approach has worked well in various transformations in providing the capability to successfully execute supply chain process transformation enterprisewide and to upgrade the professional capability of the supply chain process. A brief discussion of each of these four components is important:

Why recruit junior military officers and where can they be found? We can answer both questions (why and where) at the same time. Companies are looking for bright minds with experienced developed leadership capability. Mike Katzorke has recruited these individuals through several avenues over the years. The most successful recruiting experience for Mike came through working with Lucas Group (executive search consultants) for the following reasons:

- Only a small percentage of applicants are chosen for admittance.
- Only a small percentage of Lucas registrants exiting the military service are presented for placement to clients.

- About a third of interviewed candidates are selected for follow-up interviews.
- About a third to a half of candidates attending follow-up interviews receive offers of employment.

So, clients get the cream of the crop for organization fit, experienced and developed leadership talent, and brainpower.

Why target certain universities for hiring? Recruiting graduates from targeted supply chain schools is a proven approach especially when combined with an intern program — for both undergraduates and MBA students. These future professionals come in already having selected a supply chain career. They build up to full speed very rapidly because their educational program usually is directly relevant to the job requirements. Usually many of them continue on a career path in supply chain if the hiring company is working at being among the best in the world. (Arizona State University and Michigan State University are two of several excellent supply chain schools.)

Why hire only degreed individuals into supply chain professional jobs? This approach is almost self-explanatory. Degreed individuals raise the absolute professionalism of a supply chain team and elevate how the team is viewed in the eyes of the rest of the enterprise. How the team is viewed, of course, is extremely important in that all supply chain people are sales people, selling ideas to the enterprise and the supply chain through influence. It goes without saying that influence is greatly helped by professional credibility.

> On almost any existing supply chain team, there are team members in professional jobs who are not degreed. Although these team members are often good people, they have been trained to operate in the legacy processes, which senior leadership wants to change.

Why require ISM and/or APICS certification? Requiring ISM and/or APICS certification is designed to help people develop their capabilities in the areas of different certification programs. Certification also gives them a broader understanding of how what they do or do not do affects all the other processes in the business. Certification is designed to help them continue to succeed personally in the future and to raise the professionalism and results of the organization. All that said, most people resent this requirement at first; but experience has shown consistently that when they complete their certifications, they are proud of their accomplishments. They truly see the benefit certification has for them professionally and the team as a whole. Most companies pay for the materials and first-pass testing for the certifications.

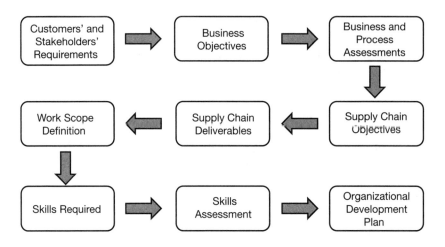

Figure 7.8. Organization Development Plan Alignment: Process from Customer and Shareholders to Supply Chain to Work Scope to Skills Assessment.

Organizational development. With a stronger team coming together through the multipart staffing approach outlined above, organizational development (OD) becomes key in building a sustainable world-class supply chain process. The trouble with the term *organizational development* is that in many organizations it means that when a training flyer comes around to process leaders, they scratch their heads and say, "Let's see. I wonder who I haven't sent to something for a while." OD should be given as serious a treatment for planning, execution, and follow-up as every other element of the supply chain strategic plan, of which it must be an integral element. How is that done? In excellent companies, OD is an integrated structured disciplined process like the one summarized in Figure 7.8. The chart in Figure 7.8 depicts an aligned OD process from customer and shareholders to supply chain work scope and the skills assessment needed to develop the overall plan:

- A skills assessment — overall and individually — is performed. Only then are group and individual development plans constructed and aggregated.
- When aggregated, the specific development plans can be prescribed for each individual and then can be rolled into a scheduled and budgeted plan for the entire supply chain team.
- Then, in each team member's monthly report, progress can be reported on the team's progress toward their OD plan, just like every other element of their deliverables.
- At review time, progress on the OD plan is part of the criteria and compensation adjustment consideration.

The opinion of the authors is that absolutely nothing is more important to transformation, morale, and resulting process performance than excellent and thorough execution of the organizational development process. Companies that want to promote high morale and loyalty, pay a lot of attention to the execution of this process.

Over the years, the authors have seen that most of the original people who were "inherited" as supply chain team members were successful with the supply chain transformation process. The old axiom "change the people or change the people" is clear. Although in the short term, changing out the people may seem more expeditious, it is really much more effective to help the people change.

CONCLUSION

A few years ago, Bill was privileged to spend some quality time with Peter Drucker at the Peter F. Drucker Graduate School of Management in Claremont, California. Both of Mike and Bill are fans of Drucker. With his 39 books and numerous articles and essays, Drucker is properly known as the "father of modern management." We would like to finish this final chapter with some appropriate ideas from Peter Drucker. He wrote the following:[7]

> Not in a very long time — not, perhaps, since the late 1940s or early 1950s — have there been as many new management techniques as there are today. ... [But] these tools are designed primarily to do differently what is already being done. They are "how-to-do" tools.

We agree wholeheartedly. We ask our readers to consider carefully the meaning of these words to their organizations.

REFERENCES

1. Treacy, Michael and Fred Wiersema. *The Discipline of Market Leaders: Choose Your Customers, Narrow Your Focus, Dominate Your Market* 1995. Saddle River, NJ: Addison-Wesley Publishing Company.

2. Porter, Michael E. *Competitive Strategy: Techniques for Analyzing Industries and Competitors* 1980. New York: The Free Press.

3. Cowley, Michael and Ellen Domb. *Beyond Strategic Vision: Effective Corporate Action with Hoshin Planning* 1997. Oxford: Butterworth-Heinemann.

4. See www.dnb.com for more information.

5. PMI. *A Guide to the Project Management Body of Knowledge (PMBOK®)*, *Third Edition* 2004. Newtown Square, PA: Project Management Institute.

6. See www.ariba.com for more information.

7. Drucker, Peter F. *Managing in a Time of Great Change* 1995. New York: Truman Talley Books/E.P. Dutton.

EPILOGUE — SOME FINAL THOUGHTS FROM THE AUTHORS

I really didn't say everything I said.
— Yogi Berra

Yogi, as you probably know, is a very quotable guy. Mike and Bill know that what we have said in this book will not be as quotable as Yogi is, but maybe we will not be embarrassed!

Mike remembers that about the time of his graduation from high school, his dad said to him: "Things will get better, things will get worse, but they will never stay the same very long." Mike believes that was sage advice and Bill agrees.

As we think back on the evolution of business performance expectations, and the associated process changes over the past 35 years, one thing is unchanging — that one thing is constant change. Building business and process strategies that are not focused both on making today's numbers and setting up the business and processes today to be competitive tomorrow is as antiquated and nearsighted as fixed fortifications were during the blitzkrieg of World War II.

Competition in the world today is, and has been for some time now, all about speed. Yet today, competition is not just about the speed of product development, or the speed of cash flow, or the speed of delivery, or the speed of inventory turns, and so forth. Competition is also about the speed of improvement — not just improvement in general, but the speed of the best improvements — improvements exactly linked in a prioritized sense to the key success factors of the supply chain and the businesses that comprise it in the eyes of the end customer of the chain and the stakeholders of each of the chain's entities.

Furthermore, this improvement focus cannot be one that looks at benchmark performance in a static sense today, but one that sets improvement plans based on where a company sees the performance of competing companies being in the future as well. Companies cannot afford plans that "shoot behind the duck" in this highly dynamic world. Simply, the pace of change and improvement makes catching up nearly impossible if a company allows itself to fall too far behind. Think about how hard GM has struggled to catch Toyota's and Honda's improvement pace (once they decided to try) — as of the time of this writing, they still are not close.

In terms of expectations, a few short years ago the financial world focused on return on invested capital and earnings. Although ROIC and earnings are still important financial metrics, the investment community is equally, if not more, focused on cash flow today. The lack of confidence in earnings reports and the type of financial reporting scams of recent months have made cash king. Customers likewise have come to expect more value for their money year after year that is driven by technology advances and productivity gains. Customers expect greater efficiencies in all processes (including the total supply chain process), producing an expectation of routine cost reduction. The once accepted annual price inflation paradigm is all but dead (unless the U.S. government brings it back with continuation of the current unprecedented deficit financing). Customers expect shorter and shorter lead times for product and new technology development as well.

The system of private enterprise competition with profit motivation has delivered on these expectations with amazing improvements — but not by doing things the same way as they had always been done, but with intelligent and integrated improvement processes and tools, linked with motivation.

The integrated improvement methodology that evolved out of programs such as the Malcolm Baldrige National Quality Award (MBNQA) helped develop improvement processes that linked enterprise process improvement efforts and the supply chain. The integrated evaluations of enterprise and process methodology and the associated results brought the largest performance and process opportunities to the surface with data-driven precision, which facilitated correct prioritization of improvements. And, in most cases, this approach yielded an ongoing process that produced continuous evaluation against the best performers and their processes. The evaluation often served as a uniting motivator for process leaders in an enterprise and for its external supply chain as well.

Specific improvements could be prioritized, quantified, and linked to process change. Then, the tools of lean and six sigma evolved with a data-centric methodology and tools of improvement that vastly accelerated results. More and more often, the best results were achieved the first time — not by trial and error, but by science. As such, the improvement process was repeatable and applicable to any needed improvement parameter set.

In the supply chain process, the Baldrige-type approach was coupled with lean and six sigma tools and methodology. The results were integrated supply chain strategic plans, integrated total cost reduction processes, mature risk management processes, and strategic staffing and organizational development processes.

Although all of the linkage and science were extremely powerful in speeding the right improvements in competing supply chains, the winners were, and are, the companies who can improve their supply chain faster than their competition. We believe the winning factor in this competition is the linked motivation of all the people in the supply chain.

Improvement processes, especially if they require broad and deep transformations, have enormous cultural implications and barriers. Barriers very often are related to individual people. Recall the old axiom of cultural change management: "Change the people or change the people." The first change obviously meant to change the way the people think and act. The second change meant to replace the seemingly unchangeable people. In any transition of significant magnitude, some of both typically are needed. In our experience, however, the latter approach is employed too often and too quickly with significant, unnecessary negative effects.

Our experience has also been that probably over 95% of the people in supply chain processes will make the desired changes in behavior, process, and results. They need only to be given an opportunity to participate in gaining a clear vision of what the organization is trying to do, why, and how and what they individually need to do to make the vision a success. They also need clear motivation, that is, "what's in it for me" or "what does this mean to me." We have found that whenever people are not transitioning in behavior, process, and results, and performance is within their control, they do not know what to do or how to do it or obstacles are in their way — or they do not want to make the transition.

The first three barriers are fairly easily fixed by leadership with better communication, education, training, listening, modeling, coaching, and barrier removal. The final group — the people who do not want to make the transition — requires a much more individualized, focused process that changes the consequences to consequences that will change the behaviors of these individuals to the desired ones. Our work experience is that the remaining few percent of people who "don't want to" can often become the most valuable contributors. The additional effort invested in these people almost always pays big dividends because not only are the don't-want-to people often some of the best contributors in the longer term, but they also are often insiders — long-term employees — and therefore influential in persuading others about the need for process and results change.

Several years ago, Mike was introduced to a process and toolset specifically designed to address these so-called "tough nuts" of supply chain transformation. Having been through numerous human relations-selected charm school exercises, Mike was highly skeptical of yet another panacea for change management related to people challenges. Aubrey Daniels introduced Mike to *Performance Management*, which has become one of his favorites. Although Mike has had many enlightening and helpful learning experiences, none has helped more than Daniels' approach[1] and Mike would like to summarize it for our readers. Aubrey Daniels says:

> *Performance Management is a systematic data-oriented approach to managing people that relies on positive reinforcement as the major way to maximize performance.*

Mike views this approach as Psychology 101 through 301, pragmatically and simply applied in a concise process to business.

Many times, Mike had tried to solve critical behavioral issues in transformation processes, but without any real individual, people-behavior analysis — but he never really had a true process to do such an analysis. *Performance Management* is as simple as ABC — antecedent, behavior, consequence. Dr. Daniels postulates that antecedents (expectations, objectives, goals, plans, and threats) do not change behavior. Antecedents may start a behavioral movement, but without linked consequences, this change usually only lasts short term. Only *consequences* change behavior. Aubrey classifies consequences as positive or negative, immediate or future, and certain or uncertain. He explains why only consequences that are positive, immediate, and certain (PICs) or negative, immediate, and certain (NIC) are really effective — that is, positive, immediate, and certain or negative, immediate, and certain.

Daniels illustrates with the example of a doctor who tells a patient: "If you don't stop smoking, you may die sooner." Daniels points out that this warning contains a consequence that is negative, *future*, and *uncertain* — and therefore highly unlikely to change behavior anytime soon. He explains that both positive and negative consequences work — sometimes equally well — but *future* and *uncertain* consequences do not. (Mike: "Had I ever thought this analytically about facilitating behavioral change? No, I used mostly gut instinct stuff. And often my gut was wrong.)

When using negative consequences, it can be helpful to remember this little tidbit: "Be careful that victories do not carry the seeds of future defeats." With positive reinforcement, people give their best because they *want to do so*. Nobody has to watch them, except to applaud. Negative reinforcement is only effective as long as people are watched adequately to sustain the behavior — possibly because they do not believe that what they are doing is the right thing to do.

For example, after the fall of the Soviet empire, while Mike was touring a manufacturing facility in the Czech Republic, one of the former factory workers told him the following: "We had a saying in the old socialist factory. We will continue to pretend to work as long as they continue to pretend to pay us."

Daniels' initial behavior analysis proceeds to a planning process that yields a simple but specific plan to elicit the correct behavior and associated performance in the toughest of cases. According to Mike, the process has worked for him with subordinates, peers, and superiors and is the most effective process and toolset he has ever encountered and utilized in solving transformation people barriers. It is simple, requires little effort to develop, and is effective.

Both Mike's and Bill's experiences are that even the most intelligent, astute supply chain design solutions, generated by the brightest leaders, can succeed and be sustained only when the more complex human behavioral challenges and their solutions are addressed and integrated into the transformation process. *What* to do is relatively easy. *How* to get it done in a large organization, much less across an integrated supply chain, is the challenge. (And, the soft stuff really is the hard stuff.)

As a senior partner with Deloitte & Touche, Bill was asked by the firm to begin a change leadership consulting practice — both as a stand-alone practice and as a supporting practice to the firm's large-scale systems implementations. In his research work to develop the intellectual capital, Bill was impressed by the research findings in this area. Much academic research has generated countless articles and books on the subject. Practitioners have added their experiences to the literature.

Aubrey Daniels' work has received recognition, and Mike has had success with it, but please recognize that significant additional research has been completed in an effort to determine the best ways to enhance performance of individuals, groups, and organizations. Suffice it to say that there are no laws of human behavior like there are laws of thermodynamics. Our suggestion to the reader is to study carefully the research on human motivation and choose to apply theories, concepts, tools, and techniques that make sense to you. You need to be able to work with whatever approach you choose.

Both of us would like to express our sincere thanks to our contributors, without whom this work would have been a series of hopefully interesting essays, but not a professional manuscript. Mike and Bill have worked together for years on some tough transformations and generally have succeeded. We have also learned much from each other and appreciate each other's capabilities and professionalism. To our readers: thanks for sticking with us. We wish you success in your supply chain transformation efforts.

REFERENCE

1. Daniels, Aubrey C. *Bringing Out the Best in People* 2000. New York: McGraw-Hill.

APPENDIX 1
THE TRANSFORMATION VISIONING PROCESS TOOL

Where there is no vision,
the people perish.
— Proverbs 29:18 (King James Version)

One of the best books on vision and visioning is by Joseph Quigley.[1] Joe includes little nuggets of wisdom regarding vision throughout his book. The following is one of his best:

Make your vision as clear as your profit goals. Profit alone is not enough to motivate your people. Expand the scope of your vision to address more of the whole person.

As the reader can probably tell from this quote, Joe, a friend of Bill Lee, is a fine person in addition to being a very bright and lucid consultant and writer. Joe discusses the role of visions and the visioning process in today's corporate world. We recommend Joe's book for serious students of transformation.

DEVELOP A VISION

Developing a vision is one of the key first steps in a supply chain transformation process. Gaining consensus and commitment to that vision is absolutely necessary for success, which is why we have the *Transformation Visioning Process Tool* in the book as Appendix 1. Our objective is to have you, the reader, focus on this process as a key tool in your toolkit for transformations. We have found the process to be extremely useful in our own experience and thus recommend it to you.

Jonathan Swift has been quoted as saying: "Vision is the art of seeing things invisible." Having the transformative supply chain vision linked to the strategic plan is important. Strategic planning is the management process of making the vision visible to the organization in ways that can be implemented. The importance of linking the supply chain vision with the company's strategic plan is a recurring theme throughout this book.

We have structured Appendix 1 a little differently from the chapters in the book. Most of the content of Appendix 1 is in the form of illustrations, with a relatively small amount of explanatory text.

Those who read Joe Quigley's book might see elements of his approach in this appendix. The visioning tool has been developed as a collaborative effort by Bill Lee, while working with numerous colleagues, clients, and critics. Bill certainly does not take credit for everything in this tool. Too many people have had a go at it. The tool has been applied in various consulting engagements. Unfortunately, memory does not permit Bill to acknowledge everyone who contributed. So, if you are one of those contributing individuals, please accept our thanks for playing a role — along with our apologies for not recognizing you by name.

THE ROADMAP

The illustrations in Appendix 1 are provided as a roadmap for readers — a roadmap to implement the visioning process — to take readers through a step-by-step series of actions along with some of the results of those actions. Our commentary accompanies each illustration.

Figure A1.1. We envision a five-step approach to managing a transformative change process as illustrated in Figure A1.1:

- Prepare for transformation
- Vision the transformation
- Benchmark the transformation
- Design the transformation
- Implement the transformation

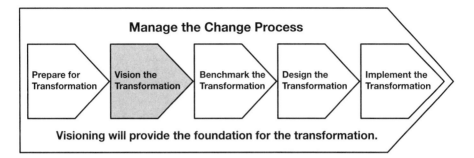

Figure A1.1. A Five-Step Approach to Managing Transformative Change: Process Visioning Is Just One Part of the Overall Project.

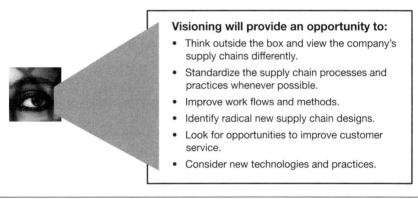

Figure A1.2. Visioning: A Forum to Encourage New Ways of Thinking about the Supply Chain.

Visioning provides the foundation for a transformation. Clearly, it is important for companies get this right.

Figure A1.2. Visioning will provide a forum for brainstorming the future *to be* process model. As shown in Figure A1.2, visioning is a structured process to encourage and assist people to think "outside the box" and view their company's supply chains differently. This appendix deals with the second arrow, *Vision the Transformation.*

Figure A1.3. A five-step approach illustrated in Figure A1.3 is the essence of the process illustrated in Appendix 1:

- Prepare for visioning.
- Conduct Visioning Session 1.
- Investigate and analyze alternative visions.
- Conduct Visioning Session 2.
- Wrap up the visioning process.

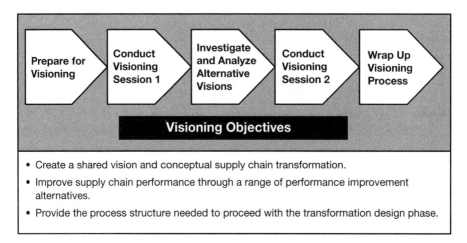

Visioning Objectives

- Create a shared vision and conceptual supply chain transformation.
- Improve supply chain performance through a range of performance improvement alternatives.
- Provide the process structure needed to proceed with the transformation design phase.

Figure A1.3. A Five-Step Approach to the Visioning Process.

Throughout this five-step approach, emphasis is on creating a shared vision of the supply chain transformation. We will take you through this five-step process.

Figure A1.4. We usually prefer to think of two primary deliverables. Both are in document form: a visioning *interim* conceptual design document and a transformative supply chain *vision* document (Figure A1.4). The first deliverable, the visioning interim conceptual design document, clearly is a work in process. We believe creating this interim document to provide a basis for further analysis and discussion is important. Without such a document, we have found that discussion and analysis tend to get off track easily, which can cause a project to go astray and to lack a clear direction. This interim document is a "thought piece" that is meant to stimulate further discussion. (The visioning interim conceptual design document is in the spirit of Bill's doctoral dissertation chair, Curt McLaughlin, who said many times: "Don't just talk with me — bring me something in writing so I can know that you have given it some thought.")

We also believe that it is important for a transformation team to create a concept of the deliverables as early as possible in the project. Having an evolving definition of what the deliverables are ensures that there is something from which the team can work as it progresses along in the project.

Figure A1.5. A number of tools are available for use in the *visioning* process (Figure A1.5). These tools are described in a variety of publications that go into much more depth than we have the space (or the motivation!) for here. Team members will utilize many of these and other tools and techniques in their visioning process. (*Wikipedia* has articles with references for most of these tools.)

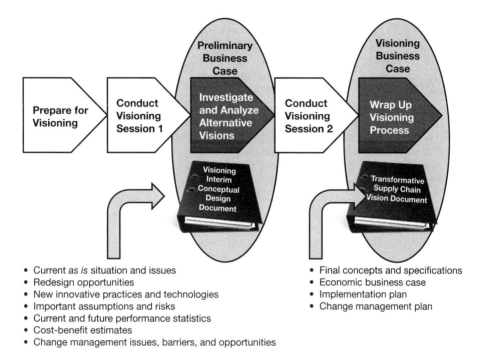

- Current *as is* situation and issues
- Redesign opportunities
- New innovative practices and technologies
- Important assumptions and risks
- Current and future performance statistics
- Cost-benefit estimates
- Change management issues, barriers, and opportunities

- Final concepts and specifications
- Economic business case
- Implementation plan
- Change management plan

Figure A1.4. Two Primary Deliverables from the Visioning Process: The Visioning Interim Conceptual Design Document and the Transformative Supply Chain Vision Document.

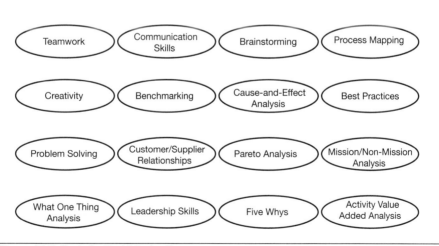

Figure A1.5. Tools for the Visioning Process.

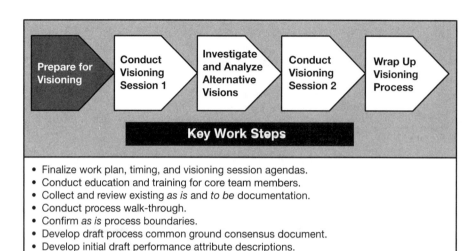

Figure A1.6. Visioning Preparation: Key Work Steps.

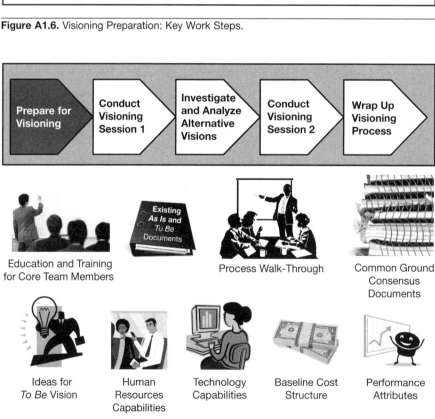

Figure A1.7. Visioning Preparation: Results.

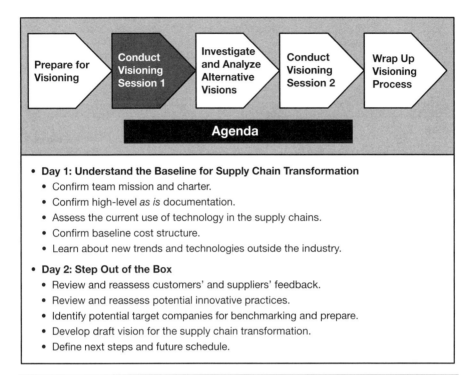

Agenda

- **Day 1: Understand the Baseline for Supply Chain Transformation**
  - Confirm team mission and charter.
  - Confirm high-level *as is* documentation.
  - Assess the current use of technology in the supply chains.
  - Confirm baseline cost structure.
  - Learn about new trends and technologies outside the industry.

- **Day 2: Step Out of the Box**
  - Review and reassess customers' and suppliers' feedback.
  - Review and reassess potential innovative practices.
  - Identify potential target companies for benchmarking and prepare.
  - Develop draft vision for the supply chain transformation.
  - Define next steps and future schedule.

Figure A1.8. Visioning Session 1: Agenda.

Figure A1.6. As outlined in Figure A1.6, getting ready for visioning entails some work. As with any project, a work plan with to-do lists, schedules, agendas, deliverables, responsibilities, resources, and so forth are needed. Education and training in the approach to visioning along with the tools and techniques used in visioning usually are necessary. Collection, distribution, and review of existing *as is* documentation sets the stage for the project. Companies often have some *to be* documentation that describes earlier attempts at supply chain improvement projects. The list of suggested key work steps in Figure A1.6 is meant to be illustrative, but not exhaustive.

Figure A1.7. The results from visioning preparation will provide baseline knowledge and documentation that can be used in Visioning Session 1. Early preparation will enable the visioning session to go much more smoothly and to be much more efficient and effective (Figure A1.7).

Figure A1.8. Many visioning sessions are designed to last for 2 days (Figure A1.8). Visioning Session 1 typically is the initial gathering of the entire team (other than a kick-off session). Frequently, the first day is "stage setting" for the team, with:

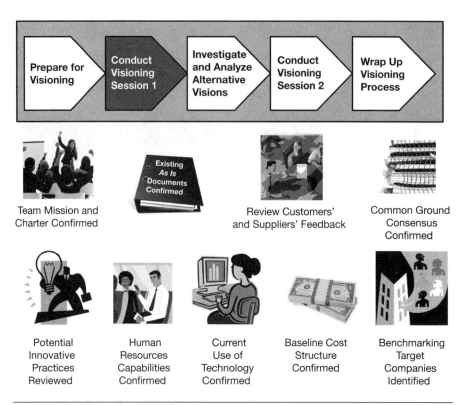

Figure A1.9. Visioning Session 1: Results.

- Discussions of the team mission and charter
- A review of high-level *as is* documentation
- Assessing the current use of technology
- Confirming the baseline cost structure
- Learning about new trends and technologies outside the industry

Some companies have an outside speaker make a presentation on what is happening outside the industry. Often companies also have an outside facilitator handle these visioning sessions.

The substance of the visioning session occurs on the second day. Frequently, contact has been made with customers and suppliers ahead of time to get their ideas and suggestions. Potential innovative practices can also be obtained through a literature search prior to the start of the sessions. The results can be presented in this session. A literature search commonly turns up references to companies that can be contacted for benchmarking visits. (See Appendix 2 for an in-depth discussion of benchmarking.)

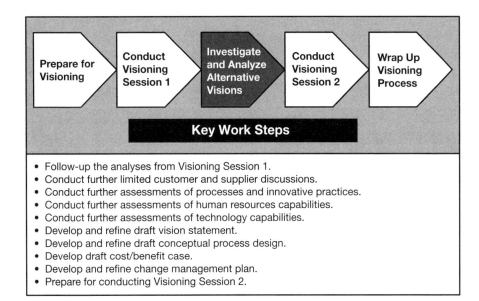

Figure A1.10. Alternatives Investigation and Analysis: Key Work Steps.

Figure A1.9. Visioning Session 1 will develop a draft process vision and define additional analysis requirements. The activities illustrated in Figure A1.9 for the session will each produce a deliverable.

Figure A1.10. This step, investigate and analyze alternative visions, likely will require the most time and resources of any of the five steps (Figure A1.10). The intention of this step is twofold:

- To use the results from Visioning Session 1 and take analyses to the next levels of depth
- To prepare for Visioning Session 2

Follow-up analyses and study usually are required at this stage of the visioning process.

Figure A1.11. The results from investigating the alternative visions will depend upon the issues that are raised in Visioning Session 1 (Figure A1.11). Some likely issues include:

- To finalize the change management plan
- To conduct further discussions with customers and suppliers
- To assess potential innovative practices for inclusion into the transformation
- To further assess the human resources and technology capabilities

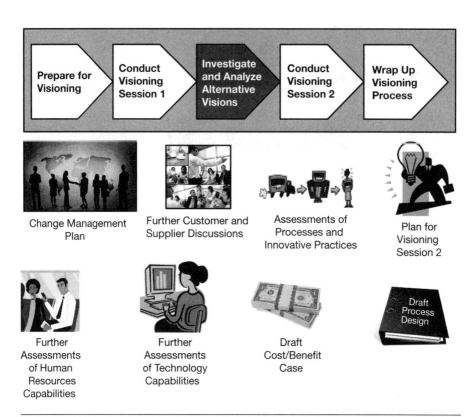

Figure A1.11. Investigation of Alternative Visions: Results.

- To develop a draft cost-benefit case
- To develop a draft supply chain process design
- To finalize the plan for Visioning Session 2

Prior to Visioning Session 2, the team needs to develop draft *to be* process designs. The 2-day Visioning Session 2 is not sufficient to *develop* the process design. Rather, it should be to *critique* the *to be* draft designs.

Figure A1.12. The economic business case depends upon the supply chain processes that will likely be included in the transformation (Figure A1.12). The business case depends on the assumptions and risks in the relevant processes, the core process cost profile, the benefits description, the operating and capital cost requirements, and the incremental cash flow and net present value of that cash flow.

Figure A1.13. Session 2 is when everything comes together into the vision for the transformation (Figure A1.13). As with Session 1, we suggest that an outside facilitator be used to help the group come to consensus on the transformative

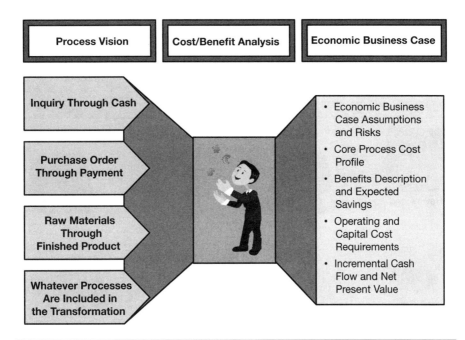

Figure A1.12. Elements that Determine the Economic Business Case.

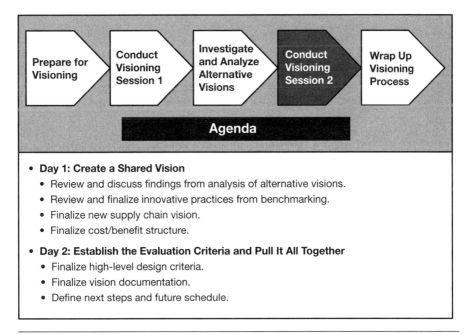

• **Day 1: Create a Shared Vision**
  • Review and discuss findings from analysis of alternative visions.
  • Review and finalize innovative practices from benchmarking.
  • Finalize new supply chain vision.
  • Finalize cost/benefit structure.

• **Day 2: Establish the Evaluation Criteria and Pull It All Together**
  • Finalize high-level design criteria.
  • Finalize vision documentation.
  • Define next steps and future schedule.

Figure A1.13. Visioning Session 2: Agenda.

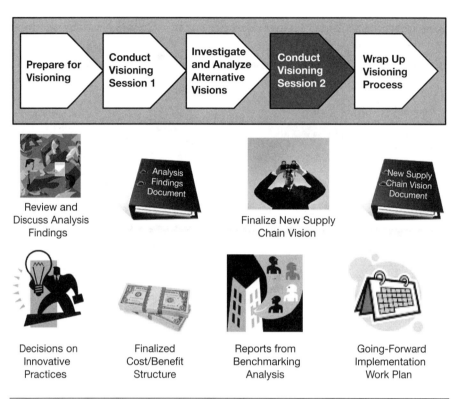

Figure A1.14. Visioning Session 2: Results.

vision. The transformative vision is likely to be significantly different from the *as is* situation, so participants may have difficulty seeing how the future could unfold.

Figure A1.14. Visioning Session 2 should result in a common vision of the transformed supply chain (Figure A1.14). This common vision should be documented in a "new" *supply chain vision document*. This document should include:

- A review and discussion of the analyses
- Decisions on innovative practices that will be incorporated
- Reports from the benchmarking analyses
- A going-forward implementation work plan

The work plan should include activities, schedules, resources, responsibilities, and so forth. It also should include a change management plan.

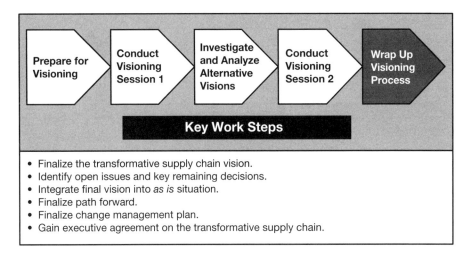

Figure A1.15. Visioning Wrap-Up: Key Work Steps.

Figure A1.15. The visioning wrap-up will occur prior to implementation. As illustrated in Figure A1.15, implementation will require:

- The final transformative supply chain design
- Any open issues and key remaining decisions
- The path forward
- The change management plan

The most important point, however, is that executive agreement must be obtained on the transformative supply chain.

Figure A1.16. The transformed supply chain document should be a complete presentation of the *to be* vision of the supply chain (Figure A1.16).

CONCLUSION

We began the discussion in Appendix 1 with a quote from Joe Quigley and we will end it in the same way. This is a message to CEOs that is very applicable to supply chain transformation:

Delegate everything else if you have to, but don't delegate the responsibility for charting or planning the corporation's future. Gaining acceptance of the shared values of the enterprise is the major responsibility of the CEO.

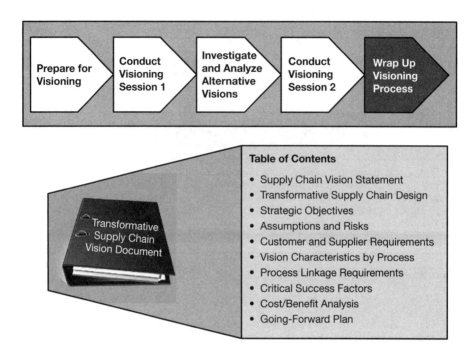

Figure A1.16. Visioning Wrap-Up: Results.

We say to CEOs: "Please pay attention to the value of your supply chain. Vision its future as an integral part of your organization and give it the attention it deserves. Please, also pay attention to the passage from Proverbs: *Where there is no vision, the people perish.*

REFERENCE

1. Quigley, Joseph V. *Vision: How Leaders Develop It, Share It, and Sustain It* 1993. New York: McGraw-Hill.

APPENDIX 2
THE TRANSFORMATION
BENCHMARKING
PROCESS TOOL

If you can't imitate him, don't copy him.

— Yogi Berra

This well-known "don't copy him" quote from Yogi Berra was said to another baseball player who wanted to hit like a member of the Hall of Fame. We believe this quote is a humorous example of how some companies try to do benchmarking — they try to copy someone else, but there is no way they can be successful merely by copying.

Another quote, from Hamel and Prahalad, also captures the cautionary tone of Yogi:[1]

Pathbreaking is a lot more rewarding than benchmarking. One doesn't get to the future first by letting someone else blaze the trail.

Hamel and Prahalad go on to say, "In this race to the future, there are *drivers*, *passengers*, and *road kill*." *Road kill*, an American term, is what becomes of little creatures that cross the highway in front of an oncoming vehicle. *Passengers* will get to the future, but their fate will not be in their own hands. *Drivers* are the innovators, or perhaps the early majority, as we discussed earlier. Too often, benchmarkers are the *passengers* or maybe even the *road kill*. Our concern: just be careful with benchmarking.

Now, please do not think that we are against benchmarking — we are not! We are all in favor of it. However, we are realistic enough to offer words of caution to our readers: please keep benchmarking in its proper perspective and recognize what it can and cannot do for you.

WHAT IS BENCHMARKING?

The American Productivity and Quality Center (APQC) is one of the world's premier benchmarking clearinghouses (see www.apqc.org for more information). APQC uses the following definition:

> *Benchmarking is the process of identifying, sharing, and using knowledge and best practices. It focuses on how to improve any given business process by leveraging proven, top-notch approaches rather than merely measuring the best performance. Finding, studying, and implementing best practices provide the greatest opportunity for gaining a strategic, operational, and financial advantage.*

We have chosen to include this Appendix 2 on benchmarking because it is needed between Appendix 1 about visioning and Appendix 3 about an assessment tool. In combination, these three tools are useful for a supply chain transformation effort. First, Appendix 1 creates a *vision* about what is possible in the future; next, Appendix 2 discusses how to *benchmark* yourself against others to determine what is feasible; and then, Appendix 3 shows how to perform an *in-depth assessment* of the *as is* and *to be* and how to develop an action plan to close the gaps. The three appendices need to be used together.

So, why benchmark? There are multiple reasons:

- To assess our performance against others
- To measure the gap that must be filled
- To develop a vision of what is possible — the *to be* solution
- To plan how to acquire or construct or implement the solution

Benchmarking for supply chain transformation is a bridge-building exercise between the *as is* and the *to be* situations. To do a good job of benchmarking, a few questions are important:

- What needs improvement?
- What should be benchmarked?

- What are the performance gaps?
- What are the goals?
- Who does the benchmarking?
- Who will be benchmarked?
- How will knowledge be discovered?
- How should the benchmarking process be performed?
- How will the data be collected?
- What are the solution options?
- How should the options be evaluated?
- What does it take to implement change?

Stork and Morgan give some good definitions and advice.[2] They also have some good ideas. We have adapted (with permission) some of their material for Appendix 2. In response to the question *what is benchmarking,* Stork and Morgan respond:

- *Benchmarking is a continuous, systematic process used to drive change in an organization. It is a practice used to identify best practices in business that lead to superior performance and process improvement.*
- *Benchmarking is a continuous, systematic process for evaluating the product, services, and work processes of organizations that are recognized as representing best practices for the purpose of organizational improvement.*
- *Benchmarking is applied to products, processes, and functions. It focuses on best practices and methods with the goal of developing changes that lead to improved customer satisfaction.*

There is much variation, of course, in the way that supply chains are organized, structured, managed, and measured. When doing a benchmarking study, our best advice: *do your homework*! Put research into decisions about the future of supply chains.

Benchmarking would be easier if there were more consistency, but this is just not the case. The biggest benchmarking difficulty that companies encounter is that they end up comparing *apples* and *oranges*. Processes, for example, reflect the context of their environment within the company. Metrics, also, are often calculated in the context of a particular process or group of suppliers or group of customers or whatever else is being measured. Understanding, within the context of a benchmarking study, just how a process works and how a particular term is being used is important. This goes as equally for the company performing the benchmarking study as it does for its target. Comparing the metrics or processes of two companies is difficult — some might even say *impossible*, although we would not go that far.

Benchmarking is used for evaluating the products, services, and work processes of organizations that are recognized as representing best-in-class practices and is intended to be used for organizational improvement. Benchmarking focuses on best practices and methods, with the goal of developing ideas for changes leading to improved customer satisfaction. Yet, emphasizing the importance of understanding what benchmarking *is not* is important:[2]

- Benchmarking is not industry tours.
- Benchmarking is not copying or adopting.
- Benchmarking is not simply catching up to competitors.
- Benchmarking is not corporate spying or counterintelligence.
- Benchmarking is not focused just on data.
- Benchmarking is not quick-and-dirty analyses.

Figure A2.1. In general, as illustrated in Figure A2.1, there are four generic types of benchmarking: competitive benchmarking, management practices benchmarking, process benchmarking, and metrics benchmarking. According to Stork and Morgan, "Competitive analysis is not benchmarking; however, some degree of competitive analysis usually is needed to establish some priorities in the benchmarking effort."[2]

> We believe the statement by Stork and Morgan makes too fine of a distinction. In his consulting relationships, Bill has been asked more times than he can remember: "Tell us about the competition in our industry — what are they doing?" Many times there are serious ethical issues in answering this type of question, especially if one actually knows the answer based on previous proprietary work. However, there are legitimate ways to get the answers, such as literature searches through publicly available information. Competitors will also frequently consent to multiclient blind studies by a recognized and respected accounting or consulting firm.

SUCCESS FACTORS

Stork and Morgan also address the question of *what contributes to success in benchmarking*:[2]

- *Companies must have a culture that allows change and breakthrough thinking in order for benchmarking to be successful. It is far too easy to be in denial and reject improvement ideas because "our business is different."*

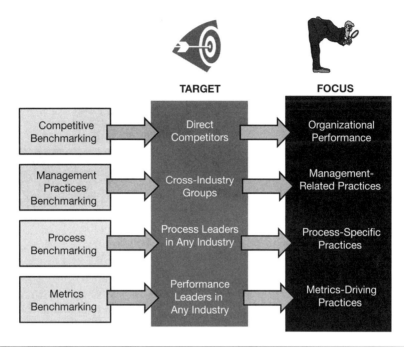

Figure A2.1. The Four General Types of Benchmarking.

- *For most benchmarking studies, learn how to ask the right questions. Learn how to ask, "What?" and "How?" and "Why?" Learn how to ask enough times until the situations are clear. This takes precedence over any "industry tour" or company presentation.*
- *Getting to the process details by asking the right questions enough times provides the secret to understanding "Best in Class" process improvements.*

Essentials. There are a few essentials to successful benchmarking. Benchmarking visits are more successful if a detailed list of questions is developed before the visit to keep the visit on track and focused. Another essential element of effective benchmarking is to establish a baseline — one that identifies the company's *as is* situation. Having a baseline is critical to developing a meaningful analysis. The next essential element is development of a survey questionnaire. Develop questions around things that need to be done, the practicalities of proposed projects, and the weak spots that definitely have to be tackled.

We say that the first success factor is commitment of top management who understands the need for change. Top management is in a position to allocate resources for benchmarking and for doing something with the information when it is obtained.

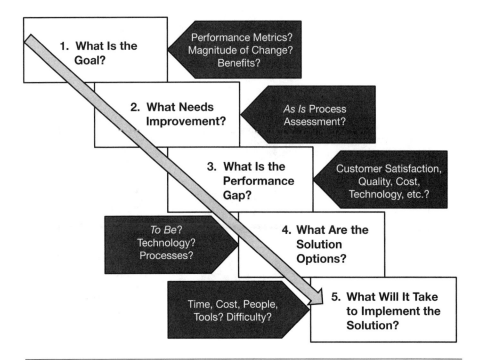

Figure A2.2. Questions that Can Help Determine Credibility.

The results of benchmarking studies should be an integrated plan; but first there is a need to understand one's own business processes and then to have a willingness to adapt existing processes to utilize some of the benchmarked learnings. Recognize that one cannot be the best in everything. Thus, learning from others is important.

Credibility. Early in a benchmarking process, an often-asked question is *how can credibility be obtained?*

Figure A2.2. Figure A2.2 provides some answers by asking questions:

- What is the goal? Is it performance metrics, the magnitude of the change, or other specific benefits?
- What needs improvement? Where in the *as is* process assessment were the needs identified?
- What is the performance gap? Is it customer satisfaction, quality, cost, technology, or something else?

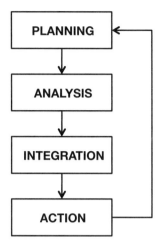

Figure A2.3. A Four-Step Benchmarking Process.

- What are the solution options? Did the *to be* visioning uncover possibilities of technology or process options?
- What will it take to implement the solution? How much time and cost, how many people with what capabilities, and how difficult will implementation be?

Ultimately, credibility in the benchmarking process will be enhanced in several ways:

- Knowledge of the benchmarking team
- Personal experience
- Company experience
- Experience of consultants (if applicable)
- Research
- Visioning process
- Assessment process
- Process models

STEPS IN THE BENCHMARKING PROCESS

Figure A2.3. Stork and Morgan advocate a four-step benchmarking process that consists of planning, analysis, integration, and action (shown in Figure A2.3).[2] Their approach is fairly standard and widely used in benchmarking efforts:

PLAN. A good benchmarking plan should answer these questions:

- Who does the benchmarking?
- What will be benchmarked?
- Who (what company) will be benchmarked?
- How will the data be collected?

ANALYSIS. The analysis step seeks to answer six basic questions:

- Does the benchmarked company outperform us? If so, how much better are they?
- Why is their performance better?
- How do they do it?
- What can be learned from them?
- How can we apply what we have learned?
- If our performance is better in some respects, how can we stay ahead or widen our lead?

INTEGRATION. The integration stage deals with two issues:

- Has or will management accept or buy-in to the findings and recommendations?
- Have new goals been clearly communicated (or will they be communicated) to all organizations involved? (Having new goals also entails developing appropriate strategies and new operating plans and goals.)

ACTION. The action stage is relatively straightforward. Answers are sought to three basic questions:

- Have work steps been identified to achieve the goals?
- Is progress being tracked?
- Is there a plan for recalibration to determine if the rate of change is still appropriate?

DOING IT SUCCESSFULLY VERSUS UNSUCCESSFULLY

Do not start a benchmarking project unless the following are available:

- A clear understanding of benchmarking — what it is, how to do it, and what the expectations should and should not be.
- A clear understanding of the goals and expectations of the senior leadership team.
- A good information base, including metrics of where the company stands currently on questions to be asked of the benchmarking hosts.

Most successful benchmarkers usually have a good handle on the fundamentals. Those who are successful in harnessing the benchmarking tool are often best identified by their serious and sensible approach to relationships. One key to success is the APQC *Code of Conduct for Benchmarking* (included at the end of this appendix). In addition to APQC, Stork and Morgan identify the following characteristics of successful benchmarkers:[2]

- They treat benchmarking seriously.
- They develop appropriate mechanisms for transferring information.
- They think of benchmarking on more than one level.
- They approach learning from others with humility.
- They have a good sense of timing.
- They have an ability to relate benchmarking to specific corporate needs.
- They recognize the absolute need to have people with the ability to change things on their benchmarking teams.
- They pay attention to building on prior knowledge and acquaintances.

Many of the most successful benchmarkers will benchmark their benchmarking. Successful benchmarkers work from the premise that in a world of continuous change, what is needed most is for them to manage change, shorten the time it takes to make positive change, and bring about change that will show results with a minimum of stops and starts.

The Japanese have been very successful at benchmarking.[2] The Japanese:

- Came to the process with specific understanding of the goals and objectives of their management
- Sent their best people
- Had a plan with specific questions to ask and specific data to be gathered
- Knew their status relative to the specific questions being asked (When better performance was found, the Japanese could focus more deeply to understand the causes of the superior performance noted.)
- Had a bias for action (Knowledge, processes, and practices were reused.)
- Studied other industries for best practices (For example, American supermarkets were the inspiration for quick-replenishment, just-in-time, and kanban techniques.)
- Had a continuous process, not just a program of visits
- Refined their process continuously in a mode of continuous improvement

There are pitfalls to avoid, however. Stork and Morgan state (and we agree) that success or failure of benchmarking is primarily a planning and execution issue:[2]

- *Delay*: Getting the project off the ground quickly is not merely good, but often critical.
- *Complexity*: The first project should be fairly simple or at least not overly complex.
- *Preparation*: Too frequently companies want to benchmark when they simply are not ready:
  - Benchmarkers need to analyze their current condition, prepare a plan for success with detailed questions to be answered, and execute that plan.
  - The type of thinking and questioning that goes into the analysis, plan preparation, and execution requires a great deal of preparation and maturity.
  - A good idea is simply not enough.

The ten deadly sins. Stork and Morgan are particularly concerned about the "deadly sins" of benchmarking.[2] (They asked that we include their ten deadly sins. We agreed to their request.) Benchmarkers need to avoid:

1. Picking a project that lacks strategic significance
2. Exhibiting a lack of in-depth preparation by those setting up the benchmarking project
3. Giving insufficient thought to staffing the project (e.g., using people who can be spared, but lack cross-functional participation)
4. Lacking adequate funding for the benchmarking project
5. Being hazy about the target company, its management, and its accomplishments
6. Overconcentrating on the metrics when developing the benchmarking project
7. Inadequately educating and training team members
8. Inadequately planning to ensure that as much as possible is learned from benchmarking visits
9. Insufficiently planning to gain interest and participation in the project from host companies
10. Inadequately preparing the inquiry or questionnaire used to focus the benchmarking project

FINDING BENCHMARKING PARTNERS

What interests benchmarking partners? Benchmarking partners need to be *convinced*. They need justification for the time to be spent in one or more of several areas:

- The potential benchmarking partner needs to be convinced that the information exchange is acceptable to the host company.
- The potential partner needs the company desiring the benchmarking project to convince them that there is significant information to be learned by both parties to the project.
- The potential candidate needs to be convinced that problems can be discussed frankly and in confidence.
- The potential candidate needs to be convinced of the potential of the benchmarking project to deliver tangible results. Information exchange is not enough. Information must be accompanied by analysis.
- The potential partner needs the promise of process improvement to be quantified (e.g., by potential cost savings).
- The potential candidate must be convinced that the project will open up opportunities for knowledge exchange and learning for promising managers.

Additionally, getting *and keeping* good benchmarking partners involves a number of confidentiality issues:

- Being really good at building benchmarking partnerships requires that some level of trust be developed between the benchmarking company and the host companies.
- For the long-term, there has to be a buildup of rapport in which people feel comfortable and free to say things "off the record."

There must also be an answer to the oft-stated question: "What's in it for me?"

MEASURING RESULTS

Measurements of improvement should be linked to strategic plans and key beliefs and value systems, not unlike the Hoshin planning linkage that was described in Chapter 7. The purpose of performance measurement linked to benchmarking is to motivate behavior that leads to continuing improvements in a variety of metrics, such as:

- Industry quality standards
- Total customer satisfaction
- Superior financial performance
- Breakthrough operating performance

The logic of good measurements is that success requires change, change requires new behaviors, and new behaviors require new measurement and reward systems. Eliminating obsolete metrics is the beginning of successful change. Installing appropriate new measures accelerates progress toward success.

SOURCES OF BENCHMARKING DATA

Benchmarking data can be obtained from numerous sources. Many are publicly available:

- Internal information
  - Competitive product analysis
  - Reverse engineering studies
  - Company resources (sales, former employees)
  - Other benchmarking studies
  - Internal experts and studies
- External information
  - Internet searches
  - Library research (books, periodicals, journals, and so forth)
  - Professional networks, trade associations, and conferences
  - Company annual reports, 10-K reports, proxy reports, and other reports publicly filed by law
  - Consultants
  - Customers
  - Suppliers
  - External experts
  - Databases

THE APQC CODE OF CONDUCT

We conclude Appendix 2 with the important *Benchmarking Code of Conduct* from the American Productivity and Quality Center (APQC). We think that the APQC code deserves serious study and observance. Adhering to this code will contribute to efficient, effective, and ethical benchmarking. Information about APQC and the APQC website follows. We recommend APQC as a superb source of benchmarking information.

APQC is an internationally recognized resource for process and performance improvement. APQC helps organizations adapt to rapidly changing environments, build new and better ways to work, and succeed in a competitive marketplace. With a focus on productivity, knowledge management, benchmarking, and quality improvement initiatives, APQC works with member organizations to identify best practices, discover effective methods of improvement, broadly disseminate findings, and connect individuals with one another and the knowledge, training, and tools they need to succeed. Founded in 1977, APQC is a member-based nonprofit that serves organizations around the world in all sectors of business, education, and government. APQC won the 2003 and 2004 North American Most Admired Knowledge Enterprises (MAKE) awards (an award based on a study by Teleos, a European-based research firm, and the KNOW network.

APQC wants the *Benchmarking Code of Conduct* to receive wide distribution, discussion, and use. Therefore, APQC grants permission for copying the *Benchmarking Code of Conduct*, as long as acknowledgment is made to APQC. Please notify and inform APQC concerning your use or application of material (APQC, 123 North Post Oak Lane, Third Floor, Houston, TX 77024). The *Benchmarking Code of Conduct* that follows is taken directly from the APQC website in compliance with APQC requirements related to reproducing the code.

BENCHMARKING CODE OF CONDUCT
Guidelines and Ethics for Benchmarkers

APQC developed and adheres to this code of conduct to:
- Guide benchmarking efforts
- Advance the professionalism and effectiveness of benchmarking
- Help protect its members from harm

Adherence to this Code will contribute to efficient, effective, and ethical benchmarking.

1. **Legality**
   a. If there is any potential question on the legality of an activity, then consult with your corporate counsel.
   b. Avoid discussions or actions that could lead to or imply an interest in restraint of trade, market and/or customer allocation schemes, price fixing, dealing arrangements, bid rigging, or bribery. Don't discuss costs with competitors if costs are an element of pricing.
   c. Refrain from the acquisition of trade secrets from another by any means that could be interpreted as improper, including the breach or inducement of a breach of any duty to maintain secrecy. Do not disclose or use any trade secret that may have been obtained through improper means or that was disclosed by another in violation of duty to maintain its secrecy or limit its use.
   d. Do not, as a consultant or client, extend benchmarking study findings to another company without first ensuring that the data are appropriately blinded and anonymous so that the participants' identities are protected.

2. **Exchange**
   a. Be willing to provide to your benchmarking partner the same type and level of information that you request from your benchmarking partner.
   b. Fully communicate early in the relationship to clarify expectations, avoid misunderstanding, and establish mutual interest in the benchmarking exchange.
   c. Be honest and complete with the information submitted.
   d. Provide information in a timely manner as outlined by the stated benchmarking schedule.

3. **Confidentiality**
   a. Treat benchmarking interchange as confidential to the individuals and companies involved. Information must not be communicated outside the partnering organizations without the prior consent of the benchmarking partner who shared the information.
   b. A company's participation is confidential and should not be communicated externally without their prior permission.

4. **Use**
   a. Use information obtained through benchmarking only for purposes stated to the benchmarking partner.

    b. The use or communication of a benchmarking partner's name with the data obtained or practices observed requires the prior permission of the benchmarking partner.

    c. Contact lists or other contact information provided in any form may not be used for purposes other than benchmarking and networking.

5. Contact

    a. Respect the corporate culture of partner companies and work within mutually agreed procedures.

    b. Use benchmarking contacts designated by the partner company if that is its preferred procedure.

    c. Obtain mutual agreement with the designated benchmarking contact on any hand-off of communication or responsibility to other parties.

    d. Obtain an individual's permission before providing his or her name in response to a contact request.

    e. Avoid communicating a contact's name in an open forum without the contact's prior permission.

6. Preparation

    a. Demonstrate commitment to the efficiency and effectiveness of benchmarking by being prepared prior to making an initial benchmarking contact.

    b. Make the most of your benchmarking partner's time by being fully prepared for each exchange.

    c. Help your benchmarking partners prepare by providing them with a questionnaire and agenda prior to benchmarking visits.

7. Completion

    a. Follow through with each commitment made to your benchmarking partner in a timely manner.

    b. Complete a benchmarking effort to the satisfaction of all benchmarking partners as mutually agreed.

8. Understanding and Action

    a. Understand how your benchmarking partner would like to be treated.

    b. Treat your benchmarking partner in the way that your benchmarking partner would want to be treated.

    c. Understand how your benchmarking partner would like to have the information he or she provides handled and used. Handle and use it in that manner.

BENCHMARKING WITH COMPETITORS

The following guidelines apply to both partners in a benchmarking encounter with competitors or potential competitors:

- In benchmarking with competitors, establish specific ground rules up-front. For example, "We don't want to talk about things that will give either of us a competitive advantage, but rather we want to see where we both can mutually improve or gain benefit."
- Benchmarkers should check with legal counsel if any information gathering procedure is in doubt (e.g., before contacting a direct competitor). If uncomfortable, do not proceed. Alternatively, negotiate and sign a specific non-disclosure agreement that will satisfy the attorneys representing each partner.
- Do not ask competitors for sensitive data or cause the benchmarking partner to feel they must provide data to continue the process.
- Use an ethical third party to assemble and "blind" competitive data, with inputs from legal counsel in direct competitor sharing. (Note: When cost is closely linked to price, sharing cost data can be considered to be the same as sharing price data.)
- Any information obtained from a benchmarking partner should be treated as internal, privileged communications. If "confidential" or proprietary material is to be exchanged, then a specific agreement should be executed to specify the content of the material that needs to be protected, the duration of the period of protection, the conditions for permitting access to the material, and the specific handling requirements necessary for that material.

REFERENCES

1. Hamel, Gary and C. K. Prahalad. *Competing for the Future: Breakthrough Strategies for Seizing Control of Your Industry and Creating the Markets of Tomorrow* 1994. Boston: Harvard Business School Press.

2. Stork, Ken and James P. Morgan. *Benchmarking: In Theory and Practice* 1999. London: Reed Business Information/Reed Elsevier.

APPENDIX 3
THE SUPPLY CHAIN
TRANSFORMATION
MATURITY
ASSESSMENT TOOL©

*I find the great thing in this world is
not so much where we stand,
as in what direction we are moving.*
— Oliver Wendell Holmes

The Supply Chain Transformation Maturity Assessment Tool© is useful for assessing where we stand currently; the progress in how far we have moved; and in what direction we are moving — as in the quote from Holmes. In those respects, the transformation maturity assessment tool is not unlike the other assessment tools presented in Chapter 2. The difference, however, is that this transformation maturity assessment tool has been developed by the authors for use in their consulting engagements. Its elements are taken from the experience of numerous companies, our research into numerous companies, and the writings of others.

> We did not originate the concept of a *maturity model. Wikipedia* provides a good description of the history and concept of maturity models (see www.wikipedia.com). We recommend that readers refer to this source for a more complete explanation.

ABOUT THE TOOL

Our tool is based on some of the ideas and structure of the *Malcolm Baldrige National Quality Award*. The tool is designed to help a company assess itself in terms of the company's *maturity* — either the entire company or a subset of processes — against the best in the world. The tool is descriptive rather than prescriptive and allows a company to score itself as *beginning, developing, or world class* in both process maturity and results. It is also a dynamic and evolving tool that normally is updated annually to reflect current thinking and practice.

> Please recognize that our tool is not a cookbook approach nor is it the only tool that is available to supply chain professionals for their assessments. As illustrated in Chapter 2, many other assessment tools are available, such as those from the Oliver Wight organization, the Supply Chain Council, and the Baldrige Award. We recommend that professionals look at all of these tools, combine them to the extent that makes sense for your organization, and then choose one to use.

The assessment tool addresses approach/deployment first and then results metrics second. When the tool is applied by experienced individuals, it provides assistance to help a business realistically determine:

- Appropriateness of the *approach* of the organization to supply chain management and whether the approach aligns with the needs of the business
- Effectiveness of the supply chain *deployment* within the organization:
  - Is repeatable, integrated, and consistently applied
  - Embodies evaluation, learning, and improvement cycles
  - Is based on reliable data and information
  - Is used to address the requirements that are relevant, useful, and important to the organization
  - Compares current performance with historical performance that can be used as a baseline for planning future performance
  - Evaluates performance relative to appropriate external comparisons and benchmarks
  - Identifies depth, breadth, and rate of performance improvements
  - Links results to important customer, market, process, and action plan performance requirements

Transformation. The assessment tool is a change enabler — a way to initiate, accelerate, and sustain transformational success. It enables the assessor to evaluate the *as is* situation, to facilitate the process of gaining cultural *acceptance*

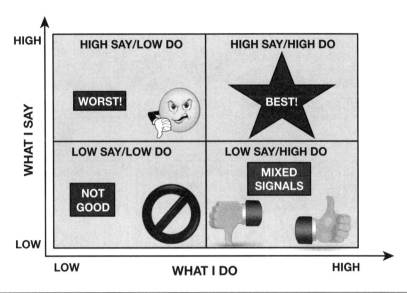

Figure A3.1. The Say Versus Do Matrix.

of the *to be* situation and to plan a *path forward* for the transformation. As we have discussed throughout this book, supply chain transformation requires all three of these.

Figure A3.1. The assessment tool also helps the communication process, somewhat like the old say/do matrix that has been around for many years and is illustrated in Figure A3.1.

Communication. In communication, we want to ensure alignment of *what I say versus what I do*. A maturity model helps as a standard or benchmark for reference, against which supply chain executives and professionals can compare their company in terms of what *good* really is. The measurement of *good* versus *not-so-good* capabilities through a maturity model helps to identify areas most in need of improvement, to organize the starting point for the transformation effort, and to determine the path forward. A maturity path helps to give a structured basis to an organization's inevitable *say/do* discussions.

Action plans. A maturity model helps to determine the focus of action plans. As we have emphasized in this book, companies typically focus first on basic internal "blocking and tackling," getting the "low-hanging fruit," and "stopping the bleeding" — to use three overworked clichés. These are the *beginning* levels in the maturity models for different supply chain processes that we will present

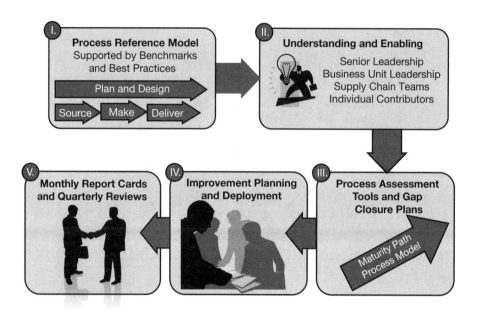

Figure A3.2. A Five-Phase Supply Chain Transformation Process Model.

in the next section. Ultimately, action plans address maturity of the supply chains by:

- Developing a generic framework process map to describe the supply chains of the business
- Accurately modeling the growth of uncertainty up and down the supply chains
- Creating a modeling approach to support strategic decision making

We now provide a number of illustrations to describe our *Supply Chain Transformation Maturity Assessment Tool.*

ILLUSTRATING THE TOOL

Figure A3.2. We suggest a five-phase transformation process model (Figure A3.2):

I.   *Process reference model:* Several process reference models were presented in Chapter 2. (The authors' favorite is the one from the Supply Chain Council.)

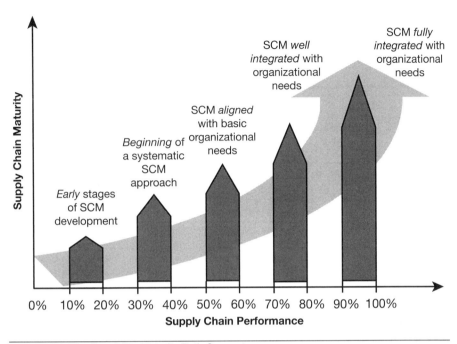

Figure A3.3. The Capability Maturity Path Concept.

II. *Understanding and enabling:* Understanding and enabling needs to occur at all levels, from the senior leadership team to individual contributors.

III. *Process assessment tools and gap closure plans:* A maturity path process model is provided for most of the processes in the supply chain.

IV. *Improvement planning and deployment:* Given the results from the *Supply Chain Transformation Maturity Assessment Tool*, a company can plan and deploy its improvement path forward.

V. *Monthly report cards and quarterly reviews:* Monthly reporting and quarterly formal reviews are important for keeping the entire transformation process on track.

Figure A3.3. Figure A3.3 illustrates the concept behind how a capability maturity path works. Note first the scoring along the bottom of the chart — from 0 to 100%. These are the scorings for each supply chain process and the result from the answers to a series of issues for each process (as will be seen in the charts in Figures A3.6 through A3.27). Note the five ranges of results:

- In the 10 to 20% point range, the result indicates the *early stages of SCM development.*

We describe the supply chain capability maturity model as follows:	
Rating	**Maturity Evaluation**
0%	No SCM or SCM-like approach is in place.
10–20%	**Initial:** Grab-bag of approaches to SCM-like decision making is used.
30–40%	**Repeatable:** The organization has implemented basic mechanisms for SCM, but the process is still just "happening."
50–60%	**Defined:** The organization has defined its SCM process well enough to start focusing on it as a means by which decisions are made. The process is documented, formally implemented, and a focus for management.
70–80%	**Managed:** At this level, SCM can be considered to be under control. This may be the most difficult level to achieve because it emphasizes a quantitative process. In addition, great resistance is often encountered because the numbers are often misused.
90–100%	**Optimized:** The organization is utilizing SCM to begin optimizing the business and to actually prevent problems from occurring. The organization, for example, is dealing with tradeoffs, such as: "How long should the backlog be to (a) not 'turn off' potential customers with increasing lead times and to (b) provide a stable and predictable production rate?" This situation implies a great deal of cross-functional and perhaps cross-geography and cross-enterprise collaboration.
Assessment is in two dimensions: approach/deployment and metrics. These general tests apply to both dimensions.	

Figure A3.4. A Capability Maturity Path Model: Five Levels of Maturity.

- In the 30 to 40% point range, the result indicates the *beginning of a systematic SCM approach.*
- In the 50 to 60% point range, the result indicates that *SCM is aligned with basic organizational needs.*
- In the 70 to 80% point range, the result indicates that *SCM is well integrated with organizational needs.*
- In the 90 to 100% point range, the result indicates that *SCM is fully integrated with organizational needs.*

The large upward-sloping background arrow portrays supply chain maturity increasing fairly steeply along the way. These scores present a quantitative-to-qualitative translation and provide talking points for discussion among executives and supply chain professionals.

Figure A3.4. A paper published by the Software Engineering Institute at Carnegie Mellon University describes a capability maturity model (see www.sei.cmu.edu/pub/document/02.reports/pdf/02tr012.pdf for a description). (Although the Software Engineering Institute's capability maturity model is directed primarily to software engineering, it is very applicable to other applications such as sup-

Approach/Deployment
• Appropriateness of the approach of the business to SCM:
• Does the approach align with the need of the business?
• Effectiveness of the SCM deployment within the business:
• Is deployment repeatable, integrated, and consistently applied?
• Does deployment embody evaluation/learning/improvement cycles?
• Is deployment based on reliable data and information?
• Is deployment used to address the requirements that are relevant and important to the organization?
Metrics
• Current performance
• Performance relative to appropriate comparisons and/or benchmarks
• Rate and breadth of performance improvements
• Linkage of the results to important customer, market, process, and action plan performance requirements

Figure A3.5. Scoring System Components: Approach/Deployment and Metrics.

ply chain management.) We also describe a supply chain maturity model with five levels of maturity — initial, repeatable, defined, managed, and optimized — as illustrated in the chart in Figure A3.4:

- *Initial:* a grab-bag of approaches to manage the supply chain
- *Repeatable*: mechanisms in place, but the process still just "happening"
- *Defined:* SCM processes that are documented, formally implemented, and a focus for management
- *Managed*: SCM processes that are under control
- *Optimized*: SCM processes that can be used to begin optimizing the business and to actually prevent problems from occurring

Figure A3.5. Our assessment tool uses two components to score a company's supply chain maturity: approach/deployment and metrics. The maturity path charts for each supply chain process illustrate these, with one for approach/deployment and one for metrics. Figure A3.5 demonstrates the thinking behind the scoring schemes.

Figure A3.6. Figure A3.6, supply chain integration (approach/deployment) is the first element of the process maturity path. We will use the chart in Figure A3.6 to describe the formatting of each of the other elements of the maturity path.

Supply Chain Integration (Approach/Deployment)

In world-class businesses: (1) all demand is aggregated across adequate planning horizons; (2) customer and supplier linking is collaborative and valued over forecasting; (3) inside-lead-time orders are managed exceptions; (4) e-business has optimized the delivery and linkage of information throughout the supply chains; data are standardized; and voice of the customer (VoC) is widely used.

0	10–30 (Beginning)	40–60 (Developing)	70–90 (World Class)	100
	The strategic plan of the business reflects supply chain management as a key strategy.	The strategic plan of the business reflects fully integrated and globally competitive supply chains with end-to-end customer focus as a strategy.	The strategic plan of the business reflects mature, collaborative, fully integrated, and globally competitive supply chains with end-to-end customer focus as a core competency.	
	Senior leadership understands integrated supply chain management.	Senior leadership understands integrated supply chain management and its importance and monitors its deployment and improvement.	Senior leadership understands integrated and collaborative supply chain management and its importance and visibly leads its continuous improvement.	
	Strategic customer and supplier relationships are identified and beginning to grow.	Strategic customer and supplier relationships are growing and are increasingly supportive of supply chain integration.	Strategic customer and supplier relationships are developed, supportive of supply chain integration, and collaboratively managed at high levels of the businesses in the supply chains.	
	Planning is underway to conduct a competitive analysis of the supply chains.	The business is beginning to conduct a competitive analysis of its supply chains in terms of customer satisfaction and costs.	The business regularly conducts a competitive analysis of its supply chains in terms of collaboration, customer satisfaction, and total costs.	
	The business is developing improvement processes to simplify, standardize, and synchronize key processes across the supply chains.	Improvement processes to simplify, standardize, and synchronize key processes across the supply chains are expanding. Speed and cost are the key focus areas.	Improvement processes to simplify, standardize, and synchronize key processes across the supply chains are mature. Collaboration, speed, total cost, and service are key focus areas.	
	Planning for statistical supply chain modeling is underway.	Supply chain models reflecting actual performance across the supply chains are being piloted.	Supply chain models are utilized. Simulations are run to plan and prioritize improvement actions toward the most significant impacts to customer satisfaction and stakeholder value.	

Figure A3.6. Supply Chain Integration: Approach/Deployment.

Supply Chain Integration (Approach/Deployment)				
0	10–30 (Beginning)	40–60 (Developing)	70–90 (World Class)	100
	Planning is underway for information sharing across the supply chains.	Information sharing is underway internally (and some externally) across organizations in the supply chains.	Information sharing internally and externally takes place in a fully integrated and optimized e-business, collaborative supply chain strategy. Databases are fully integrated across the supply chains.	
	Formal staffing and organizational development programs are beginning across all supply chains. These programs are led by human resources with some support by the supply chain organization. Senior leadership is not involved.	Formal staffing and organizational development programs are in place across all supply chains. They are initiatives instead of a strategic imperative. Human resources is actively involved. Senior leadership is aware of the initiatives.	Staffing and organizational development is a strategic imperative across all supply chains. Senior leadership understands and visibly supports the effort. The senior human resources person is a key advisor and participant in staffing and organizational development.	
	Education and training are encouraged, including membership in APICS, ISM, and other appropriate professional societies. Some new professional supply chain personnel have college degrees.	Education and training programs are in place for all supply chains. APICS, ISM, and other certification programs are encouraged by supply chain leadership. Most new professional supply chain personnel have college degrees.	Education and training are strategic imperatives across all supply chains. APICS, ISM, and other certification programs are actively in place and supported by senior leadership. A policy is in place and followed that all new professional personnel will have college degrees.	
	A formal risk management program is just beginning for some supply chains. Senior leadership is aware of the program.	A risk management program has been developed and is being implemented by supply chain leadership. Senior leadership supports the program.	A formal, mature risk management program is in place for all supply chains. The program includes risk planning, risk assessment, and risk mitigation at a minimum. Senior leadership actively reviews the program at least quarterly.	

Figure A3.6 (continued). Supply Chain Integration: Approach/Deployment.

First, notice the description of the element in the upper part of the chart. Next, notice the scoring: 0, 10 to 30 (beginning), 40 to 60 (developing), 70 to 90 (world class), and 100. The first row of the chart deals with the strategic plan. We use the first row of statements to describe the scoring:

- *10–30 (beginning)*: The strategic plan of the business reflects supply chain management as a key strategy.
- *40–60 (developing)*: The strategic plan of the business reflects fully integrated and globally competitive supply chains with end-to-end customer focus as a strategy.
- *70–90 (world class)*: The strategic plan of the business reflects mature, collaborative, fully integrated, and globally competitive supply chains with end-to-end customer focus as a core competency.

Notice that these statements get more stringent as they go from left (beginning) to right (world class).

The assessor reads each statement and selects the one that most appropriately describes the relationship of supply chain management in the company to the strategic plan. Say, for example, the first statement, 10–30 (beginning), most accurately describes how supply chain management is treated in the strategic plan — it is included as a key strategy — but *how much* of a key strategy is it? The assessor (or assessors) then must choose a score somewhere between 10 and 30. Perhaps, the choice is 17, which would indicate that supply chain management is about a third as strong as it should be.

Remember that being *approximately correct* is more important than being precise. This assessment is to be used as a guide to future action. We also suggest that the assessor, as he/she is scoring each statement, keep notes that reflect the thinking behind the scoring. Because the assessment is to be used as a guide for future action, the company needs something more than just generic statements to develop an action plan.

Returning to our example, the assessor scores supply chain management as an element of the strategic plan — somewhere between 0 and 100. We rarely expect that a score would be 0, which would indicate that supply chain management is not even mentioned or referred to in the strategic plan, nor would we expect that a score would be 100, which would indicate that the strategic plan's inclusion of supply chain management could not possibly be any stronger.

The assessor then goes through each row of statements relative to supply chain integration, choosing a score for each row in the matrix. The scoring for each row then would be averaged for a total score of the entire element in the maturity assessment tool.

Figure A3.7. Next we turn to the metrics (Figure A3.7). How well supply chain management is integrated with the rest of the organization can be ascertained by how well other parts of the organization are performing in areas which can be influenced by the supply chain. Thus, we see metrics such as fill rate, product lead times, perfect order, free cash flow, costs, and so forth. We encourage a company to add metrics that reflect their own unique situation.

> We are highly in favor of education and training opportunities being made available to supply chain professionals. Professional societies such as APICS: the Operations Management Society and the Institute of Supply Management (ISM) are two well-respected organizations which have education and training opportunities as well as certification programs. (Bill Lee is certified at the Fellow level by APICS. Although he has advanced degrees and has taught and practiced in the field for many years, Bill frequently attends APICS events such as the annual international conference to stay in touch with practices in the field.) Supply chain integration also can be measured by the level of professionalism of supply chain personnel. For example, the percent of supply chain hires who are college graduates is indicative of the professionalism of the organization — compare this percentage with engineering or finance organizations. Engineering and finance generally are held in high regard for their professionalism — typically all or almost all professional hires have college degrees.

Demand management can be defined as:

… a set of integrated tools, systems, and collaborative customer-linking processes that are used to predict, plan, communicate, reconcile, adjust, and manage the requirements, desires, and needs of customers (and customers' customers as well as customers' customers' customers) over a horizon sufficient to allow suppliers (and suppliers' suppliers as well as suppliers' suppliers' suppliers) to effectively and efficiently plan, execute, and satisfy these requirements.

Figure A3.8. In traditional businesses in the past, demand management involved (1) waiting for the orders to arrive, (2) anticipating or forecasting the orders, (3) protecting for the orders, or (4) all of the above — typically through reserve inventory. An old saying describes what was happening: "Throw the order over the wall." This saying illustrates and emphasizes the disconnection that existed between suppliers and customers. But, it's not that way anymore! Today, companies that are world class in demand management emphasize *collaboration*. Collaboration is an essential component of the statements in the demand management (approach/deployment) matrix in Figure A3.8.

Supply Chain Integration Metrics

In world-class businesses: (1) all demand is aggregated across adequate planning horizons; (2) customer and supplier linking is collaborative and valued over forecasting; (3) inside-lead-time orders are managed exceptions; (4) e-business has optimized the delivery and linkage of information throughout the supply chains; data are standardized; and voice of the customer (VoC) is widely used.

0	10–30 (Beginning)	40–60 (Developing)	70–90 (World Class)	100
	Fill rate <95%	Fill rate 95–100%	Fill rate = 100%	
	Cumulative product lead time >120% of industry benchmarks	Cumulative product lead time 120–80% of industry benchmarks	Cumulative product lead time <80% of industry benchmarks	
	Perfect order <95%	Perfect order 95–100%	Perfect order = 100%	
	Free cash flow <80% of industry benchmarks	Free cash flow 80–120% of industry benchmarks	Free cash flow >120% of industry benchmarks	
	Total supply chain costs >120% of industry benchmarks	Total supply chain costs 120–80% of industry benchmarks	Total supply chain costs <80% of industry benchmarks	
	Working capital turns <80% of industry benchmarks	Working capital turns 80–120% of industry benchmarks	Working capital turns >120% of industry benchmarks	
	Days of supply in inventory >120% of industry benchmarks	Days of supply in inventory 80–120% of industry benchmarks	Days of supply in inventory <80% of industry benchmarks	
	Education and training for all supply chain personnel supported and paid by the company	20–40 hours per year of education and training completed by all supply chain personnel	>40 hours per year of education and training completed by all supply chain personnel	
	<20% of professional supply chain personnel certified through APICS, ISM, or other similar professional societies	20–50% of professional supply chain personnel certified through APICS, ISM, or other similar professional societies	>50% of professional supply chain personnel certified through APICS, ISM, or other similar professional societies	
	<30% of professional hires into supply chain positions have 4-year college degrees	30–90% of professional hires into supply chain positions have 4-year college degrees	>90% of new professional hires into supply chain positions have 4-year college degrees; those that do not actively pursue degrees	

Figure A3.7. Supply Chain Integration Metrics.

Demand Management (Approach/Deployment)

In world-class businesses: (1) all demand is aggregated across adequate planning horizons; (2) customer and supplier linking is collaborative and valued over forecasting; (3) inside-lead-time orders are managed exceptions; (4) e-business has optimized the delivery and linkage of information throughout the supply chains; data are standardized; and voice of the customer (VoC) is widely used.

0	10–30 (Beginning)	40–60 (Developing)	70–90 (World Class)	100
	Customer-demand information process effectively forecasts and processes customers' purchase orders.	The business has moved toward a customer-linked demand management process that minimizes dependence on forecasting.	The customer demand process is fully linked and integrated across the supply chains and between all customer and supplier disciplines. Customer linking has replaced forecasting.	
	Demand is communicated primarily through firm customers' purchase orders.	Demand communication is tied to periodic ERP and is executed primarily via purchase orders. Some e-commerce is employed with customers to communicate demand information.	Rapid communications via e-business of demand information occurs across the supply chains seamlessly and in real time.	
	Product lead times are published, but inside-lead-time orders occur frequently. Expediting is a way of life.	Product lead times are agreed on and published. Orders inside lead time are measured and managed to an acceptable level.	Product lead times are collaboratively agreed on at the supply chain level. Orders and changes inside lead times are the exception and occur only after an impact analysis on the entire supply chain.	
	Clear accountability and responsibility for demand management exist. Accuracy is measured and reported.	Clear accountability and responsibility for demand management exist. Accuracy is measured, is reported, and has significantly improved.	Clear accountability and responsibility for demand management exist. Accuracy exceeds benchmark levels.	
	Overall service levels are defined, measured, and reported monthly, but not for individual customers. VoC is just beginning to be a key metric.	Service levels for key customers are well defined, measured, and reported monthly. VoC is a key metric.	Service levels for all customers are well defined and consistent with strategic customer segmentation. They are measured and reported monthly. Customer service levels meet or exceed industry and customer expectations. VoC is the primary metric.	
	Customer orders and promises are reported to the master production scheduling process.	Customer order entry and promises are integrated with the master production scheduling process.	Customer order entry and promises incorporate current available-to-promise information and are tightly integrated with the master production scheduling process.	

Figure A3.8. Demand Management: Approach/Deployment.

0	10–30 (Beginning)	40–60 (Developing)	70–90 (World Class)	100

Demand Management Metrics

In world-class businesses: (1) all demand is aggregated across adequate planning horizons; (2) customer linking is collaborative and valued over forecasting; (3) inside lead time orders are managed exceptions; (4) e-business has optimized the delivery and linkage of information throughout the supply chains; data are standardized; and voice of the customer (VoC) is widely used.

0	10–30 (Beginning)	40–60 (Developing)	70–90 (World Class)	100
	Forecast accuracy <70%	Forecast accuracy = 70–90%	Forecast accuracy >90%	
	>20% of unplanned orders and changes are in less than agreed lead time	20–5% of unplanned orders and changes are in less than agreed lead time	<5% of unplanned orders and changes are in less than agreed lead time	
	<50% of demand customer linked (versus forecasted)	50–90% of demand customer linked (versus forecasted)	>90% of demand customer linked (versus forecasted)	
	<20% of demand communicated via e-business	20–70% of demand communicated via e-business	>70% of demand communicated via e-business	
	<10% of demand results from collaborative relationships with customers	10–50% of demand results from collaborative relationships with customers	>50% of demand results from collaborative relationships with customers	

Figure A3.9. Demand Management Metrics.

Figure A3.9. Traditional demand management metrics, however, are still important to the extent that traditional approaches such as forecasting are deployed. Therefore, forecast *accuracy* is measured (Figure A3.9). (If forecasting is not used, which, of course, is preferred, and all demand thus is linked directly with customers, then the metric for forecasting is not relevant.) Collaborative demand relationships with customers are a component of the metrics. Our world-class metric of >50% in column three of the last row of Figure A3.9 may not be totally accurate because we are not sure of what the true amount of genuine collaboration is in reality. However, we believe the 50% metric is at least realistic.

Figure A3.10. Just as in demand management, a primary issue in supply management is collaboration — and the resulting linkage (Figure A3.10). We like to think of supply management as being the other side of the demand management coin. We believe that all too often companies seem to naturally want much closer partnering relationships with customers than they are willing to have with suppliers. *This is not the case for world-class companies.* We have a saying that we use frequently: "Your suppliers are your suppliers because they can do things that you cannot, or do not want to, do — treat them accordingly as key members of your supply chain." Most people have also heard this saying: "A chain is only as strong as its weakest link." The supply base (or at least a portion of the supply base) frequently is the weak link in a supply chain.

Optimization of the supply base is a more up-to-date (and nicer) way of saying *rationalization* of the supply base. Although we used *rationalization* in the past, the word eventually came to mean simply reducing the number of suppliers. *Optimization* (in spite of the fact that we really do not care for the term except in a mathematical optimization sense) means obtaining the *best* suppliers, not just a smaller number of suppliers. (Of course, we all know that the process of obtaining the *best* suppliers naturally will result in *fewer* suppliers.)

Figure A3.11. Traditional supply management metrics are still very important, such as on-time delivery, quality, lead time, and productivity gains (Figure A3.11). However, of increasing importance are the formal linkages with suppliers, including e-business. Here, too, collaborative relationships are moving to the forefront in the importance of supply management.

We also admit to not liking the term *sales and operations planning* (S&OP). We do not even like the term *sales, inventory, and operations planning* (SIOP) that some companies use. (Bill Lee admits to liking the more academic term *aggregate planning* that is seen in most academic textbooks. He also admits, however, that part of this is the fact that he wrote his doctoral dissertation on the subject! New terms, *integrated business management* and some variations of that term, are beginning to be used. We'll see how they catch on. We're all in favor.) We do admit that the more comprehensive definition of S&OP (which we prefer) extends beyond the generally accepted boundaries of the supply chain. However, this definition should not be too bothersome if one accepts the notion that linkage and collaboration are important determinants of supply chain success.

The well-known *Oliver Wight Class A Checklist* defines the purpose of S&OP as follows:[1]

> *To establish an integrated business management process that realigns company plans in response to change, including the integration of financials. It drives gap-closing actions to address competitive priorities, upper-quartile performance and to deliver management commitments. It deploys the business strategy.*

This definition is much closer to our view of what S&OP really is, but it still does not encompass the completeness of our concept. Ling and Goddard wrote what has become perhaps the classic book on S&OP. They liken S&OP to an orchestra.[2]

Supply Management (Approach/Deployment)				
In world-class businesses, supply management includes (1) strategic collaborative long-term relationships across the entire supply chain; (2) strategic improvement plans, including monthly supplier performance metrics; (3) supplier development and integration; (4) automation optimizing e-business to minimize labor-intensive transactions and other waste and to maximize process and data linkage and speed.				
0	10–30 (Beginning)	40–60 (Developing)	70–90 (World Class)	100
	The company's leadership is aware of and supportive of strategic supplier initiatives.	The company's leadership meets occasionally with leadership of strategic suppliers.	The company's leadership meets regularly with leadership of strategic suppliers to build collaborative relationships.	
	The company's product and nonproduct purchasing activities are developing strategic partnerships, key relationships, and commodity leverage. A core strategic supplier base is identified.	The company's purchasing activities are deploying segmentation of strategic partnerships, key relationships, commodity leverage, and routine purchases. Key resources are occasionally focused on strategic purchases to accomplish a specific objective.	The company's purchasing activities are driven by linked strategic planning and segmentation among strategic partnerships, key relationships, commodity leverage, and routine purchases. An integrated total cost reduction process is linked and mature across the supply chain. Strategic, third-party logistics, low-cost economy sourcing, and total supply chain aggregation are some key elements of the strategy. Key selected and developed resources are focused on strategic and key purchases.	
	Long-term relationships are sought with strategic and key suppliers.	Long-term relationships are established with some strategic and key suppliers and are based on continuous improvement.	Long-term collaborative relationships are sought with all strategic and key suppliers and are based on continuous improvement.	

Figure A3.10. Supply Management: Approach/Deployment.

Ling and Goddard begin their book with a quote from Sir Thomas Beecham, a British conductor:

There are two golden rules for an orchestra: start together and finish together.

	Supply Management (Approach/Deployment)			
0	**10–30 (Beginning)**	**40–60 (Developing)**	**70–90 (World Class)**	**100**
	Supplier suggestion programs are in place to reward suppliers who contribute cost-saving ideas.	Selected suppliers are introduced to the product design and development process based on their willingness to contribute improvement ideas.	Strategic and key suppliers are fully integrated early in a collaborative product design and development process and product targets are openly shared.	
	Supplier improvement and education and training programs exist to drive overall supplier improvements.	Supplier improvement and education and training programs exist to drive overall supplier improvements. Suppliers join with customer's company teams to improve product performance, quality, and cost.	A mature, comprehensive, and integrated supplier improvement and education and training program is driving continuous improvement in supply chain performance. Suppliers join with internal teams to improve product performance, quality, and cost.	
	A process for supply base optimization has been formulated.	The supplier base is being optimized consistent with requirements of the business.	The supplier base is optimized consistent with strategic business objectives, leverage, global competition, and risk management.	

Figure A3.10 (continued). Supply Management: Approach/Deployment.

An orchestra is a very good analogy for S&OP — to get everyone to play together. It is not just that an orchestra needs to start and finish together — but that it needs to play the entire piece together.

The term S&OP has been around for many years and now is accepted terminology. Yet the practice of S&OP now is much larger than just *sales* and *operations* planning. When done well, S&OP also includes other functional areas such as product development and finance.

Figure A3.12. Notice the first and third rows of statements in the sales and operations planning (S&OP) (approach/deployment) matrix in Figure A3.12. These statements emphasize the importance of *all* functional areas. A truly collaborative S&OP process will indeed include all functional areas.

Supply Management Metrics				
In world-class businesses, supply management includes (1) strategic collaborative long-term relationships across the entire supply chain; (2) strategic improvement plans, including monthly supplier performance metrics; (3) supplier development and integration; (4) automation optimizing e-business to minimize labor-intensive transactions and other waste and to maximize process and data linkage and speed.				
0	10–30 (Beginning)	40–60 (Developing)	70–90 (World Class)	100
	Supplier on-time delivery <90%	Supplier on-time delivery = 90–99%	Supplier on-time delivery >99%	
	Supplier quality >2500 PPM	Supplier quality = 2500–150 PPM	Supplier quality <150 PPM	
	Supplier lead time >120% of industry benchmarks	Supplier lead time = 120–100% of industry benchmarks	Supplier lead time <100% of industry benchmarks	
	Supplier productivity gains <7%	Supplier productivity gains = 7–12%	Supplier productivity gains >12%	
	<50% of purchases supplier linked	50–90% of purchases supplier linked	>90% of purchases supplier linked	
	>25% of purchases communicated via e-business	20–75% of purchases communicated via e-business	>75% of purchases communicated via e-business	
	<10% of purchases results from collaborative relationships with suppliers	10–50% of purchases results from collaborative relationships with suppliers	>50% of purchases results from collaborative relationships with suppliers	

Figure A3.11. Supply Management Metrics.

Figure A3.13. In terms of the metrics for S&OP, notice that the first two rows of the matrix in Figure A3.13 contain traditional supply chain metrics. The last three rows contain metrics that are indicative of the entire business plan. We believe this is as it should be. Part of the S&OP process is to ensure product delivery to customers — yet an equally important part is to focus on the overall business plan.

Figure A3.14. The master production schedule (MPS) (approach/development) matrix in Figure A3.14 links S&OP with enterprise requirements detail planning (ERDP) and includes rough-cut capacity planning (RCCP). As we sometimes say, the MPS implements S&OP — the sum of the MPS aggregates to S&OP and S&OP disaggregates to the MPS. The MPS then disaggregates to the

Sales and Operations Planning (S&OP) (Approach/Deployment)

In world-class businesses, S&OP: (1) is owned and chaired by the business leader; (2) aggregates and balances demand and supply; (3) performs rough-cut capacity planning (RCCP) at the family level; (4) reconciles business plans monthly into a singular plan; and (5) requires adherence to a policy that collaboratively defines clear roles and responsibilities.

0	10–30 (Beginning)	40–60 (Developing)	70–90 (World Class)	100
	S&OP-like processes take place in each functional area. Coordination and integration of plans are informal.	The business leader owns and chairs the monthly S&OP process.	The business leader owns and chairs the monthly S&OP process, including an executive S&OP meeting at which all functional plans are reconciled into a single collaborative business plan at an aggregate level.	
	The S&OP-like processes do little to balance demand and supply. Supply is expected simply to meet demand.	The S&OP aggregates and balances some demand and some supply. Not all product families are included.	The S&OP aggregates and balances all demand and all supply, including original equipment plus all spare parts, repair and overhaul components, and so forth.	
	The monthly S&OP process discusses the business plans for most functional areas. Gross discrepancies are identified and modified. Little accountability exists for meeting the plan.	The monthly S&OP process yields one singular business plan for sales, production, distribution, inventory, supply chain, new product development, finance, and other key areas of the business. Some accountability exists for meeting the plan.	The monthly S&OP process yields one singular business plan for sales, production, distribution, inventory, supply chain, new product development, finance, and other key areas of the business. Accountability for meeting the plan lies with the business leadership.	
	An explicit S&OP policy exists and generally is followed. Little accountability exists for following the policy.	An explicit S&OP policy exists and generally is followed. Collaborative cross-functional roles and responsibilities are not consistently fulfilled.	An explicit S&OP policy exists and is followed. Collaborative cross-functional roles and responsibilities are clearly defined and consistently fulfilled.	
	Significant changes to the S&OP during the monthly cycle are discussed among the functional departments.	Changes to the S&OP during the monthly cycle are approved at lower levels in the functional departments.	Changes to the S&OP during the monthly cycle are rare and require business leader approval.	
	RCCP is being performed on an ad hoc basis.	RCCP is performed on a periodic basis as part of the S&OP process.	RCCP is consistently performed monthly at the family level as part of the S&OP process to ensure that S&OP creates a realistic load on key resources and suppliers. Rate-based planning is extensively used.	

Figure A3.12. Sales and Operations Management: Approach/Deployment.

Sales and Operations Planning (S&OP) Metrics

In world-class businesses, S&OP: (1) is owned and chaired by the business leader; (2) aggregates and balances demand and supply; (3) performs RCCP at the family level; (4) reconciles business plans monthly into a singular plan; and (5) requires adherence to a policy that collaboratively defines clear roles and responsibilities.

0	10–30 (Beginning)	40–60 (Developing)	70–90 (World Class)	100
	Plan linkage — RED (meaning the following generally do not apply): • Sales plan = S&OP production plan + FGI plan = shipment plan = revenue plan • S&OP production plan = MPS = build plan = demonstrated capacity	Plan linkage — YELLOW (meaning the following generally apply and are becoming part of the culture of the company): • Sales plan = S&OP production plan + FGI plan = shipment plan = revenue plan • S&OP production plan = MPS = build plan = demonstrated capacity	Plan linkage — GREEN (meaning the following absolutely apply and are integral to the culture of the company): • Sales plan = S&OP production plan + FGI plan = shipment plan = revenue plan S&OP production plan = MPS = build plan = demonstrated capacity	
	<80% of unplanned orders and changes are within time fence policies	80–95% of unplanned orders and changes are within time fence policies	>95% of unplanned orders and changes are within time fence policies	
	Sales revenue = business plan ±20%	Sales revenue = business plan ±10%	Sales revenue = business plan ±5%	
	ROIC <80% of industry standards	ROIC = 80–100% of industry standards	ROIC >120% of industry standards	
	Free cash flow <80% of industry benchmarks	Free cash flow = 80–100% of industry benchmarks	Free cash flow ≧100% of industry benchmarks	

Figure A3.13. Sales and Operations Management Metrics.

detail planning process. Simply put, the MPS specifies the following in a manufacturing enterprise at a top-end item level:

- *What* will be produced?
- *How many* or *how much* will be produced?
- *When* it will be produced?
- *Where* it will be produced?

Figure A3.15. The metrics from the MPS generally relate to how well the above four questions are executed (Figure A3.15).

Enterprise requirements detail planning (ERDP) used to be called *materials requirements planning* (MRP). MRP is a term which is generally credited to Joe

Master Production Scheduling (MPS) (Approach/Deployment)

In world-class businesses, MPS: (1) supports the S&OP production plan whereby the sum of the MPS by family equals the sum of the S&OP by family; (2) maintains realistic schedules with zero due; (3) reconciles to the RCCP whereby demonstrated capacity equals the MPS requirement; (4) allows changes within the framework defined by the MPS policy; (5) consistently measures compliance of on-time completion to the MPS; and (6) instills action to improve in a collaborative fashion.

0	10–30 (Beginning)	40–60 (Developing)	70–90 (World Class)	100
	An approved MPS policy exists, but is not followed consistently.	An approved MPS exists and is followed.	An MPS policy exists, is followed, and is incorporated into the culture across all disciplines.	
	MPS compliance is consistently measured and reported.	MPS compliance is consistently measured and reported and is improving.	MPS compliance is consistently measured and reported and has reached benchmark levels.	
	RCCP is performed on an ad hoc basis.	RCCP is performed on a periodic basis as part of the MPS process.	RCCP is consistently performed monthly at the end-item level as part of the MPS process to ensure MPS creates a realistic load on key resources and suppliers.	
	Changes to the MPS are controlled.	Changes to the MPS are controlled at the functional level. Most past-due orders are rescheduled. Rate-based planning is expanding.	MPS extensively reflects a rate-based planning process. Changes to the MPS are controlled by policy. Whenever any order shows a potential delay, all measures are taken to prevent the delay. Only as a last resort are orders rescheduled with new realistic due dates.	
	MPS is compared to the S&OP production plan monthly.	MPS is reconciled to the S&OP production plan monthly. The sum of the MPS by family equals the sum of the S&OP by family.	MPS is driven by the monthly S&OP production plan, and the sum of the MPS by family equals the sum of the S&OP by family.	
	MPS data are sometimes used for customer order promising inside lead time.	MPS data is used as a key input for customer order promising inside lead time.	MPS governs customer order promising inside lead time.	
	MPS information generally is available to demand management for order promising on request.	MPS is always available to demand management for order promising on request.	MPS is linked and in continuous communication with demand management for order promising and available-to-promise information.	

Figure A3.14. Master Production Scheduling: Approach/Deployment.

Master Production Scheduling (MPS) Metrics

In world-class businesses, MPS: (1) supports the S&OP production plan whereby the sum of the MPS by family equals the sum of the S&OP by family; (2) maintains realistic schedules with zero due; (3) reconciles to the RCCP whereby demonstrated capacity equals the MPS requirement; (4) allows changes within the framework defined by the MPS policy; (5) consistently measures compliance of on-time completion to the MPS; and (6) instills action to improve in a collaborative fashion.

0	10—30 (Beginning)	40—60 (Developing)	70—90 (World Class)	100
	MPS performance <85% of the time	MPS performance = 85–100% of the time	MPS performance = 100% of the time	
	Overdue backlog >15%	Overdue backlog = 15–2%	Overdue backlog <2%	
	MPS = demonstrated capacity <90% of the time	MPS = demonstrated capacity 90–98% of the time	MPS = demonstrated capacity >98% of the time	
	MPS schedule changes = time fence policies <80%	MPS schedule changes = time fence policies 80–97%	MPS schedule changes = time fence policies >97%	

Figure A3.15. Master Production Scheduling Metrics.

Orlicky, who actually coined the term around 1960, although he did not publish his book until 1975.[3] Joe was with IBM and was seeking ways to help IBM sell computers to manufacturing companies. The preface to Joe's book contains the following:

> *The number of MRP systems used in American industry gradually grew to about 150 in 1971, when the growth curve began a steep rise as a result of the "MRP Crusade," a national program of publicity and education sponsored by the American Production and Inventory Control Society (APICS).*

Bill Lee actually put one of the first MRP systems into a Rockwell valve plant beginning in 1967 using an IBM 360-30, which had fewer capabilities than his mobile telephone does today! You may have seen one of these IBM machines in a museum. An IBM 360-30 took up an entire room and required special air conditioning.

Originally, MRP was strictly *materials* requirements planning in manufacturing enterprises. Since its origins, however, MRP has grown to include manufacturing resource planning (MRPII), a term coined by Oliver Wight in the early 1970s. Ollie actually published a book in 1981, which had a major impact in the global manufacturing industry.[4] Ollie became rich and famous — he was on the cover of *Fortune* magazine and flew his own business jet! Yet, Ollie is reputed to have said something along the lines of: "I made a mistake. By calling it *manufacturing* resource planning, I was referring to the entire manufacturing *enterprise* and not the manufacturing function." So people misunderstood and insisted that MRP did not include all the other functions of the manufacturing business, such as finance and accounting, product development, sales and marketing, and so forth. Of course, you know the rest of the story. Today we use the term *enterprise requirements planning* (ERP) in recognition that MRP deals with the entire enterprise — and not just the manufacturing enterprise either. ERP has been applied in all sorts of organizations. But, that is enough historical trivia. Back to work!

What we call enterprise requirements detail planning or ERDP is distinguished from MRP, MRPII, and ERP in three ways:

- MRP deals with *materials* only.
- MRPII deals with all the *functional areas* of the manufacturing enterprise.
- ERP is a more encompassing term than just the *detail* planning to which we refer in ERDP.

Figure A3.16. ERDP is a process that translates the MPS and other demand information into valid supply chain requirements to be utilized in maintaining supply and demand alignment. At the detail level, ERDP includes detail materials requirements for suppliers, manufacturing, and distribution. Simply put, ERDP:
- "Explodes" the MPS through the bills of material
- Determines the net requirements by subtracting the on-hand and on-order information from the gross requirements
- Back-schedules the requirements by their lead times
- Presents time-phased net requirements

Of course, ERDP is more complex than this simple list, but you get the picture (Figure A3.16).

Figure A3.17. We say that ERDP is a tool to provide planning information. ERDP generally is not an execution tool. We prefer our vision of world-class companies as *lean* enterprises wherein planning is with ERDP and execution is with some form of pull signals that say, in essence: "We need some more; please give it to us." ERDP provides detailed requirements information and maintains alignment of supply with demand. ERDP metrics generally fall into well-known supply chain metrics which indicate that the processes are working correctly (Figure A3.17).

Enterprise Requirements Detail Planning (ERDP) (Approach/Deployment)

In world-class businesses, ERDP: (1) synchronizes supply and demand; (2) effects a closed-loop schedule reconciliation process; (3) provides planning information to internal and external supply chains; (4) utilizes appropriate scheduling techniques; and (5) consistently includes detailed capacity planning.

0	10–30 (Beginning)	40–60 (Developing)	70–90 (World Class)	100
	An approved ERDP policy exists, but is not followed consistently. Collaboration and coordination of plans are not consistent.	An approved ERDP exists and is followed.	An ERDP policy exists, is followed, and is incorporated into the culture across all disciplines. It facilitates collaboration and coordination of plans.	
	ERDP takes detailed demand information and schedules or reschedules supply in support of demand.	ERDP is performed, details demand, and schedules/reschedules supply in support of demand. A rate-based planning capability is being implemented where appropriate.	ERDP effectively synchronizes supply and demand within established policies on a daily basis. A rate-based ERDP capability exists and is utilized extensively.	
	ERDP exception and action messages are measured and consistently taken care of within an established time frame.	ERDP exception and action messages are measured and consistently taken care of within an established time frame. Action message volume is decreasing.	ERDP exception and action messages are measured and consistently taken care of within an established time frame. Action messages are minimized.	
	Some appropriate (value-dependent, etc.) material planning and signaling techniques are utilized, such as kanban, point-of-use, and two-bin systems.	The use of appropriate (value-dependent, etc.) material planning and signaling techniques is expanding, such as kanban, point-of-use, and two-bin systems.	The use of appropriate (value-dependent, etc.) planning and signaling techniques is strategically employed, such as kanban, point-of-use, and two-bin systems.	
	ERDP filters exist to dampen exception messages consistent with established supply chain policies.	ERDP filters effectively dampen exception messages consistent with established supply chain policies.	The need for ERDP filters has been eliminated by supply chain maturity.	
	ERDP exists as a closed-loop process, but feedback mechanisms are not always employed.	ERDP usage is moving toward a closed-loop process, and the due date usually equals need date.	ERDP is a strong closed-loop process in which the due date always equals the need date.	
	Inventory and bills of material accuracy are at acceptable levels.	Inventory and bills of material accuracy are approaching benchmark levels.	Inventory and bills of material accuracy are at benchmark levels.	

Figure A3.16. Enterprise Requirements Detail Planning: Approach/Deployment.

Enterprise Requirements Detail Planning (ERDP) Metrics

In world-class businesses, ERDP: (1) synchronizes supply and demand; (2) effects a closed-loop schedule reconciliation process; (3) provides planning information to the internal and external supply chains; (4) utilizes appropriate scheduling techniques; and (5) consistently includes detailed capacity planning.

0	10–30 (Beginning)	40–60 (Developing)	70–90 (World Class)	100
	Data accuracy (all ERDP elements and bills of material) <95%	Data accuracy (all ERDP elements and bills of material) = 95–100%	Data accuracy (all ERDP elements and bills of material) = 100%	
	Material available at start date <95%	Material available at start date = 95–100%	Material available at start date = 100%	
	Percent of inventory excess and obsolete >5%	Percent of inventory excess and obsolete = 5–1%	Percent of inventory excess and obsolete <1%	
	Dollar receipts = inventory plan <90%	Dollar receipts = inventory plan = 90–97%	Dollar receipts = inventory plan >97%	

Figure A3.17. Enterprise Requirements Detail Planning Metrics.

As companies move from beginning to world class in internal supply chain (ISC) scheduling, the objective is to eliminate some of the poor practices from the past. Why is it that the traditional product delivery systems have problems?

- We have seen the symptoms:
  - Products delivered late
  - Large inventory positions of the wrong products
  - An almost constant state of emergency in which the *best* materials people are actually *best* at firefighting and taking care of emergencies
- We have heard the excuses. Pick one or more:
  - Poor demand forecasts
  - Unreliable suppliers
  - Poorly maintained equipment that breaks down
  - People being sick or on vacation
  - The order being mishandled
  - The customer changing the order

We have also heard: "Federal Express and UPS are our preferred suppliers!" So, what has been the traditional preferred way to deal with these symptoms and excuses?

Guess. Guess (some would say *forecast*) what demand will be several months into the future due to the cumulative lead times:

- How much attention was given to the forecasting process?
- Was employee compensation tied to forecast accuracy?
- Were forecasts giving a distorted picture of true demand based on collaborative data?
  - Stocking plans and distribution and/or retail promotions?
  - Overbooking in anticipation of seasonal shortages?
  - Monthly or quarterly close of the accounting books?
  - Annual shut-down periods?
  - Model phase-outs and new product introductions?
- Is there a mechanism for capturing actual point-of-sale demand data?

Pick a number. Pick one number for the production plan (call it the MPS) with a zero plus-or-minus margin for error:

- Were discrete orders given to perhaps hundreds of suppliers based on this one-number estimate?
- What is the one thing known with certainty about a demand forecast? It is wrong!

Use a set rate. Load the supply chain at a set rate and schedule far out into the future:

- Are capacity and materials reserved to handle routine exceptions?
- Are each supplier's products scheduled to arrive "just-in-time" for production?
- Are manufacturing plant managers rewarded for overhead absorption and work-in-process inventory turns based on monthly accounting closes?

Make decisions on the fly. Make *make-or-buy* decisions on the fly depending upon whether current load exceeds or falls short of manufacturing capacity and/ or whether a supplier comes in with a special price on certain products.

- Is make-or-buy a strategic decision based on analytical study of different commodities?
- Do make-or-buy decisions reflect the company's core competency?

Figures A3.18 and A3.19. See Figure A3.18 to get a sense of our views of the traditional versus current world-class performance. Notice how the ideas of cultural change, lean, flattened bills of material, and so forth have been incorporated to distinguish current world-class approaches from traditional approaches. As for the metrics (Figure A3.19), they are short, simple, and focused on execution.

Distribution is the process that links the supply source (usually manufacturing) to the demand source (usually the customer) in the supply chain. Distribution usually is for finished goods inventory, but also can include aftermarket and service items.

Since Andre Martin wrote the second edition to his groundbreaking book in 1990, distribution resource planning (DRP) has become the generally accepted approach for managing distribution inventories.[5] Martin uses the following description:

> One way or another, every non-service company is part of a "marketing channel" [We prefer use the term supply chain.] or industrial pipeline, which consists of retailers, wholesalers, distributors, and manufacturers who do business with one another.

The purpose of distribution and distribution planning is to help a business place the right products in the right location at the right time to:

- Maximize customer satisfaction
- Minimize inventory levels
- Minimize transportation, manufacturing, and warehouse costs
- Achieve seamless communication of demand
- Provide an integrated approach toward management of demand

Traditional distribution frequently is made difficult by sales promotions that often override service level and inventory turn considerations. A typical traditional distribution system:

- Is not linked by a flow of information from the retailer through the supply chain to the manufacturer and its suppliers
- Gives suppliers a very limited view (if any) of what is happening at the retail level
- Provides little or no information that can be used for production planning

Figures A3.20 and A3.21. About two decades ago, the term *continuous replenishment* (CR) came into common usage. Since then, continuous replenishment has been replaced by the term *collaborative, planning, forecasting, and replenishment* (CPFR) — CPFR is intended to enhance the supply chain by emphasizing the importance of collaboration and cooperation all along the supply chain. Sharing of information in a collaborative manner is the key (Figure A3.20). CPFR originated in 1995 in an initiative begun by Wal-Mart and a few other

Internal Supply Chain (ISC) Scheduling (Approach/Deployment)

In world-class businesses, ISC scheduling is preceded by a make-or-buy process that is formal, strategic, and owned by the business leader. The make/buy process is based on core competency and collaborative economic decisions. The ISC scheduling process: (1) maximizes the utilization of rate-based pull systems; (2) uses simple scheduling techniques; (3) replaces physical inventories with cycle counting; (4) utilizes flattened bills of material; (5) eliminates informal prioritization processes; and (6) maintains accurate bills of material, routings, and inventory records.

0	10–30 (Beginning)	40–60 (Developing)	70–90 (World Class)	100
	ISC scheduling has begun utilizing simple scheduling and tracking methods.	ISC employs simple scheduling and tracking techniques supportive of lean, rate-based planning, visual signals, kanban, scheduling boards, etc.	ISC has effected a cultural change to lean ISC techniques and processes and is supported by rate-based planning, visual signals, kanban, scheduling boards, etc.	
	ISC capacity planning is utilized.	Effective ISC capacity planning is extensively utilized.	Effective ISC capacity planning is an integral part of how ISC is managed.	
	Bills of material and routings accuracy has reached acceptable levels.	Bills of material and routings accuracy has reached acceptable levels and is being continuously improved.	Flattened bills of material and routings are accurate, match the optimal ISC processes, and are extensively used.	
	Informal authorization and prioritization techniques (hot lists, shortage reports, etc.) are gradually being phased out through use of formal processes and systems.	Informal authorization and prioritization techniques (hot lists, shortage reports, etc.) have generally been phased out through use of the formal processes and systems.	Authorization and prioritization techniques are based on pull systems.	
	A pilot program to employ point-of-use material delivery (i.e., direct delivery to the ISC location) is underway.	Point-of-use material delivery is expanding	Extensive use of point-of-use material delivery is deployed to the maximum appropriate level.	

Figure A3.18. Internal Supply Chain Scheduling: Approach/Deployment.

Internal Supply Chain (ISC) Scheduling (Approach/Deployment)

0	10–30 (Beginning)	40–60 (Developing)	70–90 (World Class)	100
	Key stocking locations focus on inventory record accuracy for high-dollar items. Physical inventories are conducted less frequently while cycle counting begins to take hold.	Inventory record accuracy is measured at all stocking locations. Cycle count systems supplement physical inventories.	Inventory accuracy is established at benchmark levels.	
	All materials transactions have been analyzed and targeted for elimination throughout the ISC process.	Automated materials transactions are employed throughout the ISC process to eliminate non-value-added effort and to speed delivery of materials and information.	An automated materials tracking system has resulted in an accurate, high-velocity, efficient process of moving materials throughout ISC.	

Figure A3.18 (continued). Internal Supply Chain Scheduling: Approach/Deployment.

Internal Supply Chain (ISC) Scheduling Metrics

In world-class businesses, ISC scheduling is preceded by a make-or-buy process that is formal, strategic, and owned by the business leader. The make/buy process is based on core competency and economic decisions. The ISC scheduling process: (1) maximizes the utilization of rate-based pull systems; (2) uses simple scheduling techniques; (3) replaces physical inventories with cycle counting; (4) utilizes flattened bills of material; (5) eliminates informal prioritization processes; and (6) maintains accurate bills of material, routings, and inventory records.

0	10–30 (Beginning)	40–60 (Developing)	70–90 (World Class)	100
	MPS performance <85%	MPS performance = 85–100%	MPS performance = 100%	
	WIP inventory accuracy <95%	WIP inventory accuracy = 95–100%	WIP inventory accuracy = 100%	

Figure A3.19. Internal Supply Chain Scheduling Metrics.

Distribution (Approach/Deployment)				
In world-class businesses, distribution: (1) plans and optimizes the entire distribution network; (2) maximizes customer satisfaction while minimizing inventory and cost; (3) systematically aggregates and feeds distribution demand to S&OP; (4) runs DRP as an integral part of a collaborative supply chain; (5) requires DRP to be reconciled through the S&OP process; (5) eliminates informal prioritization processes to balance supply and demand; and (6) maintains accurate customer and inventory records.				
0	10–30 (Beginning)	40–60 (Developing)	70–90 (World Class)	100
	Distribution has begun a cultural change program to effect collaborative and cooperative customer/supplier relationships.	The cultural change program is well underway, with some collaborative and cooperative customer/supplier relationships established.	Distribution has effected a cultural change to collaborative and cooperative customer/supplier relationships.	
	The distribution network design has evolved to serve demand points in what appeared at the time to be the optimal manner. No formal network optimization techniques have been used.	The distribution network is evolving to reflect an optimal design to connect supply and demand points. Quantitative network optimization techniques have been introduced to begin establishing the optimal design.	The distribution network is well defined with optimal and alternative service points for demand. Quantitative network optimization techniques were used to establish the optimal configuration.	
	Distribution capacity planning is utilized.	Distribution capacity planning has begun to impact network efficiency.	Effective capacity planning is an integral part of how distribution is managed.	
	CPFR techniques are being implemented with customers. Benefits are beginning to show.	CRFP techniques are being used actively and beginning to show substantial benefits.	CPFR techniques are well established and providing substantial benefits.	

Figure A3.20. Distribution: Approach/Deployment.

companies, consultants, and software suppliers. CPFR is in primary use in fast-moving consumer goods industries. Metrics for distribution deal primarily with customer service implications of the supply chain (Figure A3.21).

Logistics in a business sense evolved from the military in World War II, when there was an enormous need to move people and material on a global stage. Today, logistics, first and foremost, is a provider of service for the physical movement of goods from origin to destination and, as such, is an important part of the supply chain.

Businesses use the terms *inbound* logistics (moving *in* from the supplier) and outbound logistics (moving *out* to the destination). They also use the term

Distribution (Approach/Deployment)

In world-class businesses, distribution: (1) plans and optimizes the entire distribution network; (2) maximizes customer satisfaction while minimizing inventory and cost; (3) systematically aggregates and feeds distribution demand to S&OP; (4) runs DRP as an integral part of a collaborative supply chain; (5) requires DRP to be reconciled through the S&OP process; (5) eliminates informal prioritization processes to balance supply and demand; and (6) maintains accurate customer and inventory records.

0	10–30 (Beginning)	40–60 (Developing)	70–90 (World Class)	100
	Informal authorization and prioritization techniques (hot lists, shortage reports, etc.) are gradually being phased out through use of the formal processes and systems.	Informal authorization and prioritization techniques (hot lists, shortage reports, etc.) have generally been phased out through use of the formal processes and systems.	Authorization and prioritization techniques are based on pull systems.	
	Distribution requirements planning has been introduced and is being used extensively in distribution planning.	Distribution demand requirements from DRP are used in the S&OP and MPS processes.	Distribution demand requirements from DRP are integrated and reconciled with the S&OP and MPS processes.	
	Collaboration, cooperation, and linkage are being established for some key customer/ supplier relationships.	Implementation of collaboration, cooperation, and linking are well underway and beginning to show quantitative results.	Collaboration, cooperation, and linking are well established for customer/ supplier relationships. Significantly improved results have occurred.	

Figure A3.20 (continued). Distribution: Approach/Deployment.

reverse-flow logistics for product repair, recycling, and even remanufacturing activities. Another business term is *third-party logistics*. A so-called third-party logistics (3PL) provider contracts with a company (or a group of companies in combination) to perform logistics functions. These functions typically consist of (at a minimum) warehousing, pick and pack, and transportation. Comprehensive arrangements can call for a more extensive set of activities, possibly including even customer development. Accenture has coined the term *fourth-party logistics* (4PL) to designate an integrator that assembles the resources (possibly including one or more 3PLs) and bundles them with intellectual capital usually in the form of software.

Distribution Metrics				
In world-class businesses, distribution: (1) plans and optimizes the entire distribution network; (2) maximizes customer satisfaction while minimizing inventory and cost; (3) systematically aggregates and feeds distribution demand to S&OP; (4) runs DRP as an integral part of a collaborative supply chain; (5) requires DRP to be reconciled through the S&OP process; (5) eliminates informal prioritization processes to balance supply and demand; and (6) maintains accurate customer and inventory records.				
0	10–30 (Beginning)	40–60 (Developing)	70–90 (World Class)	100
	Actual performance = plan <85% of the time	Actual performance = plan 85–100% of the time	Actual performance = plan 100% of the time	
	Overdue backlog >15%	Overdue backlog = 15–2%	Overdue backlog <2%	
	Distribution demonstrated capacity = plan <90% of the time	Distribution demonstrated capacity = plan 90–98% of the time	Distribution demonstrated capacity = plan >98% of the time	
	Fill rate <100%	Fill rate = 97—100%	Fill rate = 100%	
	Finished goods inventory days of supply >110% of specific industry benchmarks	Finished goods inventory days of supply = 110–90% of specific industry benchmarks	Finished goods inventory days of supply <90% of specific industry benchmarks	

Figure A3.21. Distribution Metrics.

Figures A3.22 and A3.23. The extent of the logistics function in a given company depends a great deal on the nature of the industry and the company's strategy (Figure A3.22). For example, companies that are highly cost sensitive may use 3PL more extensively under the presumption that 3PL will be more efficient in performing these tasks. For the most part, satisfying customer demand is paramount, whether that demand is for quick response, low costs, or for other needs in which logistics plays a part. Metrics are standard for customer-focused supply chain activities (Figure A3.23).

Companies increasingly are recognizing that supply chains do not end with selling and delivering products to customers. These companies understand the importance of:

- Operating a sustainable supply chain
- Accepting returned products
- Recycling used materials into new products

The three terms of *sustainability*, *returns*, and *recycling* have different meanings, of course, but we have chosen to use them together. We prefer to encompass

Logistics (Approach/Deployment)

In world-class businesses, logistics: (1) minimizes or avoids the storage of finished goods once they leave the ISC process; (2) employs smaller and more frequent shipments so that supply chain inventory is minimized; (3) ensures that production and replenishment are synchronized with customer demand; (4) analytically plans optimal shipment loads, sequences, and transportation modes; and (5) maintains strategic relationships with key transportation and third-party logistics suppliers.

0	10–30 (Beginning)	40–60 (Developing)	70–90 (World Class)	100
	A continuous replenishment process linking customer demand directly to warehouse inventory in a pull process is underway.	A continuous replenishment process is expanding, and automation is underway using industry-standard information flow tools is underway.	A collaborative, cooperative, and continuous replenishment process is mature and automated, including maximum use of industry-standard information flow tools.	
	Automation of warehouse operations (receiving, put away and storage, retrieval, and staging and shipping) is underway.	Automation of warehouse operations is expanding.	Automation of warehouse operations is at benchmark levels.	
	Flow-through distribution and cross-docking is underway.	Flow-through distribution and cross-docking is expanding.	Flow-through distribution and cross-docking are employed to the maximum appropriate degree and are at benchmark levels for the industry.	
	A supplier-managed inventory strategy is developed and deployment is underway.	A supplier-managed inventory strategy is developed and deployment is expanding.	Supplier-managed inventory and strategic third-party logistics strategies are utilized to the maximum appropriate levels consistent with business objectives. Fourth-party logistics suppliers also may be used in certain circumstances.	
	Cycle counting has begun to replace the physical inventory.	Cycle counting is replacing the physical inventory.	Cycle counting has replaced the physical inventory.	
	A transportation policy exists.	A transportation policy exists and is becoming embedded in the operational culture. Clarity of roles, responsibilities, and metrics is improving.	A transportation policy exists and has become embedded in the operational culture. Clarity of roles, responsibilities, and metrics is clear.	

Figure A3.22. Logistics: Approach/Deployment.

Logistics Metrics				
In world-class businesses, logistics: (1) minimizes or avoids the storage of finished goods once they leave the ISC process; (2) employs smaller and more frequent shipments so that supply chain inventory is minimized; (3) ensures that production and replenishment are synchronized with customer demand; (4) analytically plans optimal shipment loads, sequences, and transportation modes; and (5) maintains strategic relationships with key transportation and third-party logistics suppliers.				
0	10–30 (Beginning)	40–60 (Developing)	70–90 (World Class)	100
	Distribution fill rate <95%	Distribution fill rate = 95–100%	Distribution fill rate = 100%	
	Order fulfillment cycle time >120% of industry benchmarks	Order fulfillment cycle time = 120–100% of industry benchmarks	Order fulfillment cycle time <100% of industry benchmarks	
	Distribution cycle time >120% of industry benchmarks	Distribution cycle time = 120–100% of industry benchmarks	Distribution cycle time <100% of industry benchmarks	
	Distribution cost >120% of industry benchmarks	Distribution cost = 120–100% of industry benchmarks	Distribution cost <100% of industry benchmarks	

Figure A3.23. Logistics Metrics.

the entire range of the meanings of these three terms. Therefore, in this appendix, we are particularly concerned with an issue that is variously referred to as sustainability, return, and recycle.

Over the past several years, society and business have become increasingly intertwined. As a result, two questions are relevant for every company:

- What are the characteristics of a sustainable company?
- What are the implications for every company that has a supply chain?

Sustainability. The term *sustainability* has become increasingly popular. A website sponsored by Chevron discusses sustainability, obviously from an energy standpoint (see www.willyoujoinus.com for a good explanation). In 2006, for example, 35% of the energy consumed in the world economy was by manufacturing and industry. Dow Jones also publishes the *Dow Jones Sustainability Indices*:

> [Sustainability] is a business approach that creates long-term shareholder value by embracing opportunities and managing risks deriving from economic, environmental and social developments. A defined set of criteria and weightings is used to assess the opportunities and risks deriving from economic, environmental and social developments for the eligible companies.

A major source of information for Dow Jones is a questionnaire, which is completed by companies participating in the annual review. Additional Dow Jones sources include company and third-party documents as well as personal contacts with analysts and companies. We recommend the Dow Jones website for further information (see www.sustainability-index.com).

Returns. The Supply Chain Council (SCC) includes *return* in its Supply Chain Operations Reference® (SCOR) model (see www.supply-chain.org). Under the return element of their model, SCC includes the return of defective products, MRO products (maintenance, repair, and overhaul), and excess products. SCC also includes the business rules for management of return activities, performance indicators, data collection, return inventory, capital assets, transportation, network configuration, regulatory requirements and compliance, and supply chain return risk. Additionally SCC includes processes associated with returning or receiving returned products for any reason. These processes extend to post-delivery customer support. Consistent with the SCOR model, SCC considers the *plan, source*, and *deliver* of returned goods.

Recycling. As most consumers already know, *recycling* has become a big deal (and a big business) in the last few years. Many consumers are now being asked to separate their own garbage for recycling. Those who study recycling tell us that, aside from the "save the planet" considerations, there are also enormous economic considerations in recycling. For example, the website for Waste Management encourages individuals as well as companies to recycle (see www.wm.com). The website for Dell has the following statement (see www.dell.com):

> *We are pleased to offer you the opportunity to recycle your unwanted Dell-branded product for free. Plus, if you buy a new Dell desktop or notebook and select the free recycling option at the time of purchase, we will recycle your old PC and monitor at no cost to you (even if it isn't a Dell-branded product.)*

> Although there may be others, we are not aware of another assessment tool for supply chain maturity that includes a sustainability/return/recycle section that stresses the economic value as ours does. We believe this feature of our tool is important for supply chain transformations.

Figures A3.24 and A3.25. The approach/deployment matrix in Figure A3.24 for sustainability/return/recycle begins with the highest levels of the organization and the need for strategic decision making and rigorous cost/benefit analyses for sustainability, return, and recycle programs. Furthermore, the supply chain for both the supply of recyclable materials and the demand for products made with recycled materials is a key element in supply chain transformation.

Sustainability/Return/Recycle (Approach/Deployment)

In world-class businesses, sustainability/return/recycle: (1) refer to almost every facet of the business of a company; (2) are not just buzzwords used for public consumption; (3) are often taken to include environmental, social, and economic dimensions; (4) involve the practical processes of making used materials into new products to prevent waste of potentially useful materials; (5) are not without economic benefit; and yet (6) require decisions to be made at the strategic level.

0	10–30 (Beginning)	40–60 (Developing)	70–90 (World Class)	100
	Support for sustainability, return, and recycle programs is beginning to be seen throughout the business. Support is building among the senior leadership team.	Decisions are being made at the senior level that sustainability, return, and recycle programs make sense for the organization and that they will be actively and visibly supported by the senior leadership team.	Decisions have been made at the strategic level that sustainability, return, and recycle programs will have a visible commitment from the senior leadership team. An executive champion has been empowered and incentivized to lead the effort.	
	Elements of a rigorous cost/benefit analysis are in place and generally show a positive net present value. Various elements of the program are being developed to enhance the economic benefits.	A rigorous cost/benefit analysis is being performed showing a positive net present value. Various elements of the program have been developed and are in place showing positive results.	A rigorous cost/benefit analysis has been performed showing without doubt that the sustainability, return, and recycle program has a positive net present value. The senior leadership team actively shows its visible commitment to the program(s) as making good business sense.	
	A return/recycle process is beginning as a strategic initiative that has an economic benefit objective.	A return/recycle process is well underway with collaborative and cooperative efforts in place with supply chain partners on both the supply and demand side.	A collaborative, cooperative, and continuous return/recycle process is a mature part of the firm's overall sustainability initiatives.	
	An adequate, stable supply of recyclable material is being developed with encouraging results.	An adequate, stable supply of recyclable material has been developed and the appropriate supply chain is in place.	An adequate, stable supply of recyclable material is in place, including provisions for collection, sorting, transportation, and storage.	
	An adequate, stable source of demand for recycled product is being investigated with encouraging results.	An adequate, stable source of demand for recycled products has been developed and the appropriate supply chain is in place.	An adequate, stable source of demand for recycled products is in place. The appropriate supply chain is achieving planned results.	

Figure A3.24. Sustainability/Return/Recycle: Approach/Deployment.

Sustainability/Return/ Recycle Metrics

In world-class businesses, sustainability/return/recycle: (1) refer to almost every facet of the business of a company; (2) are not just buzzwords used for public consumption; (3) are often taken to include environmental, social, and economic dimensions; (4) involve the practical processes of making used materials into new products to prevent waste of potentially useful materials; (5) are not without economic benefit; and yet (6) require decisions to be made at the strategic level.

0	10–30 (Beginning)	40–60 (Developing)	70–90 (World Class)	100
	Percent of appropriate personnel that have been educated and trained in sustainability, return, and recycle processes <80% of industry benchmarks	Percent of appropriate personnel that have been educated and trained in sustainability, return, and recycle processes = 80–120% of industry benchmarks	Percent of appropriate personnel that have been educated and trained in sustainability, return, and recycle processes >120% of industry benchmarks	
	Cost/benefit analyses show a positive net present value <80% of the company's standard hurdle rate, which indicates the economic benefits of the program	Cost/benefit analyses show a positive net present value = 80–120% of the company's standard hurdle rate, which indicates the economic benefits of the program	Cost/benefit analyses show a positive net present value >120% of the company's standard hurdle rate, which indicates the economic benefits of the program	
	Percent of recycled material in the company's products <80% of industry benchmarks	Percent of recycled material in the company's products = 80–120% of industry benchmarks	Percent of recycled material in the company's products >120% of industry benchmarks	
	The stable supply of recyclable material <80% of the company's needs	The stable supply of recyclable material = 80–120% of the company's needs	The stable supply of recyclable material >120% of the company's needs	
	The stable demand for recycled products <80% of supply for the foreseeable future	The stable demand for recycled products = 80%–120% of supply for the foreseeable future	The stable demand for recycled products is >120% of supply for the foreseeable future	

Figure A3.25. Sustainability/Return/Recycle Metrics.

Current Supply Chain Process Maturity	Scoring				
	0	10–30	40–60	70–90	100
Supply chain integration					
Demand management					
Supply management					
Sales and operations planning					
Master production scheduling					
Enterprise requirements detail planning					
Internal supply chain scheduling					
Distribution					
Logistics					
Sustainability, return, recycle					

Figure A3.26. Current Supply Chain Process Maturity: Scoring Approach/Deployment Assessments.

Current Supply Chain Metrics Maturity	Scoring				
	0	10–30	40–60	70–90	100
Supply chain integration					
Demand management					
Supply management					
Sales and operations planning					
Master production scheduling					
Enterprise requirements detail planning					
Internal supply chain scheduling					
Distribution					
Logistics					
Sustainability, return, recycle					

Figure A3.27. Current Supply Chain Metrics Maturity: Scoring Metrics Assessments.

The metrics matrix begins by assuming that appropriate personnel within the organization will need to be educated and trained in sustainability, return, and recycle processes (Figure A3.25). We have found that the costs and benefits of education and training are not necessarily intuitively obvious. Thus some personnel may believe that the education and training program is a *feel-good* activity or that it is being done in order to be politically correct. They may not realize that such programs, if done well and properly, usually yield a positive net economic benefit.

Figures A3.26 and A3.27. Two matrices are used for scoring the results of the *Supply Chain Transformation Maturity Assessment Tool.* Figure A3.26 is for scoring the approach/deployment assessments. Figure A3.27 is for scoring the metrics assessments.

THE TOOL IN REVIEW

The Supply Chain Transformation Maturity Assessment Tool is a comprehensive, integrated business assessment that drives meaningful improvements in supply chains. The tool can be used to strengthen planning by focusing improvement resources on critical capability gaps — a focus that is on organizational capability and business results. The assessment drives improvement through using three steps:

Organize. A 2-hour meeting to:
- Select appropriate people to participate in the assessment
- Review the business goals and issues in the assessment
- Plan data collection
- Develop a communications plan

Assess. Off-line by individuals and subteams for 2 to 3 days to:
- Fill out assessment forms
- Agree on key strengths, areas for improvement, and scores
- Develop recommended actions

Review and plan actions. Business leadership in a 1-day offsite meeting to:
- Conduct debriefing of subteams
- Identify key gaps and suggested actions
- Prioritize and plan actions based on business impact and strategy
- Launch action plans

THE FINAL TASK

Figure A3.28. Figure A3.28 illustrates the final task of the *Supply Chain Transformation Assessment Tool*. Rank each of the eight supply chain processes that are contained in the tool from high to low on two dimensions: *impact* on the supply chain maturity and performance and *difficulty* of implementation. This ranking will allow the team to place each process into the appropriate quadrant of the 2 × 2 matrix shown in Figure A3.28. The following four priorities will likely result:

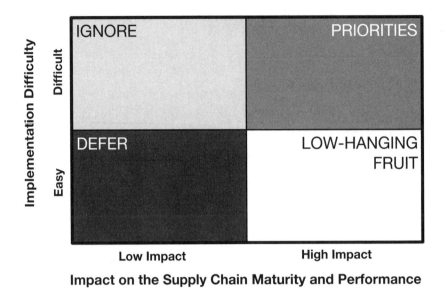

Impact on the Supply Chain Maturity and Performance

Figure A3.28. The Four Likely Priority Categories Resulting from Ranking the Eight Supply Chain Processes.

- *High impact/easy implementation*: Fix the LOW-HANGING FRUIT first because of the high impact with minimal effort.
- *High impact/difficult implementation*: Provide adequate resources for the PRIORITIES because of their high impact, but difficult implementation.
- *Low impact/easy implementation:* DEFER these processes until a later time because of higher priorities.
- *Low impact/difficult implementation:* IGNORE these processes because addressing them is not likely to be worth the effort, at least not in the short run.

CONCLUSION

Appendix 3 has presented the *Supply Chain Transformation Assessment Tool* for your use. We have tried to provide sufficient guidance and examples to enable you to apply the tool to your organization without undue difficulty. We hope you find it useful.

REFERENCES

1. The Oliver Wight *Class A Checklist for Business Excellence, Sixth Edition* 2005. New York: John Wiley & Sons.

2. Ling, Richard C. and Walter E. Goddard. *Orchestrating Success: Improve Control of the Business with Sales and Operations Planning* 1988. New York: John Wiley & Sons.

3. Orlicky, Joseph. *Material Requirements Planning: The New Way of Life in Production and Inventory Management* 1975. New York: McGraw-Hill.

4. Wight, Oliver W. *MRPII: Unlocking America's Productivity Potential* 1981. New York: Oliver Wight Limited Publications/John Wiley & Sons.

5. Martin, Andre J. *DRP: Distribution Resource Planning, Second Edition* 1990. New York: Oliver Wight Limited Publications/John Wiley & Sons.

INDEX

A

ABC segmentation analysis, 85, 86–87,
    153. *See also* Third-party logistics
Accenture, 233
Accuracy issues, bullwhip effect and, 80
Acquisitions. *See* Mergers and
    acquisitions
Action plans, 39–40
Adoption curve, management fads and,
    22–24
Aftermarket products, 46, 116
Aggregate-level planning activities, 47,
    221
Aircraft on the ground (AOG), 46
Alignment, strategic plan and, 102, 109
AlliedSignal, 100
American Production and Inventory
    Control Society (APICS), 218, 226
American Productivity and Quality
    Center (APQC), 192, 203
Analysis, framework for, 28–32
    cash-to-cash cycle and, 29–30
    competition and, 30
    DELIVER component, 31
    MAKE component, 31
    PLAN component, 29, 30–31
    RETURN component, 29, 31
    SOURCE component, 31
AOG. *See* Aircraft on the ground
APICS certification, 166, 167

APQC. *See* American Productivity and
    Quality Center
APQC *Code of Conduct for
    Benchmarking*, 203–206
    completion, 205
    confidentiality, 204
    contact, 205
    exchange, 204
    key to success, 199
    legality, 203–204
    preparation, 205
    use, 204–205
Ariba Inc., 154, 159
As is state of supply chain processes,
    49–50
    As Is → Path Forward → Continuously
        Improve model, 57
    as is/to be performance measures, 71
    benchmarking and, 192
    change imperative and, 52
    consensus and, 71
    current processes and, 47
    determining the, 54
    documentation of, 183
    gap closure and, 70, 192
    SCOR and, 30
Assessment methodology, 33–43
    objectives and, 34
    sample metrics for, 42
    six-step approach in, 34

249

Original equipment manufactured. *See*
    OEM products
Orlicky, Joe, 6, 7, 224
Outsourcing, 9, 148
Overall cost leadership model, 138
Over-forecasting, future demand and,
    47–48

P

Parts, standardization of, 5
Parts and service, multiple supply chains
    and, 127
People-oriented levers. *See* Phased
    approach
Performance improvement, behavioral
    change and, 57
Performance Management, 174–175
Phased approach, 57–60
    action research model, 57
    behavioral change levers and, 56–60
    *As Is → Path Forward → Continuously
    Improve* model, 57
    Scout → Enter → Diagnose model, 57
    Unfreeze → Move → Refreeze, 56, 57
PLAN component, analysis framework,
    29, 30–31
Planning/deployment management,
    92–93
PMBOK (*A Guide to the Project
    Management Body of Knowledge*),
    157–158
Policies, price increases and, 90
Porter, Michael, 10, 138, 221
Power, James D, IV, 123–124
Problems. *See* Assessment of supply chain
Process-based business model, 102
Procure-to-pay process, 53
Procurement, nonproduct, 132
Product delivery systems, traditional, 229,
    231–232
    decisions on-the-fly, 232
    guessing about demand, 231
    production plan and, 231–232
    set rate, using, 232
Product development requirements, 46
Product differentiation, 138–139

Product families, aggregate level planning
    and, 47
Product leadership model, 138
Product life cycles, 130–132
    long life cycle, 131
    nonproduct procurement, 132
    short life cycle, 131
Profit generation, 89
Programmatic management of change.
    See Phased approach
Progress monitoring, 94–95. *See also*
    Metrics
Project Management Institute (PMI), 157
Project teams, in six-step change
    management, 67

Q

Quarter-by-quarter decision making, 16, 17
Questionnaires, assessment and, 32–33
    Baldrige checklist, 32–33, 50
    Oliver Wight Class A Checklist, 32
    SCC framework, 33
    supply chain integration and, 37
Quigley, Joseph, 177, 178, 190
Quotes, misconceptions about change, 58

R

Rationalization of supply base, 220
RCCP. *See* Rough cut capacity planning
Recycling, 241
Red Adair story, special demand
    requirements and, 49
Remanufacturing, items for, 46
Reorganization, in supply chain processes,
    92
Replenishment inventory, 86–87
Requests for proposal (RFPs), 45
Requirements, orders and, 79
Resistors, change and, 63
Results orientation program, 71
RETURN component, analysis
    framework, 29, 31
Return on invested capital (ROIC)
    game change and, 88
    improvement focus and, 172
    trapped cash and, 77
    as understood priority, 78

risk management and, 157
sequence and, 102–103
as STRAP, 103
strategic linkage, levels 1-4, 139–141
strategic questions and, 96
Strategic staffing/organizational
development, 165–168
aligned OD process, 168
degreed individuals, 166, 167
four-part approach, 165–166
ISM and/or APICS certification, 166
junior military officers, 165–167
organizational development (OD), 168
targeted universities and, 166, 167
Strengths/weaknesses/opportunities/
threats. *See* SWOT analysis
Suppliers, multiple supply chains and, 127
Supply base, cash flow leak and, 79–80
Supply chain
before term existed, 89
corporate strategy and, 20
delegation, transformation and, 190
as misnomer, 10
purchasing and, 101
Supply chain collaboration, 100. *See also*
Collaborative supply chains
Supply Chain Council (SCC)
assessment tools and, 208
returns and, 240–241
SCC framework, assessment and, 33
supply chain models and, 28
Supply chain integration, 36, 37
Supply chain linkages, 112
Supply chain management (SCM)
definition of, 11
entire supply chain and, 7
evolution of, 10
introduction of, 9
Supply Chain Operations Reference (SCOR)
adaptation of, 30
development of, 28
four levels of, 32
knowing the *as is* and, 50
returns and, 240, 241
SCC framework and, 33
Supply chain risks. *See* Risk management
process

*Supply Chain Transformation Maturity
Assessment Tool©, The*, 207–246
about the tool, 208–210
assessor, scoring and, 216
capability maturity path concept,
211–212
demand management and, 218, 219–220
distribution metrics and, 238
distribution systems and, 232–233,
236–237
ERDP and, 223, 224, 228–231
final task, 245–246
five-phase process, 210–211
forecast accuracy and, 218, 220
ISC scheduling and, 234–235
logistics and, 233, 237, 239, 240
metrics and, 216–217, 224, 240
MPS and, 223, 227–228
optimization of supply base, 220–221
priority categories, eight processes
and, 245–246
recycling and, 241
returns and, 240–241
S&OP and, 221–226
scoring system components, 213
supply chain integration (approach/
deployment), 213–216
supply management and, 220, 222
sustainability and, 238, 240–243
tool in review, 244–245
traditional product delivery systems
and, 229, 231–232
Sustainability, 238, 240–241
of change, 91
recycling and, 241
returns and, 240–241
SWOT analysis, 39, 40

T

Taylor, Frederick W., 5
Team. *See also* Internal/external team
in integrated total cost reduction
process, 161
leadership team, 36
project teams, 67, 68
Team dynamics, 63
Technology, innovation and, 17–18